D0480433

Toothing Stones
Rethinking the Political

Toothing Stones
Rethinking the Political

edited by

Robert E. Meagher

THE SWALLOW PRESS INC.
CHICAGO

First Edition

Published by
The Swallow Press Incorporated
1139 South Wabash Avenue
Chicago, Illinois 60605

This book is printed on recycled paper

IBSN (cloth) 0–8040–0566–4
IBSN (paper) 0–8040–0567–2
LIBRARY OF CONGRESS CATALOG CARD NUMBER 75–189197

One change always leaves a toothing-stone on which another may be built.

—MACHIAVELLI

Contents

Introduction

Robert E. Meagher

"One change," writes Machiavelli, "always leaves a 'toothing-stone' on which another may be built." [1] A toothing-stone is an irregularity in the edge of a wall which allows for its extension. In building a stone wall, if one were to leave a plane surface, any further construction would have nothing to tie onto, thus being discontinuous with the other. Similarly, in the affairs of men, one never begins altogether afresh. Descartes saw it as a manifest imperfection that we are all children before we are mature and in control of our affairs and that cities and the law-governed lives of cities never proceed from the mind of a single, sovereign architect. The lives of the dead and of the living and of the not-yet-alive are complicit and tangled; their stories intermingle and depend upon one another. They form a wall, some portions of which lie in decay and other portions of which are even now being set in place; they form a continuum that circles and traces out the wanderings of our common lives. One never begins afresh.

> It requires bucketsful of blood and centuries of history to lead to an imperceptible modification in the human condition. Such is the law. For years heads fall like hail, Terror reigns, Revolution is touted, and one ends

up by substituting constitutional monarchy for legitimate monarchy.[2]

It is always a matter of toothing-stones, "leadings" toward and from, a dialogue that spans past and future and, at the same time, locks us within our own mortal time and energies.

The energies recorded within this volume are almost uniformly those of persons whose lives and words have unfolded within the academy. At the risk of quite evident oversimplification, I would suggest that the space which exists between the polis and the academy is a generation gap. Consider the posture of parent to child and of child to parent. A child is desperately imitative of parental appetites and prejudices and mannerisms; and yet a child represents a challenge to his elders. A mirror image is always a challenge to the original, an occasion of oblique self-confrontation, a reminder of the irreversible and ambiguously prolific character of one's own life. And yet a child never simply imitates and thus always offers a subtle critique or caricature of the part he is given to play. Childhood is the time of futilely endless questioning. Clearly the scope and depth and sheer multitude of a child's questions, if ever honestly engaged, would break one's stride forever and suspend indefinitely the orderly progression of adult concerns which must meet the incessant press of very real necessities and claims. The academy is the place of youth, both metaphorically and, in fact, literally, in our society. While it often seems a mere immature mimic of the larger whole, it remains a source of irony, disillusionment, righteous or perhaps more often self-righteous anger, and of occasional hope. The academy is not precisely a microcosm, nor a measuring device of one sort or another, nor a hermitage. Rather, it is that place and time, that moment, where and when each stone is set in place; it marks the passage from the private to the public, where and when one is most desirous and yet most lucidly despairing of ever beginning afresh with one's life. It is a place of toothing-stones where the unfinished, the questionable, and the inevitable converge to form human fate.

This volume, variously in each of its essays, represents a response to a problem, a question, which raises itself among us daily and which, no doubt, admits of a variety of formulations. However, more comprehensively than any peculiar formulation, it is the radically problematic and questionable character of our common lives that occasions and grounds the inquiries pursued here. The following six paragraphs are what I initially wrote to each contributor, inviting his or her response; they form the immediate, common occasion and context for the ideas, concerns, and hopes shared in these pages.

"We have witnessed in modern times and in recent years the corruption and trivialization of the public realm and the consequent withdrawal into privacy and intimacy. Martin Heidegger has expressed the altogether pervasive modern perception of public life when he claims that the light of the public darkens everything. This withdrawal is understandable although unfortunate; it means that we generally ask too little, indeed almost nothing, from public life and expect too much, indeed almost everything, from private life. Such is surely the movement, whatever its pace and progress, a movement which may leave political life to the corrupt and the quixotic and consume private life with unqualified demands for meaning and fullness beyond its scope. What is at stake in such a movement is not a particular political issue but the political dimension itself. The level of this analysis, rather than its particular conception and formulation, is perhaps representative of the essays which are to compose this volume. These essays might ask whether serious, long-term engagement in political life is already irrevocably passe and if not, what the sources and aims of such engagement might be. In these essays, one might wonder what would have to enter the public realm, what would have to be held up and hoped for, for the approaching presidential election [November 1972] to be challenging and compelling for what is best rather than for what is worst in our common lives. As matters stand, five or six million newly enfranchised youth may only widen, rather than fill, the gaps left by their disillusioned and spiritually disenfranchised fellow-voters. That one party and candidate will win is predictable, whereas it is quite possible that our country will know only unyielding night for still another four years regardless. It is this darkness of long-settled moral fatigue and confusion which calls into sheer questionableness the peculiar claims of any likely candidate and which formulates a central query of this book: engagement in or disengagement from the concerns and responsibilities of political life.

"It is to this decay of the public realm and the consequent withdrawal from political life into private life, or to the same problem variously formulated, that the contributing essays will address themselves. What this suggests is the location and scale of the problem to be considered, without limiting either the possible formulation of the problem or its possible resolutions. Clearly one's conception of a problem and one's constructive proposal for its resolution are inseparable. In every formulation of a problem there is already the embryonic presence of its possible resolution. Consequently, I wish these forethoughts not to force upon this volume a particular definition of the contemporary crisis in political life and the consequent withdrawal into private life any more than to weight its response to that crisis. Rather, I wish only to suggest the range of that crisis—i.e. that it encompasses the whole of political life rather than a part or dimension of it. The question for many, and in particular for this volume, is not a specific malfunction or misdemeanor which complicates involvement in political concerns, but instead a general collapse or pervasive misconception of political life which precludes or at least questions the integrity and significance of any involvement at all.

"Further, I might suggest, as a possible concern for these essays, that not only engagement in political life, but also the character and quality of that engagement is a critical matter during the remaining months prior to the primaries, conventions, and the election itself. The public realm and political life have been periodically renewed and illumined by the play of false lights and the shouts of empty voices. Apathy and despair are occasionally vulnerable to brief amusement and curious excitement, which is to say that garish political spectacles always have their captive audiences. Perhaps words of caution in this regard would be appropriate. One might ask, quite generally, what form and degree of integrity is proper and necessary to a political campaign, a summons to political life. One might ask whether there might not occasionally be greater defeats than losing. The focus of these essays, then, will fall upon the most fundamental, substantive concerns, responsibilities, and prospects of any future political campaign.

"Whether unfortunate or not, it is descriptively accurate, I think, to say that for all but a small fraction of citizens, political life is cyclical and approaches a significant level at best once every four years. In an election year, involvement in political life, at least to the point of attention and discussion, is ordinarily widened and intensified. However, it is questionable whether that attention and discussion are illuminating, edifying, and enriching, or even any longer interesting. What are the appropriate, as distinct from the actual, concerns of contemporary political life? What would have to be discussed and resolved upon to allow for intelligent and moral participation in public life? It is my perception that it is particularly in an election year that the appropriate concerns of political life are trivialized and perverted. Caution, strategy, theater, and divisive pressure replace honest, serious debate. With an illusion of clarity and decisiveness—which is merely an imposed confusion of issues and reduction of options—each voter is encouraged and left no alternative but to calculate his immediate self-interest.

"The concerns of this volume are not merely the peculiar concerns of a particular election year; rather, its concerns are the deepest and most appropriate concerns of political life as they are reflected in or suppressed by the contemporary political situation. Its proper speculations are not, for instance, who will win on what issues in '72; but perhaps what it would mean to really win at all in '72. It is to those who at least wonder whether there is anything decent, significant, or serious any longer at stake in the events and deliberations of political life that these essays are to be addressed. For there are many whose hopes and expectations have been reduced from public to private, or from common to personal, dimensions. Can one any longer speak of or hope for national decency, honor, integrity, justice, meaning, or peace? Or have these become necessarily private concerns able to be raised and resolved at best within the confines of an individual life or of a small communal nucleus?

"Some of the contributors to this volume may argue that the only thing wrong with the political whole precluding hopeful participation is its present leadership. Others would argue that the common or public life of our nation has broken down progressively as it has departed from the conception of its founders. Still others would locate the seeds of final fragmentation and collective selfishness within our nation's founding documents. What all of these have in common is their sense that American life has in some pervasive way broken down and ceased to function with minimal adequacy. Some would maintain that its renewal may be looked for in electoral politics, whether within or outside of the present two-party system, others in educational reform, others in extra-institutional moral or spiritual conversion, and still others not at all. In the interim or remnant, one might argue that a decent, hopeful private life is still possible though impoverished, while others would deny this and suggest that private and public life, the life of the part and the life of the whole, are so inseparable that the individual life is necessarily cast into the darkness, confusion, and polluting stagnation of the streams of our common life—which have ceased to flow."

Men surely differ, as this volume attests, in the formulations they would offer for the distinction between the public and the private and for the appropriate relationship between the two. However, most generally, all would assume, I think, that in a sound, vigorous nation there would be a harmony between public and private concerns, a well-suitedness of the one to the other. National well-being and unity would seem to require that the life of the individual find its bearings, support, recognition, and even completion in the life of the community. Our own national experience, quite to the contrary, points at least for the moment to a radical disharmony between the public and the private. Public concerns appear at worst antithetical and at best indifferent to private concerns, to the individual's concern for a lighted space in which to live a decent, full life. It is this quite available, in fact unavoidable, experience of the sundering of the public and the private to the point where it seems that one must opt between them (unless, by chance, one's own most personal leanings are in the direction of public life or unless, by design, public life is diverted to personal gain) that occasions these admittedly diverse reflections upon *the political*—that point or space where public and private converge and converse. And surely any proposed articulation of what is currently wrong in this regard is already a suggestion of what ought to be right.

What this volume recognizes is that concern for the political is noticeably heightened during periods of national campaigns and elections for public office. Hence such periods are presumably privileged and particularly disposed for considerations of the political both in its highest conceivable perfection and in its immediately experienced practicalities, a spectrum roughly spanned by this volume. Still, what this volume (without gainsaying its contributors) does *not* assume is an identity between the political and "politics" understood as that complex phenomenon which reaches some fulness of being and expression every four years.

Rather, it is tolerably clear that the ranging scope of this volume as a whole represents a questioning if not a denial of any restriction of the political to "politics" and so of political or public life to "elected public office." In one of the most brilliant reflections upon the political in our tradition, Sir Thomas More presents Utopia as a state in which all things are common and nothing is private. (Contrastingly, it might be and has been argued in this volume that in America all things are private and nothing is public.) In Utopia, what is central to and effectively constitutive of its political life is shared deliberation regarding *the* preeminently public thing, the comprehensive good which is most properly common and thus most properly the concern of the common or public life of all Utopians, namely, happiness, fulness, or well-being (all attempts at the Greek *eudaimonia*). *The* political activity, then, is seen as the essentially communal endeavor to understand and articulate human well-being which is presumed to be *the* public thing, the *res publica*. (Again, in clear contrast to this, is the American, not to say exclusively American, consecration to the essentially private character of happiness in conception, articulation, and realization.) The endeavor that is this book might be seen as a somewhat scattered and not fully lucid (shared beginnings are never fully communal or conscious) attempt to expand the meaning of the political to its appropriate scope and to inquire into the properly political, to inquire into the *res publica,* the common thing or things the possession or anticipation of which constitutes and nourishes our common lives. The endeavor that is this book is itself, then, a political act at a moment when such action might be particularly visible and, it is hoped, fruitful.

I am deeply grateful to those who have joined so graciously and thoughtfully with me in pursuing this discussion which I initiated nearly a year ago. The ensuing experience of admittedly remote dialogue has been often rich and sustaining. It is the common hope of all of us who have thought and spoken in these pages that our words might cast some light and clarity, rather than further darkness and confusion, upon the experience of our common, troubled lives. The very most we might say in retrospect and in looking before us is that:

> We have not overcome our condition, and yet we know it better. We know that we live in contradiction, and do what is needed to reduce it. Our task as men is to find the few principles that will calm the infinite anguish of free souls. We must mend what has been torn apart, make justice imaginable again in a world so obviously unjust, give happiness a meaning once more to peoples poisoned by the misery of the century. Naturally, it is a superhuman task. But superhuman is the term for tasks men take a long time to accomplish, that's all.[3]

Notes

1. Niccolo Machiavelli, *The Prince,* trans., A. Robert Caponigri (Chicago: Regnery, 1963), p. 24.
2. Albert Camus, *Notebooks 1942-1951,* trans., Justin O'Brien (New York: Knopf, 1965), p. 119.
3. Albert Camus, "The Almond Trees," in *Lyrical and Critical Essays,* ed., Philip Thody, trans., Ellen Conroy Kennedy (New York: Knopf, 1968), p. 135.

I

For as Long as it Takes

Allard K. Lowenstein

Perhaps the first thing that might be said is that all the problems that have borne down on us for so long as a people now are at some turning. When we consider the lawlessness and violence on our campuses and in our streets over the past several years, I think that it is important to clarify the sequence of that lawlessness which the President and Vice-president have seen fit to condemn. While I imagine that I have condemned lawlessness as much as any person, I think it's important to remember that, in fact, what has produced the kind of atmosphere in the United States that can turn young people against their government in such bitterness that they would march on other young people wearing its uniform, which has become a sadly common affair, is not something planted from some alien place. It's not conspired into or organized by "kooks." Rather, it's something done to our people, to our young people especially, by our government. And that's an atrocious fact, which our government ought to recognize and remember. It isn't something that could have been done by anyone but our government. Because our kids, our people, grow up loving this country, caring about it as much as any generation ever has, and more than most; and they find themselves in a situation where all the things that they love, and all the things which they are told are true, seem not to be true. And so, their tremendous sense of gratitude for being American, and their fidelity to the traditions and heritage of this country, are precisely what lead to hostility, resentment, and frustration and, finally, to outbursts of protest and, occasionally, even of violence, which then produce a wave of repression and even of killings, which are then justified as necessary and appropriate responses to arbitrary violence. And that's the sequence.

It wasn't random children gone crazy under foreign sedition that ran up against guns at Kent State and Jackson State. They were not lunatics who were poisoned by money to turn against their own people. Those young men and women, whose disillusionment and depression resound all over this country, in every university and most schools, are the most dedicated, the most concerned, the most generous, the most hopeful of our own future generation, who have somehow, in the period since 1963, been made to feel so sour about what their government does and says that they are now in a condition that leads to the kind of events that have marked the past few years and have scarred the memory of our people with such moments as Kent State and Jackson State.

Now all of this needs to be understood by the President and the Vice-president, because if they don't understand it, and if all they think that they need do is to pin libellous labels on people they don't care for, people who don't agree with them, then they are, in fact, going to wreak extraordinary havoc on this country. They are virtually going to lose for us our sons and our daughters. They are going to refuse their loyalty, their love of country, their spirit, and their generosity. They are going to turn these into something embittered and negative; they are going to make of our people a country that cannot stand. Because a house divided in that fashion cannot stand.

There was a quote from Vietnam some time ago, after the

events at My Lai; a colonel was asked about the complaints of some of the draftees about those events. What he said was: "The young are idealistic; and they don't like man's inhumanity to man. But as they get older, they will become wiser and more tolerant." I suppose that if one could summarize the horror-show of the last few years in one paragraph, it would be that.

The side of the ledger that we don't talk about enough, the fact that we don't face clearly enough, is the extraordinary, altogether tangible fact that the feeling of frustration with this country's policies and its failures is now not limited to the groups usually cataloged "young" and "poor" and "black." That frustration reaches now throughout the country; if we regroup and take it on ourselves to explain why things are as bad as they are to all the other people who know they are as bad as they are and who are being misled into thinking that they are this bad because of something that has to do not with the way the country is led, but with the way the protesters complain about the way the country is led, then we can, with rather extraordinary dispatch, I think, change the direction of this country.

On every one of these questions, the war, poverty, racism, pollution, on the questions that afflict the American people, we happen to be standing for what is right, we happen to be standing for the interests not just of the minorities, not just of the young, but for the interests of the American people. That's the fact. We ought to stop pretending it's not the fact; we ought to stop acting as if we have to hoodwink them. It's the Nixon administration that has the problem of hoodwinking the American people. And it was the Johnson administration that had to hoodwink them. And it was the American people who said "no" to the Johnson administration, when they realized that they were being hoodwinked. And why in the world is it necessary now for all of us to act as if somehow we're all licked? Why is it necessary to pretend that somehow or other the hope has gone out of the change we sought to make in 1968 and came just up to the point of making? It is nonsense. We need only get the facts to people about the situation. They are not boobs.

Put the facts about the situation into the information booth in every state, and we'll discover how quickly people will come back to where they were in 1968 when they were turning against those who misled them and were trying to find leadership that would in fact end wars and right our serious wrongs. So I hope that in understanding what the facts are and instead of just talking to each other all of the time, escalating our own miseries and frustrations, we will remember just exactly what power is represented by people, ordinary people like ourselves, who did so remarkable a job in 1968. I hope that we don't go on with the self-pity that I hear from every side that says "We've been trying to change the system for years and nothing works" as if we've been storming the Bastille with bare fists. It was three months in 1968; it began in New Hampshire with McCarthy in March and ended in Los Angeles on June fifth. That was what we did then. There were three months of effort, which was not extreme, either. And yet there followed a most profound change in the attitudes of this country, there followed for the first time the possibility of reuniting our people in a program that would make sense. All this was taken away by bullets.

And that's part of the story. For it's obvious that the problem we face now, in near despair, is not because we failed then, but because we succeeded and yet nothing changed. And that's where this terrible gap comes. It was Hannah Arendt who once said that what drives people from being *engagé* to *enragé* is the sense that words have lost their meaning and that nothing one does is consummated, because there is always some way in which it can be distorted. It's that sense, I think, of distortion that interrupts the achievement and makes it all so sour.

It's honest to say that we don't know whether, if the right leaders had come along and not been taken away when we needed them most, we could have salvaged the country. What would have happened in the United States in 1933 if Franklin Roosevelt had been assassinated and we would have had to cope with the depression and John Garner at the same time? I don't know; thank God we never had to find out. But it surely isn't clear or certain that we can't succeed, because, in fact, a measure of success was nearly had a few seemingly long years ago. In a very, very clear way this country turned. And it's my judgment that if we get back into this with the effort that we're capable of making, with the facts that are on our side, we can effect a similar turn again. Are we such summer soldiers that whenever it looks like something will change only slowly and with great difficulty, we immediately opt out of trying to change it at all and leave the state to the things we see happening when we quit? I just don't believe that. There's too much at stake in this whole test, this whole turning that we're at, to allow such a response.

In conclusion, I wish to quote two things. The first is from John Gardner who made a very remarkable speech some time ago in which he said:

> As we enter the 1970s, there are many curious aspects of our situation, but none more strange than our state of mind. We are anxious but immobilized. We know what our problems are, but we seem incapable of summoning our will and our resources to act. We see the murderous threat of nuclear war. We know our lakes are dying, our rivers growing filthier. And we have racial tensions that can tear the nation apart. We understand that oppressive poverty in the midst of affluence is intolerable. We see that our cities are sliding towards disaster. But these are not problems that stop at our borders; problems of nuclear war, or population, or environment are impending planetary disasters. We are in trouble as a species. But we are seized by a kind of paralysis of the will that becomes a waking nightmare. . . . Systemic inertia is characteristic of every human institution and is overwhelmingly true of

this nation as a whole. Our system of checks and balances dilutes the thrust of positive action. Competition of interests inherent in our pluralism acts as a brake and the system grinds to a halt. Madison designed it in such a way that it simply won't move without vigorous leadership.

That's democracy and not a cult of personality. It says that individuals matter and that great individuals can inspire other individuals to do things they might not otherwise do, so that cumulatively individuals can make a difference. That's what the history of this country has shown. And that is, of course, what we know in our hearts is not now happening.

These next words were spoken several years ago in Indiana by Robert F. Kennedy on the day that Martin Luther King was killed. We recall them now with the very haunting sense that everything said then is so much more true now than it seemed to be then.

> Some Americans who preach nonviolence abroad fail to practice it at home. Some who accuse others of inciting riots, by their own conduct invite them. And some look for scapegoats, some for conspiracies; but this much is clear, violence breeds violence, repression wins retaliation. And only a cleansing of our whole society can remove this sickness from our soul. But there is another kind of violence, slow but just as deadly, destructive as the shot or the bomb in the night. This is the violence of institutions, indifference, inaction, and slow decay. This is the violence that afflicts the poor and poisons relations between men because their skin is different colors. This is the slow destruction of the child by hunger in schools without books and in homes without heat in the winter. So that really we are asked to look at our brothers as aliens, men with whom we share a city but not a community, men bound to us in common dwelling but not in common effort, men who learn to share only a common fear, only a common impulse to meet disagreement with

force. What we need in the United States is not division or hatred or violence, but love and wisdom and compassion toward one another, and a feeling of justice toward those who still suffer within our country, whether they be white or whether they be black. My favorite poet was Aeschylus who wrote: "In our sleep, pain, which we cannot forget, falls drop by drop upon the heart until, in our own despair and against our will, comes wisdom through the awful grace of God." So let us dedicate ourselves to what the Greeks wrote so many years ago, to tame the savageness of man and to make gentle the life of this world. Let us dedicate ourselves to that and say a prayer for our country, for our people.

The President, I think, would do well to note that we who oppose his policies are not bums but men, that we are not cops but neither are we cop-outs, that we are alien neither to this land nor to its Constitution. We are, on the contrary, the heart of this land and the pillars of its Constitution. We are a vital part of the broad, intelligent mind and powerful pulse beat, with reason and compassion, which courses all the way back through our history from a hundred far-off shores and through two hundred extraordinary years. We are Washington, Jefferson, and Madison, the Adamses, Robert E. Lee, Lincoln, and Whitman, Holmes and Audubon, La Guardia and Einstein. We are Woodrow Wilson, Norman Thomas, and Wendall Wilkie, Franklin and Eleanor Roosevelt, and, yes, Dwight Eisenhower. We are John F. Kennedy, and we are Martin Luther King; and we are Robert F. Kennedy. We are Ethel Kennedy and Charles Evers; we are Shirley Chisholm, David Harris, and Caesar Chavez. We are grieved, and we are wounded. We are alive and we are tough; and we have just begun to fight. We are in the Valley Forge of the American spirit; but we have been to Valley Forge before, because America has been to Valley Forge before, and we are part of what is best in America. We are going to survive these perversions of America during the past years to become one nation, indivisible, with liberty and justice for all, one nation where we can eat grapes and sing joyous songs and be able at last to love justice and still love our own country. We are the majority; and we shall no longer be silent. We shall march henceforth not to taps but to reveille. And soon our country shall march not to war but to stop war. We are in the battle to reclaim this country that we love so very dearly. And we are in the battle for as long as it takes to reclaim it. We speak both for our children and to them when we say that we shall prevail.

Accounting for a Political Generation

Elinor B. Bachrach

Ask not what your country can do for you; ask what you
can do for your country.   JOHN F. KENNEDY

This was the rallying cry for a whole generation of young people,
myself among them. The torch had been passed to us, we knew,
and we were eager to take it up. Politics was exhilarating and
fascinating, and public service an honor and a challenge not to
be passed over lightly. And yet within a few years our generation was to become hopelessly split and confused, and by the
end of the decade our reflections on political life—whatever our
ideological stripe—tended to be cynical and bitter.

When I speak of a generation here, I am referring to a
political generation. The concept of a political generation is certainly overworked and may be questionable in itself. Quite
possibly every person finds that the tide of history flowing by him
coincides neatly with the currents of his own life. Nonetheless,
I think that the concept has some validity, especially so long as
one recognizes that political generations are very short, perhaps
no more than five to ten years. Furthermore, I believe that my
political generation, more than any other, embodies the dilemmas
of present-day political life. The conception of politics with
which we grew up was vastly elevated during the Kennedy era,
and then foundered on the rocks of Vietnam. We rode both the
crest and the trough. The preceding generation was largely co-

opted into the system before it was seriously questioned; the succeeding one has felt free to reject the system. My generation was intensely attracted to political life and then progressively alienated from it in the course of just a few years, in the first stage of political maturity. Both the approach and the avoidance remain strong forces in our lives. Thus, I think that an examination of the experiences of my political generation and an analysis of some of the forces operating within them, provide a good vehicle for considering the condition of current American politics.

To be more specific, the generation I am talking about was born during or immediately after World War II but remembers none of it, went to high school in the latter part of the 1950s, and attended college in the early 60s. Basically I am talking about an elite group within that generation—those who went to college, and often to graduate school as well, since that was, after all, the thing to do. Although we would never have put it that way, we fancied ourselves the ruling class; indeed, we had every reason for thinking so. Education was, after all, the great opportunity in American society, and we were all getting the best of educations at our various colleges.

Eisenhower Administration: Childhood

We were small children during the Joseph McCarthy era; probably the first and largest amount of television violence we were exposed to at that tender age was the Army-McCarthy hearings. We went to school at the height of the Cold War. Nuclear war was explained to us as a distinct possibility; we learned pathetically to "duck and cover" under our desks should an atomic bomb chance to drop on us. We were taught to think in terms of good and evil; only much later did we realize how deeply that lesson had been absorbed. Grandfather Eisenhower, our President, was good; Communism was bad. If you got mad at a kid you were playing with you called him a dirty Communist. Somehow in memory the Eisenhower era seems to go well with childhood. It flowed along comfortably and securely, except for some brief flurries when the President was sick and you were told that someone awful named Richard Nixon might become President in his stead. And even if you were from a Stevenson family, as many of us were, and if you were sternly told not to "like Ike" too much, it really was difficult to imagine anyone else being President. For the most part, politics was happily "out there," and you could just let it drift past you.

Then came the 1960 election and its preliminaries, when we were at the end of our high school years or just beginning college. All of a sudden politics was all around us, and it was exciting and interesting. We were caught up in it, or so it seemed at the time. We certainly were activists compared to our predecessors, who were becoming known as the "apathetic fifties" generation. Most of us did nothing more than follow the course of the campaign, watch the conventions and the debates, argue the relative merits of Nixon and Kennedy. But we felt involved, and somehow we felt it was all for our benefit when Kennedy won.

Kennedy Administration: College Years

And so our hero became President, or the President became our hero. It's hard to say which; the latter may be nearer the truth. He was our hero in part because he was like us, so we fondly hoped. He was clean cut, well educated, Ivy League, and he surrounded himself with people like himself—or maybe like us, as we hoped one day to be. Because certainly it seemed that there could be nothing better than to be associated with a Presidential administration, particularly one which combined power and style.

For me and a number of others he was especially a hero. We were the ones who trooped off to jobs in Washington at that time, all of us budding Senators or Cabinet members or diplomats. The power and the glory were all around us, so we could almost grab it ourselves. Even more, there was idealism. Great things were going to happen, great wrongs righted; and we would witness it, and perhaps in the near future even contribute to it. Of course we knew enough to be cynical about Congress— a bunch of obstructionist old men running things, conservative Southerners most of them. But a few reforms could take care of that.

The time was the summer of 1963, the summer before the fall of everything. Civil rights was the big thing. George Wallace stood in the schoolhouse door, Medgar Evers was killed, and President Kennedy gave an inspiring speech and submitted legislation to insure that injustice and inequality would no more hold sway. We were going to raise up the blacks, by God, and incidentally reform the South. The March on Washington in August 1963, for which we considered ourselves lucky to be present, seemed to show that black and white together would indeed overcome.

Civil rights . . . that was the start of it all. Not that it was a new idea, but at that point it really caught fire, although then only figuratively. Its implications were enormous, much greater than we realized at the time. Black and white were equal, we knew that. But if black and white, then why not poor and rich, young and old, even female and male. And ultimately if it were wrong for whites to kill blacks in the South, was it really right for them to kill browns in South Vietnam?

No one talks about civil rights any more. Nor do today's young white college students rush down South to register black voters and tutor black students, as we did. Now they do their marching in the cities of the North. What we did then smacks of paternalism. But it was a beginning, at least for us. And the idea was dynamite. Civil rights was equal rights was everyone's rights, and that started us all thinking, and kept us doing so.

Then our whole world was shattered. November 1963, and our hero was assassinated. The one constant factor, the pole around which the political turmoil revolved, was gone. It seemed that the world had gone dark.

In the shock of President Kennedy's death we also forgot the earlier assassination, that of Ngo Dinh Diem. He was, after all, an unpleasant character, and Vietnam was a long way away.

Johnson Administration I: Vietnam

So Lyndon B. Johnson became President. We really couldn't bear it, although we decided to put up with it. He talked so corny, and he was a Southerner, and really he had no class. However, we had to admit that we were lucky, that there could have been a considerably worse V-P. We defended him quite fiercely in the Presidential election the next year against the amiable but war-mongering Barry Goldwater.

In the summer of 1964 I went again to Washington, this time to work at the Agency for International Development in the State Department. I had become fired with concern for the problems of underdeveloped countries and wanted to consider seriously a career with A.I.D. There I met many other students, all of us wanting to bring enlightenment and gain to less fortunate areas of the world—and also quite sincerely not wanting to be paternalistic, much less imperialistic.

A number of things happened that summer. The Civil Rights Act of 1964 was finally passed, although too late to really be considered a "memorial" to John F. Kennedy. It outlawed discrimination of various sorts, including discrimination in employment on the basis of race, color, creed, national origin, or even sex.

That summer, too, I was made more aware than ever before of how handicapped I was in seeking a career. Forget about the Foreign Service, State Department people advised me. After all, I'd want to get married, wouldn't I, and then I would lose my job. Well . . . no, said the A.I.D. official addressing the whole group of summer employees (including some carefully selected blacks), our overseas career programs are not really open to women, but we'd love to have you as a secretary—you might work your way up.

Finally, that was the first summer in which the problem of Vietnam was really tangible and hung over all of us. The situation was so confusing, the rights and wrongs so difficult to pin down, the guerrilla warfare situation so unaccustomed and perplexing. Then came the Tonkin Bay crisis and the Tonkin Bay resolution. Most of us were rather relieved at the time, however disquieting the whole thing was. The circumstances seemed clearer and at least we were doing something—satisfying the American need for action. Surely North Vietnam would back down soon, and a solution would be found.

Most of us, I think, accepted the Vietnam war in the early stages, although not without some ambivalence. It is this which demarcates us so clearly from the succeeding generation. There was much in our backgrounds which pushed us to do so. Although we had learned to disparage rigid Cold War attitudes, we nonetheless had a basic distaste for Communism and the loss of human freedom it seemed to entail. Even more, we were brought up with a certain faith in the basic morality of American foreign policy and particularly in the justness of the wars which America chose to fight. True, the Korean War was the most recent and also the most dubious, but we really had no firsthand recollection of it, and our parents' most vivid memories—passed on to us—were of World War II. Their views of war were colored by images of Munich and Hitler and the "final solution"; they were caught up in the idea that the U.S. had to take a stand against totalitarianism, fascist or Communist. These were the ideas passed on to us, and reiterated by political leaders. Given our background and a certain amount of trust, it was hard for us to break away.

But break away we did, bit by bit, at our own rates of progress. For me it happened in the first year after Lyndon Johnson's re-election, but gradually and piecemeal. Most of us had talked ourselves into supporting Johnson's candidacy whole-heartedly, despite our gut feelings, on the grounds that he would not widen the war in Vietnam and would pursue enlightened domestic policies for the betterment of all—and also because Barry Goldwater was so frightening. However, in those first few months of the second term it became apparent that Johnson was not winding down the war, but was in fact escalating it. The first real breaking point for me came in April 1965, when President Johnson announced that he was increasing troop commitments and bombings in Vietnam and also proposed a billion-dollar development plan for Southeast Asia. This combining of an actuality of increased U.S. military intervention with the sweet promise of economic aid, the hypocrisy of saying you want only to help underdeveloped countries to be better off when in fact you are expending boundless resources essentially to destroy one such country, was to me wholly unacceptable.

European Interlude

After graduating from college in June 1965, I went abroad for what became ultimately a period of two years. In doing this I was not unlike the rest of my generation, many of whom went into the Peace Corps, or, like me, went off to Europe to do various things. And some, of course, went abroad in the armed services. I felt a real need to go away for a while and try to get some perspective on American society and American political problems, such as Vietnam. Probably it was something of an escape as well. For example, I no longer had to confront the Vietnam war on the front page of every newspaper; it was tucked away on the inside pages instead.

One thing one couldn't escape was being an American. In a way I became an American then for the first time. Before then I had been a New Englander, a college student, a member of various small categories; now I was forced to be the composite American. Everywhere one was confronted with questions and criticisms of American society and politics—materialism, racism, Vietnam. Sometimes people defended what America was doing, saying for instance that it was definitely a good thing that she was taking a stand against Communism in Vietnam; and those statements could be more upsetting than the blanket and often rather mindless condemnations.

Thus I found I had to talk and reflect more about the U.S. than I ever had before, and at a time when I was more confused about what was happening and what I really believed than ever before. The tendency is, I think, to defend one's country more vehemently abroad than at home. You feel more isolated in a foreign context, and somewhat ganged-up on; attacks on your country seem more like personal attacks as well. Furthermore, people often try to provoke, by making their criticisms as extreme as possible. So I found myself instinctively trying to counter their arguments, while at the same time beginning to agree with some of them more and more.

I traveled extensively in Eastern as well as Western Europe, reflecting and talking about the similarities and differences of the societies. I lived for a while in Paris, where I read about the first bombing raids into North Vietnam; then I worked for some time in London, and heard there about the race riots in Detroit and Newark and the commitment of half a million American troops to the Vietnam war effort. My parents sent news that one person from my home town had been killed in Vietnam—a boy from one of the two black families in the town.

By this time I had decided definitely to reject the idea of a career in government work; in fact I rejected politics as well. For a time I seriously considered rejecting the U.S. completely and staying in Europe, but I decided ultimately that that was not tenable. What then could I do? Like many of my generation I decided to return to the private world of the university.

Johnson Administration II: Graduate School, Chicago, the 1968 Elections

I returned to the U.S. rather alienated and dispirited, only to find that many of those who had stayed in the country had become even more so. Furthermore, there was a new radicalism underway, which had only barely begun before I left, with the establishment of the Students for a Democratic Society. While I had been turned off the idea of working for the government, they had rejected the whole system—the economy and society as well as the polity. To many people younger than I, undergraduates in particular, the government and the military as well as the Vietnam war were so obviously corrupt that they could not conceive of anyone's ever supporting them. The feelings we had in the Kennedy era would have been to them incomprehensible, I think. Thus I, and many other "liberals" of my young age, came to feel suddenly old and tainted. Yet in another sense I felt more innocent than they. It was on the South Side of Chicago, at the University, in a carefully maintained white community surrounded by the black ghetto, that I first really learned something about racial deprivation, police brutality, and political corruption.

Chicago was where it all converged—the race problem, the Vietnam war, the election campaign, the malaise of American political life. Even closer to home were the radical student move-

ments, sit-ins and marches, and a fundamental questioning of
the values of academic life and the mission of the university.

Eugene McCarthy announced his candidacy for President
on a peace platform in Chicago in December 1967. Many of us
went down to the Hilton Hotel and heard his speech, standing
either in the ballroom—or most of us—in the basement under
the ballroom; and we felt a new optimism, despite our cynical
inclinations. At least the attempt was being made, a battle was
being launched on the home front to oppose President Johnson's
war in Vietnam. Thus began the endless and painful campaign
year of 1968.

By March and April the campaign had come our way
again, with the Presidential primaries in Wisconsin and Indiana
and the amazing progress of the McCarthy candidacy. Many of
us from Chicago participated actively in the campaigns in the
two states, with even some of the most radical types cutting their
hair and going "clean for Gene." Johnson's bowing out of the
race was a stunning triumph, even though his proxy, Hubert H.
Humphrey, did declare his candidacy fairly soon thereafter.
Robert F. Kennedy's tardy entrance into the fray caused some
ambivalence, and divided the ranks of campaign volunteers, but
on the whole it was another welcome sign of change. His candidacy inevitably brought back memories of the past and some
of the subsequent disillusionment too.

April also brought the assassination of Martin Luther King,
and Chicago became a city of fear and flame. Rioting and
destruction occurred in the black ghetto areas, especially on the
West Side, and no one knew how far it all would spread.
Ironically but predictably, while the white population trembled,
it was the black ghetto dwellers who suffered all of the pain and
violence and destruction. Chicago took on the air of an occupied
city. Troops marched through nearby streets in my area, army
vehicles moved down the boulevards, and every highway bridge
held National Guardsmen with ready guns. Police cars were

everywhere. Mayor Daley surveyed the scene from a helicopter and issued his "shoot to kill" order. But then in a few days it all dissipated, leaving behind only shells—of burned-out buildings, of still-smoldering bitterness.

Later in April a peace march through downtown Chicago turned out to be a misnomer for the people involved. Chicago policemen pushed the marchers around, clubbed them on their heads and elsewhere (one friend got his hand broken—from holding it up to shield his head), arrested them indiscriminately, and packed them off to jail, all the while taking care to remove their own badges so that they could not be identified. It was said that the police were acting under orders from Mayor Daley and that they were practicing for the Democratic Convention, scheduled to take place in Chicago in late August.

Then in early June the unthinkable happened, the awful repetition. Robert F. Kennedy was shot. "Robert Kennedy's death has broken our politics," wrote a commentator at the time, expressing perfectly what all of us felt. To have dreamt the dream of the Kennedy era and then seen it crumble, and now to re-enact the same terrible denouement with another Kennedy, who—by extraction and by his own force of personality—revived the feel of the dream, that was unbearable. Yet another assassination, in an America still reeling from the first two.

Into the summer the campaigns limped. Eugene McCarthy and George McGovern, the latter standing in for Kennedy, saw hard-won primary votes snatched away by entrenched local forces. The pathetic aura of Nelson Rockefeller's late and costly drive for the Republican nomination only reinforced the inevitability of Richard Nixon. This was confirmed in Miami in July. Politics was mired in apathy and idiocy, and many of us had little spirit left for the fight. Meanwhile, preparations for the Democratic Convention proceeded.

In Chicago in late August all the groups collided. Within the Amphitheater the forces of McCarthy/McGovern were overwhelmed by the established ranks of Humphrey supporters, even unto the Vietnam plank in the platform. But very few of us were on the inside. Many more were outside, in the street, in front of the same Hilton Hotel where the McCarthy movement started. From all over the country they came—New Left radicals, pacifists, despairing liberals, Yippies. They carried out their acts of protest, some dignified and some less so, and they were clubbed and gassed and seized by the Chicago police, in a shocking demonstration of extralegal brutality. Welcome to Chicago— Richard J. Daley, Mayor—the signs read.

That it should come to this—Richard M. Nixon and Hubert H. Humphrey. After all the turmoil and the shouting, here we were, presented with two white Anglo-Saxon males, of middle age and middle class and middle-of-the-road party lines, distinguished only by the elephant and the donkey, two vice-presidents from discredited administrations whose policies we had repudiated. Despair, fatalism, estrangement, exclusion— these were what we felt.

Richard Nixon's victory was sad but expected. Most of us were so weary of the election and of politics that only the closeness of the vote kept us at our television sets on election night. By and large we voted for Humphrey, by default, although some refused to compromise and went for Socialist-Labor or the Peace and Freedom party. That over with, trying to hide from ourselves that we were in for at least four years of Nixon, we turned inward and tried to avoid talking or thinking about politics.

Nixon Administration: Retreat, Radicalism, Reconsideration

National political life, then, seemed barren. At the same time, however, the politics of university life attained national prominence. Student protests on campuses across the country focused on curriculum, admissions policies, hiring practices, discipline, the entire power structure of faculty and administration. Also under attack were universities' investment portfolios, their involvements in government-sponsored research, their relationships with the communities surrounding the campuses, their treatment of minority groups on their own campuses. Student demands, student sit-ins, student strikes became part of the texture of university life in the late 1960s, providing yet another dimension to the growth in political consciousness and social activism.

In early 1969 there was a long student sit-in and strike at my own university which polarized the campus and created great bitterness. The immediate cause was the firing of a sociology teacher who was both a radical and a woman. Many students claimed that her dismissal was rooted illegitimately in her sex and her political radicalism. Among the complex facets of this controversy, one of the most important for me, and many like me, was the sharpening of the issue of women's liberation. I had personally encountered discrimination, particularly on the job market. The main benefit which the women's liberation movement offered was that it raised these problems from the realm of the personal to the realm of the political and revealed the pervasive patterns of discrimination running through the society. Once that consciousness is there, then one's whole manner of perceiving and acting in society is changed.

Autumn 1969, and the ghosts of the Convention and the sit-in reappeared in Chicago. Radicalism reached its most blindly destructive and self-destructive point as the Weatherman faction of the SDS, many of the University of Chicago exiles and some from my generation, went rampaging through the streets of the plush Near North Side, hitting out at windows and policemen and inspiring only bewilderment and rage among the general population.

At that same time in Chicago there began the trial of the

"Conspiracy 8," as the leaders of the Convention demonstrations were called—until Black Panther Bobby Seale was "purged" and they became the "Conspiracy 7." They were charged with violating the newly framed federal law against crossing state lines to incite a riot. The trial was a farce from beginning to end, all four months of it, and a travesty of American justice. On the one hand, it showed the total paranoia of the U.S. Government toward radical protest movements and indicated that its response was solely to condemn and repress, not in any way to heed, the criticisms. On the other hand, the antics of the defendants in the courtroom, while amusing and symbolically effective, were disturbing in their implications of institutional decay throughout the system, even to the courts of justice. Judge Julius Hoffman's obvious bias against the defendants, carried to the point of malevolence, did nothing to reassert confidence in the system. In the end, they locked up the defendants and cut off their hair and sold it at auction at a Republican party dinner, but they silenced neither those particular leaders nor the movement itself.

In late April 1970, President Nixon announced that U.S. and Vietnamese troops had invaded Cambodia. The rationale was an appalling one—that extending the conflict to another country would hasten our withdrawal from the Vietnam war. Hostility toward Nixon and his government reached an all-time high and continued to mount. Protests broke out at universities all over the country, and when the smoke had cleared from the National Guardsmen's guns, four young students at Kent State lay dead. Jackson State accounted for two more dead. Student strikes were called and protests broke out within all segments of the population. To me, recovering from illness and taking my doctoral examinations, the whole situation had an air of feverish unreality, and possibly that perception was quite accurate. Feelings of urgency and need for action ran high; it was invigorating, but also saddening, because one knew that the momentum could not be sustained. One salutary effect of the protests at the University of Chicago was to reunite students and faculty, who were pretty much unanimous in opposition to the Nixon move. Established professors could deplore the actions of the Administration, while radical students could applaud reactions in Congress and the Cooper-Church amendment.

Despite the excitement of the Cambodia crisis, however, I was becoming weary of university life, and estranged from it. It was all so small and self-centered and divorced from the outside world. The question then nagged at the back of one's mind : what jobs would be available to us, with the best of academic training but no real job experience.

At the same time, I had to admit that I was no longer interested in student politics. I had never really been a part of the student movement. Whereas I could accept some of the radical criticisms of American politics and society and indeed felt that there was much that was wrong and needed changing, I very often could not accept the radical tactics or their general and ill-defined conclusion that we had to tear it all down and build anew, or for that matter the unfounded arrogance with which they presented these conclusions. Revolutions, I felt, were drastic remedies, with incalculable and often harmful side effects. Systems are too valuable and too difficult to build up just to dispense with them if they are in trouble; it seems better to me to tinker with them than to overthrow them. In the end, one's position is a matter of personal taste and conviction about how far the system has decayed and how salvageable it is. My temperament and training were such that I balked at rigid and extreme positions on any issue, up to and including giving up on the American political system as hopelessly compromised and corrupt. If I were to work for change, it would have to be within the system, not out in the streets or in the cellars. Many of my generation have, I think, come to similar conclusions : after considering alternatives, they have decided to work within the system, however distasteful elements of that system may seem at times.

After much soul-searching, I decided to leave the university for a while. I wanted to get a job, to gain some work experience and give some structure to my life, and also hopefully to overcome some of the societal and psychological barriers that being a woman presented to professional achievement. The logical place for a political scientist to look for a job was Washington, the city which was so important to me in my college years. Coming back into the world of organized politics was rather a shock to me, after having spent so many years in an atmosphere of academic radicalism. Then again, I started work during the Mayday demonstrations and was thereby reassured that bureaucratic placidity could and would be occasionally disturbed.

I was fortunate in my search and found an interesting and stimulating job working as a legislative assistant to a Maine Congressman, doing research and writing position papers and analyses of legislation. So I can now combine my political inclinations with some of my academic skills. Perhaps I've sold out, but it's basically on my own terms. And at least this way I may get a chance to take part in the decision-making process, rather than only being its victim.

Conclusions

A number of thoughts come to me in surveying these recollections of politics in recent times. The most personal one is that I have learned not to try to make final judgments anymore, either about the viability or decay of American politics or about the course of my own life. Rather I intend to adjust my actions to my perceptions as I go along, while maintaining a strong and expanding set of basic values. At present I am working actively in the political system, but I may at some point return to academic life. The tension between academic life and political concerns will always exist in me, as it does in many persons I have known, but I think that potentially it can be a creative force.

A more general impression is that of the recurring tendency in American politics to see things in terms of good and evil, black and white, with no shades of gray. My political generation recognized this tendency and deplored it in examining such things as American attitudes toward Communism. And yet we have been guilty of the same fault in analyzing the politics of our own time. Kennedy was good; Johnson and Nixon are evil. This is the impression given, despite the strengths and shortcomings of all three Administrations. Vietnam was made into the absolute evil of our time, whereas in fact it might better be seen as the greatest misapprehension and misfortune. It demonstrates the dangers of simplistic and inflexible attitudes applied to complex and changing situations and of confusion over principles and priorities. We would do well to recognize that there are numerous shades of gray, that situations change over time and so do we, and that constant reassessments and readjustments of policy are essential to the good operation of political life.

In addition, I think we have a tendency to search for heroes, for great men to lead our country and single-handedly solve our nation's problems. And if we can't have heroes, then we will turn around and have villains, around whom we can unite in opposition. John F. Kennedy was our hero, and filled that role to our satisfaction—almost irrespective of his actual accomplishments. After he died, we did two things. First, we had to build him up as a great myth, and then ultimately we had— almost as senselessly—to tear the myth down. Both of these were costly and needless exercises. We tried to make Lyndon Johnson into a hero to fill the gap left by John Kennedy's death, and then when he disappointed us, we turned on him mercilessly and made him a villain. Richard Nixon we considered a villain from the start, even though he is really far too mediocre to suit the role.

Now we face another Presidential election, and again we are looking for a hero. We are afraid we may not find one, at least not one who will last; so we conclude that something is desperately wrong with a political system that is not producing heroes. Perhaps we should instead question our wanting one. In a time of conflicting group interests and changing priorities, possibly we could better use a compromiser, an honest broker rather than a charismatic leader. It might be more beneficial to try to strengthen and make more representative of popular interests other centers of power, such as the Congress, rather than look to a single man to solve everything, which is a basically undemocratic solution.

Finally, I would like to take issue with any contention that Americans are retreating into private life and abandoning through despair a commitment to political life. If we expand our notion of political participation to include actions outside of established channels of political parties and government, I think we will find that participation is running at a high level in the U.S. today. There is a wide range of issues which have engaged people's attention and active concern on a broad scale—issues such as the environment, consumer protection, the Vietnam war, and the arms race. In addition, we should take into account the expanding political consciousness and activism of different groups within the society, groups which heretofore have been largely voiceless and powerless—poor people, blacks, women, students. This expansion of the vocal electorate may be the most significant development in recent American politics. Some of these groups act mainly outside and even against the established system, but it can be said that they are also, indirectly if not directly, influencing the system in certain ways and thus having an impact on our political life. Furthermore, much of this activity is beginning to feed back into the channels of regular political life. The Black Caucus in Congress is an example of this; so is the establishment of the Women's Political Caucus in anticipation of the 1972 elections. Thus, perhaps one can see a certain cyclical tendency in the development of the political movements of the 1960s as well as in the lives of the political generation which came to maturity during that time.

My generation now covers a wide political spectrum. You could say that it runs from Bernardine Dohrn and Angela Davis to Barry Goldwater, Jr., and even Lt. William Calley. Doubtless every political generation includes members of every ideological strand. What I do think is more peculiar to my generation is that we participated in and in many cases directed the first real revival of left-wing politics in the U.S. in several decades. The preceding generations concentrated on the Cold War and affluence and more generally on maintaining the status quo of the post-World War II period. The current youth generation is left-wing, on the whole, but they inherited their radicalism and a ready-made critique of American politics. My generation spanned the gap. We lived through a gradual and painful disillusionment with American politics after a rather complacent upbringing and an optimistic early adulthood in the brief Kennedy period. We launched the movements and worked out the ideologies. Some of us went off to the New Left, to head the great radical movements of the 1960s and to try to change the system, or even to blow it up. Others of us hovered on the fringe of regular politics, working in the peace movement and opposing President Johnson, but nonetheless ready to work in the regular political campaign process for a candidate who represented our beliefs. Most of us were involved as well in one or more of the great social group movements that grew up in our early adulthood : civil rights or black power, the poor people's campaign or the student sit-ins, or women's liberation.

Ask not what your country can do for you ; ask what you can do for your country.

I think in the end that we did ask and answer that question, although not in the expected way. We started off thinking more or less that we were going to spread the blessings of American democracy at home and abroad and instead found ourselves questioning the foundation and assumptions of our political system. It has been a painful but ultimately a valuable experience, and it has fixed rather than curtailed our engagement in political life, whatever course that commitment may take.

A Dream Gone Rancid

John G. Hessler

Distinguished members of the platform, fellow classmates, parents, faculty, friends:

By way of prologue, I would like to read to you a poem which I wrote perhaps a month ago. I see in it all I could ever bring myself to say of the love, the hate, the hope, the fear, the sadness I feel over Notre Dame. It seems to me in place here. I have called it, "Leaving Notre Dame. A defiance."

> the green shoots of willow bud early
> water from rising streams
> stands in ditches   in fields of coming wheat
> as in the rice paddies of the Yangtze
>
> in ancient China
> men esteemed their men friends best
> they wept at partings
> wrote love poems in place of letters

Originally delivered as Valedictory address, May 22, 1971, University of Notre Dame.

among our people
in this time
in this country it is forbidden
to do either

There is so little I can say, that I can say truthfully. Words
are treacherous things. All over the world, in every country, in
every language, in every time, words have been the instruments
of murder and violence and destruction. Words kill people. Even
as I stand here under this flag, even as I am speaking, people are
dying at the hands of one or another of a whole series of
unspoken lies for which our flag has come to stand. The whole
texture of lies we call our way of life has killed thousands of
people, made life less than worthless to countless more. If the
words which stick in our mouths were only empty that would
not be so bad. But they are tongued with poison; they are lethal.
There was a time, we are told, when this flag stood for a great
dream of union and peace. That dream has long gone rancid.
There has since been the time of the stench of slaughtered
buffalo carried for miles on the wind across the prairie. There are
even now unholier stenches still in more recent fields. It does
not help to weep when they play the national anthem.

I am speaking to you of lies. It has become a commonplace
to shudder at the profound wasteland of modern life. Demented
visions of our waste and loss and loneliness attend us everywhere.
The proliferation of urban concrete uglinesses, the fouling of the
environment have become stock sources of lamentation. Violence
in the streets and campuses of our land is only the same, at last,
as violence in the fields and hamlets of Vietnam. Billions of
dollars have been burned away in heartbreaking games of conquest. Eighty years ago we subdued the final frontiers of our
continent, but we have not ceased to seek new conquests with
which to stuff our hollowness. We have chased our lengthening
shadows across the horizon; we have left our vain footprints on

the lifeless shores of the moon. Even our vast system of super-highways, the triumph of engineering and technology, the pride of congressmen and businessmen and housewives, are only the externalization of our troubled psyche writ large. Like the fibers of our being stretched to an awful pitch, we have strung out roads across the continent and are busy racing up and down them, back and forth to nowhere. There is no more eloquent, no silenter, no sadder witness to the fruitlessness of our lives than the rusted frame, smashed glass, twisted metal of a wrecked automobile—multiplied as this vision is, endlessly, in the junk-yards across the country.

I am speaking to you of lies. In Washington the play-actors of our own ignorance and incompetence gather daily, pathetically intent on maintaining our glorious dream, our way of life. Few eyes remark the gathering darkness, few voices admit our nightmare perpetrations. The very air is heavy with a rhetoric of power, the barrenness of which no one seems to recognize. Yeats might have been speaking of us when, in his poem, "The Second Coming," he said :

> The best lack all conviction, while the worst
> Are full of passionate intensity.

Shall we attribute our commitment to this course of world, national, and personal destruction to blindness, or to depravity? Our leaders are only fools or demagogues or scapegoats.

Unconscious almost of alternatives, we live in a moribund culture. Disgust is our familiar companion. Faced by the disjunction between those lies the culture blares at us, and by what we know even as we know the blood which is dying in our veins, faced by this disjunction, we are seized with fear, seek escape in some absolute ordering action, whatever it may be. Some of us cultivate God, a refuge of ages, a shore against time. Others of us cling to our friends and to the possibilities of human intercourse, finding strength in the touch of their bodies. Still others are forever implementing the Revolution, moral, social, or aesthetic. Some of us find less satisfactory ordering activities even than these. Some withdraw into private drug-fed fantasy worlds. Others commit suicide. Still others of us go mad. There is little wonder really that young people in their disaffection are more inclined simply to drop out than to try to offer any creative solutions of their own. Simple refusal to participate in the placid murderousness of our age is in itself a powerful and constructive action. Some people may call this morbidness; I call it rage for the truth, unwillingness to look at things other than as they are. I cannot and will not cast a rosy haze over the past, nor will I paint rose-colored pictures of the future. To live without hope is perhaps to be a moral coward. But to live by false hope is to be a fool. I ask not for orientations, for compromises with life, for the lies by which we go on living. I ask for vision.

I am speaking to you of lies. It is not sweet and just to die for the fatherland. We have not got to make the world safe for democracy. We have not got insure the self-determination of the peoples of Southeast Asia. We have not got to be murdering mankind in pursuit of crazy illusions. It is not sweet and just to die for anything.

I cannot send you out with the usual blessings and good wishes. I cannot tell you if you go out and make lots of money you'll be happy. I cannot tell you if you give it all away you'll be happy. It is not our lot to be happy. Everything is falling apart. We have killed too much to get where we are. We have come too far and there is no way back. I feel helpless and compromised. I can only hope that somehow, somewhere, you will find some measure of justice and humaneness in your lives. I trust in that, insanely. There is an animal hope beyond hope, and I have that in you. I only wonder, in twenty years, if we live that long, when our children ask us, even as we are asking our parents now, what we were doing while our government was carrying off this carnage, then, when none of the marching and burning and rioting and demonstrating will seem excessive or irresponsible, then, when the world is no better, when they ask us what we did to stop the murder of innocent human beings, when we think of our years at Notre Dame, and of the very little we have had the courage to do, then, when we have come to live by our own set of lies, excuses, extenuations, then, what will we say to them? I wonder, will we ask ourselves ever why we did not stop this goddamned war?

I had thought I might end by singing a song with you, but I haven't the power or the voice left to do that. Instead I am going to read to you a poem. The poem is about lies. It was written over fifty years ago by an Englishman in the trenches of the First World War. His name was Wilfred Owen. Here, then, is his poem:

Bent double, like old beggars under sacks,
Knock-kneed, coughing like hags, we cursed through sludge,
Till on the haunting flares we turned our backs,
And towards our distant rest began to trudge.
Men marched asleep. Many had lost their boots,
But limped on, blood-shod. All went lame, all blind;
Drunk with fatigue; deaf even to the hoots
Of gas-shells dropping softly behind.
Gas! Gas! Quick, boys!—An ecstasy of fumbling,
Fitting the clumsy helmets just in time,
But someone still was yelling out and stumbling
And floundering like a man in fire or lime.—
Dim through the misty panes and thick green light,
As under a green sea, I saw him drowning.
In all my dreams before my helpless sight
He plunges at me, guttering, choking, drowning.
If in some smothering dreams, you too could pace
Behind the wagon that we flung him in,
And watch the white eyes writhing in his face,
His hanging face, like a devil's sick of sin;
If you could hear, at every jolt, the blood
Come gargling from the froth-corrupted lungs,
Bitter as the cud

Of vile, incurable sores on innocent tongues,
My friend, you would not tell with such high zest
To children ardent for some desperate glory,
The old Lie : Dulce et decorum est
Pro patria mori.

In the manuscript that poem is dated August 1917. A little over
a year later Wilfred Owen was killed in those same trenches by
enemy fire. A bare week after that the Armistice was signed.
Wilfred Owen knew the truth. He saw the lie. But the lie was
too strong. And it killed him. The people of England did not
mark much his passing.

II

Slough of Unamiable Liars, Bog of Stupidities

Joseph M. Duffy

Rage is not the best disposition for the conduct of intellectual discourse, but I am not certain the present subject can be effectively intellectualized. That subject, as I understand it, is the relationship of the individual to the political life of this time in America. In what fashion, the question seems to be, can private ideas of order contribute to and be solidified in the public good? What rigors of public good take precedence over private ideas of order? How does the political realm—the nomination and election of officials, the management of government—serve to enforce or block the relationship between public and private concepts of order? What reconciliation of means to ends is possible for a community of men through participation in the political process as we have come to know it in the United States in recent years? Because of the evident dilapidation of this process, the present discussion seems to require not so much intellectualizing as a leap of faith or a collapse into despair. Rage seems as calculated to motivate the one as the other, and it is with rage, therefore, that I try to set down my views during this Presidential election year.

With his usual felicity and accuracy of phrasing, Henry James wrote that to be an American is "a complex fate." What is interesting here is the assumption of the individual's involvement with destiny. Like their country, Americans are especially "fated" to succeed or fail at some purposeful endeavor while others simply are or live or exist. James' phrase suggests a grandiose view of the person and his space before a universe which is more concerned with than indifferent to him. Because of its origins, location, size, and variety, expectations have always been high about this country and its inhabitants. These expectations have been centered around America's claim to innocence and youth, its promise of freedom of movement and thought, and its offer of abundant physical opportunities for new life. Americans have perennially been captivated by their own national mythology, and sometimes they have been imprisoned by it. This often attractive mythology is not, it is true, without a basis in reality, but like all abstracting tendencies it blurs distinctions and erases complexities. The antiquity and corruptibility of the human species, the errancy of reason and the force of passion, the enormity and strangeness of physical space and the frailty and shortness of human life—all suggest a less pristine view of any gathering of men, including Americans.

Nevertheless, this nation's past both refutes any special claim to eminence and election by its inhabitants and also gives sustaining instance of their aspirations towards uniqueness. The meanness and violence of the westward movement and the fratricidal slaughter of the Civil War exist side by side with a quest for Edenic liberty and a compassionate urge towards social brotherhood; the corruption of American politics roils the spring of political idealism; and what James in another place called the imagination of disaster tilts with speculative optimism. Moreover, this country's classical literature reflects the discord of the American experience straining against the national myth: the melancholy, pessimism, and awareness of unbreachable limits in the work of Hawthorne, Melville, Twain, and James challenge the vivacity and expansiveness of Cooper, Emerson, Thoreau, and Whitman. Although the sun was but a morning star to Thoreau at Walden Pond, an eternal confidence man put out the light of experience for the old god and the hapless riverboat passengers in Melville's *The Confidence Man*. Even if a cold eye cast on the universe does not allow for such discrimination, Americans have often felt it to be a complex fate to be what they are; tantalized by a mythology which is a dream of prelapserianism and face to face with an actuality which is no more than the common lot of man. At no time has this division been more apparent and more agonizing than at present when the mythology is most exploited by those most deeply mired in the reality. Richard Nixon, appearing on television to justify the Cambodian invasion with an American flag shining in his lapel, epitomizes the manipulation of the myth to embellish the most ruthless political acts.

In any discussion of the prospects for participation in the political life of this country, the issue of American involvement in the Indochina war is paramount. I take this to be the case no matter what change in the character of that war may occur before the publication of this essay. For almost a decade the war in Vietnam, Cambodia, and Laos has been a central fact of life for Americans as well as a metaphor for the difficulties of our national existence. The war has exacerbated the economy, hindered social change, and shadowed almost every aspect of our private and public lives. No doubt it will prove to be a greater watershed than the Civil War in the history of the American consciousness and political tradition. For this morally vile and endlessly prolonged conflict and the lies and hypocrisies used by public men over the years to justify it give grave witness to the final spoilage of the image of America as a country providentially selected for dominance over the other places of the earth. Hopefully, with the passing of this spurious radiance, certain traditional virtues will not also disappear into the light of common day.

It is not melodramatic to say that the United States has waged a racist-imperialist war in Asia. In fact it is a more just evaluation than to call the war a mistaken endeavor on the part of a variety of well-intentioned persons. Clearly America would not have entered the war—all other political considerations aside—if Vietnam were a small country in Europe. Or, if such aggression could be conceived, the titanic bombing, the immense defoliation, and the indifferent massacre of old people, women, and children are unimaginable. Only a remote land separated from the western and white tradition could be incinerated with such mechanical casualness. Only non-whites could be drenched with napalm or sprayed with razor-sharp fragments from anti-personnel bombs. The concept of "Vietnamization" could not have been enunciated with such suave reasonableness if it were not Asian blood that was to continue to hemorrhage while the United States paid for and managed the dying.

Even though some of it—certainly not all—has occurred in the past, this violence must be spoken of because its meaning does not diminish. Unless we understand the meaning of our actions, this country's chances of recovery from its sickness will be even fainter than they now seem to be. We need to confront our capacity for brutality—our national crime—as it has been evidenced in Asia and see that brutality in the context of our great national power. Despite the elaborate fictions woven to deceive the world (and especially the American electorate), the war was planned and carried out as an assertion of America's powerful will to dominance in international affairs. Although our aggression was and still continues to be masked by the policy-makers of several administrations as a gesture of American concern for an endangered people, the basically imperialist nature of the war can no longer be disguised. Even the late charade over the number of presidential candidates in the South Vietnam elections resulted in vulgar attempts to induce General Minh to remain on the ballot because "Mr. Nixon wanted him to."

Nearly fifty thousand Americans have been killed, countless times that number of Asians have died, and three countries have been ravaged in order to justify America's pride in its own eminence. That is the grievous understanding we have to live with. That is the subject our history will be dealing with from a later and more dispassionate vantage point than ours.

We cannot be unaware of the future we are designing even though our lives will be silent to it. As a vastly powerful country with at least the ordinary human proneness towards vicious behavior, we need to discover a means of handling our power in positive fashion—perhaps of turning that power inward and using its energy to change society. For if we recognize the disastrous use we have made of our power as an instrument of foreign policy, we must simultaneously recognize that within our society this power has been exercised not with such calculated brutality—we have not yet come to the point of being at war with ourselves—but with similar indifference to human welfare. The questions then arise whether such power as ours can ever be humane in its effects and whether such a society as ours can ever be made humane. If the answer to either question is unconditionally negative, the expectations for the future of this country become intolerable because being Americans we must live with our power and being neither gods nor beasts we must live within society.

Rather than speak of the large environmental and cultural problems which weigh down our national climate with almost vindictive substance, I would rather limit my discussion to the problem of the poor. If, in this abundant and powerful country, the right of some of its inhabitants to exist with certain human prerogatives intact—the possibility of self-esteem, the assurance of economic tranquillity, the opportunity for equal and joyful contact with others—is not upheld, the rights of all are diminished. By ignoring or dealing inadequately with the captives of the slums, the inhabitants of anachronistic rural pockets, the migrant workers, and the aged poor, society makes life less livable for all of us. It may be that the war with its evidence of our indiscriminate violence abroad has also compelled us to notice the strains of savage discord at home. In both cases political attempts to suppress the real nature of our activities and to disregard the real condition of our lives warrant a reappraisal of the chances for ameliorative change within the established order.

While the attitude of the present administration is to abolish the poor by ignoring their fundamental problems, the forces of social and economic discrimination would kill them by limiting their chances of mobility in housing, education, employment, and even consumption. Those who do not exist as a class in the social imagination can ultimately be made not to exist as individuals if basic economic and social rights are indefinitely withheld from them. Although the government is willing—through taxation— to subsidize the construction of huge planes which are neither needed for use nor wanted except by those who build them, it will not prevent hundreds of children from dying annually of lead poisoning caused by swallowed paint flakes. In comparison with the great expenditure of resources required to support industry, however, a simple and cheap control of paint content would preserve the lives of mainly black slum children. But government policy and concern are inextricably linked with the fates of giant corporations and conglomerates. In this bloated corporate enterprise the capitalist system manifests its real power rather than in the small holdings cherished in American myth : a system proficient in the manufacture of instruments of warfare and of inferior and superfluous products for beguiled consumers. But capitalism, like the government its serves and which serves it, can only let the poor die since they are largely non-taxable and they notoriously underconsume.

A long time ago William Blake, who understood the suffering of a people already damaged by industrial greed and imperial ambition, described the injustice of a society where the prosperity of some was enjoyed at the expense of pain to others:

> Then the groan & the dolor are quite forgotten & the
>   slavegrinding at the mill
> And the captive in chains & the poor in the prison, &
>   the soldier in the field
> When the shattered bone hath laid him groaning
>   among the happier dead
>
> It is an easy thing to rejoice in the tents of prosperity
> Thus could I sing & thus rejoice, but it is not so with
>   me!

Nor can one sing in the present tents of prosperity while the
groans can be heard from the withered land outside. The radical
assault Blake made on the life-denying manacles which privileged
institutional structures forge to chain the human spirit is still
convincing today. It is hard to live together in a society where
quantitative replies are officially sanctioned as answers to qualitative questions about human imperatives. But for those who
are neither poets nor prophets and who are not content with
simply repeating the words of poets and prophets, alternative
courses of action seem dismally limited.

Certainly no one would expect that by acting in a conventionally political manner—by engaging in all the procedural
skirmishes that lead to elections—citizens could compel this
government to alter its foreign policy or remedy economic and
social inequities. The government is too far away, its powers are
both too large and vaguely articulated, and its managers are too
entrenched, intractable, and evasive for the voices of citizens to
make any significant impression. At best a bad administration
like this one would be succeeded by one only less bad. And
probably a majority of Americans have been rendered dim and
sullen by their chaotic freedom to purchase unneeded and
unsatisfying goods and by the control exercised over their
opinions and prejudices by morally sterile government officials.

Nothing holds this society together except the inadequate improvisation of the national will by political and economic entrepreneurs interested in nothing more serious than their own perpetuation. When the source of influence and power is so shallow and tainted, it is idle to speculate about the renewal of society under traditional political leadership and through traditional political means. That high office can be held by figures so little fitted—intellectually, imaginatively, and morally—for the complex understanding of human activities as the members of the present administration is dismaying; but that their meretricious expression of that power should provoke so little opposition from the public raises perplexing questions about the nation's chances for recovery.

This essay, which is a response to the present condition of American life and to those who oversee and are responsible for that condition, takes its title from part of Ezra Pound's Canto XIV:

> The slough of unamiable liars,
>   bog of stupidities,
> malevolent stupidities, and stupidities,
> the soil living pus, full of vermin,
> dead maggots begetting live maggots,
>   slum owners,
> usurers squeezing crab-lice, panders to authority, . . .

Since the theological conviction of hell which underlies this passage is no longer operative either as a source of terror or as a promise of retributive justice for the enemies of God (and of man), it is not possible to have the medieval satisfaction of consigning Richard Nixon and his associates to the peculiarities of eternal damnation. What is left for the contemporary man who surveys the political leadership of his country—those unamiable liars with their malevolent stupidities—is the dregs of frustration, intense contempt turned rancid by a sense of inability even to act imaginatively on his judgments. Many Americans who think about this country not in terms of old myth or of past literature but as urgent present reality—a gathering of individuals with personal and group responsibility for their history—regard President Nixon (like Lyndon Johnson and other government, military, and business leaders) as a criminal figure who engages in large deceptions of the country he heads and who is responsible for enormous violence done to the lives of his own citizens and much more to others and to their land. Nevertheless, in the absence of an answering heaven, there is no punishment for such crime.

The majority of Americans have not, of course, made this judgment on Richard Nixon. But if it is allowed that such a judgment can be made and held not only by underground and revolutionary figures but by persons otherwise considered responsible members of society, then the ramifications in the total thinking of these individuals will also have to be considered. Because society through the government has broken a tacit agreement with its members not to involve their consciences in morally unacceptable activities, the individual is compelled to assume personal responsibility for all his actions and to withdraw support from society by refusing, if necessary, to countenance not only the practices but also the laws of that society. In that case, the individual will becomes dominant over the social will and accepts only as much of society's values and society's laws as are morally applicable to all persons on all occasions. Although he will remain unpersuaded by official slogans about "law and order," by official attempts at prosecution or political blackmail, or by outraged reaction from his fellow citizens, the dissenter is not free to do what he likes, but rather is free to do what he judges right despite the prevailing ethic. His view of the universe remains unchanged, but the once familiar aspect of his immediate environment has been acutely transformed. The conditions accounting for this drastic assertion of the individual will must reveal a society in extreme turbulence, in decline, or in breakdown. But that is precisely the prospect at the present time where a national policy that is either lunatic or disgusting is advanced by government leaders and condoned by the majority of the populace. If public conduct as practiced in this country were the norm for private life, the result would be chaos in human relationships. Caprice, mendacity, and guile would replace consistency, trust, and candor so that each individual would be isolated from the other just as individuals are now isolated from their government. It makes no sense, therefore, to recommend patience or to urge acquiescence to a system that is either indifferent to or persistently betrays the values which impel men to commit their human fortunes to a community in order to extend and deepen their relationships.

Recently a former student, one of the most intellectually gifted and humanly responsible young men of his graduating class, wrote me about the work he was doing among the poor in a western city. Describing the children who are his main concern, he observed that "even the violence, the genius of thievery incarnate in the kids . . . becomes constructive because revolutionary." Since my friend is a pacifist and an honest, warm, and honorable person, many will doubtless find it incredible that he should accept the violence and thievery and, more remarkable still, put them in a favorable revolutionary context. What may seem equally incredible is that I share his feelings. If I do not admire the conduct he describes, neither do I condemn it; for I see in it tormented evidence of the vitality of the individual, an assertion of his will to live in the face of an oppressive environment. By becoming a threat these children must at least come to the attention of a society that would prefer to ignore them. A good society will learn to make use of their energy and transform it; a bad society will breed the revolutionaries it deserves. In recent years the inclination of this society has been to throttle the energy of the poor and the young. It will pay with its future for such denial.

Perhaps now my position on the coming election is becoming apparent. I am an American, one of many, whose assenting social consciousness is separated from the larger society in which I live. For that society's quality is dominated by futile and violent foreign adventurism and by a wasteful and discriminatory economic system. Because there appears to be an indissoluble alliance between government and corporate enterprise and consequently between American foreign policy and its domestic economic and social institutions, conventional political action appears to offer little possibility of fulfilling the actual needs of people as opposed to the illusory demands propositioned by imperialist shibboleths and commercial slogans. The very term "political," now far removed from its Greek sense of exercising the rights of citizenship along with others on a common issue, has come to signify the partisan, selfish, devious, and crafty. When Richard Nixon is described as the complete political animal, the implication is that his opportunistic gestures and actions have been bleached of all feeling for human values. The bleak arrogance, the implacable mediocrity, the sense of hidden motives, the inhibited physical behavior which gives the impression of a man so little at home even in that most familiar space, his own body, point up the vast impersonality, barrenness, and inaccessibility of this most political man. Nor is the President a unique example of the kind, for the men around him reveal the same rusty absence of burnish—the lustrelessness of success without reputability, dryness without wit, sharpness without fineness, competence without wisdom or even sense.

Other men, it may be suggested, can be summoned up who will respond to this country's need in a time of troubles. But the prospect of strong new leadership seems unlikely for the coming Presidential elections. Despite the experience of the 1968 convention in Chicago, the machinery of petty connivance has already begun to operate to fill the Democratic delegation with party "regulars." And throughout the country, desperate efforts are being made to disenfranchise student voters mainly by dingy plunderers of countless backwater fiefdoms who imagine that the young are lusting to invade their ramshackle seats of power. Inevitably, the choice of the Democrats will be a survivor of the debacle of the Johnson administration, someone associated with the old style Cold War power policy at the international level and with palliative liberal social measures in the domestic area. A Presidential package will likely be made up to appeal to timidity and fear among a wide spectrum of the electorate, and little attempt will be made to consider the deepest needs of the country. Although politics has been said to represent the art of the possible, that scepticism is no longer persuasive after all the compromises have been made by one side.

Consequently, some of us find ourselves part of what can broadly be called a resistance group which has no faith in the possibilities of political reform unless society itself is literally re-formed. The members of that total resistance which is made up of organized and unorganized groups exhibit a diverse range of attitudes and activities, but all share a common alienation from the conventional methods of political action. For some, the image of a revolutionary with a gun is terrible, but his desire to destroy society in order to create a new one can be understood if not accepted by all. What can be neither understood nor accepted is the point of view of those who think this country is capable of renewal within its present political and social structure. Whatever their political convictions may be, those who do possess this confidence are aligned with the establishment—an awkward and banal term, but probably inevitable here. As a basic political and ideological discrimination, this country may be divided into the majority who belong to the establishment and the minority who belong to the resistance. An editor of the *New York Times* may approve as little of John Mitchell as I do of the revolutionary, but he must be placed on the same side of the ideological line with Mitchell as I must with the revolutionary.

In view of this distinction, it may seem a paradoxical conclusion to say that I believe in the negative value of voting because I wish to prevent or at least postpone a revolutionary crisis in this country. Some candidates and some programs are less harmful than others and may in fact prepare the way for radical change without widespread violence. Some members of Congress are admirable—William Anderson and Walter Mondale, for example—and others of similar calibre may now and then be elected. Above all, I plan to vote because I fear, on the one hand, violent revolution (which is the last and most questionable means of changing society) and, on the other, extreme political and social repression (which would perpetuate a degenerate social order). The Nixon administration has no respect for the civil and social rights of Americans; it has indeed no regard for the human person, no sense of the complex texture of individual and community experience. It would like to achieve a viscous amalgam—an objectified mass of speechless figures materially sated and humming listlessly while some men die and the restless moral energies of all men are stopped. Since the power of repression is immensely more urgent than the threat of revolution, I think with concern of the appointments to the Supreme Court and to the lower federal courts which will be made over the next several years. A revolutionary with a gun may, as I have said, present a terrible image. More terrible still is the image reported in *Newsweek* of Warren Burger opening his door to reporters one spring night holding a gun in his hand. At every level, justice is ambiguously doled out in the United States, but the clarity of the Chief Justice's decision to take up a gun before going to his door is an appalling insight into his version of reality.

In a dark time, the best that can be aspired to is the achievement of a perilous truce among warring factions in our society—the precarious restraint of the nihilism of a few and the nihilism of the many. The keeping of this peace, which need not be so civil nor so docile as to be confused with acquiescence to the establishment, should enable the resistance to enlarge its numbers through personal and public encounters. Since there is no prospect of a viable third party in the foreseeable future, a less formal organization is necessary to win over members of the two major parties and especially to enlist new voters so that both groups can in turn work tacitly or overtly for resistance against the established order. The path ahead is arduous, the outcome is uncertain, and the adventure is not for the volatile or modish. It is worth the effort, however, when the alternatives lead to chaos or to petrification. At the same time it must not become a journey into a labyrinth of temporizing since the forbearance of the oppressed is not perpetual.

The pettiness and irrelevance of much of conventional politics pall before the problems of our society; yet these very problems shrink before the capacity of modern man to cope imaginatively and technically with his universe. Present work in astrophysics and microbiology dramatically involves the exploration of the macrocosm and the microcosm, the discovery of worlds beyond worlds and worlds within worlds. This scientific questing which is the poetry of our time gives a sense of marvellous perspective to human cares, but its genius also testifies the opportunity man has to realize his legitimate dream of a better life on this planet. Against such a background, the parochial vacuity of the American myth is verified in the lilliputian stature of Richard Nixon as he urges the mass purchase of American over foreign cars in tribute to a resurgence of "the pioneer spirit." Or the tendency of the "straight" American way to trivialize everything it encounters is displayed in the photograph of the astronaut rigidly saluting the American flag on the moon. The human imagination can liberate its energies to achieve more generous, flexible, and expansive concepts of man and his fate. Men owe more to each other in the solitudes of their individual mortality and in the solitude of the race flaring momentarily in this chamber of ungaugeable space. That they should continue to live in a debasement they themselves create is an occasion for pity and wonder and rage.

In Defense of Politics

William Pfaff

The question at the heart of our political crisis is this: what do we have a right to expect from political action and reform? It is the inveterate question of modern politics because never before this century has society been so intricately and powerfully interdependent, and never has the material power of organized society been so immense.

Before World War I, the *distance* between state and individual remained very great, the lives of people predominately influenced by local and private circumstance, by the caprice of race and inheritance, by the impersonal and apparently unalterable forces of class, religion, marketplace, weather, disease. Politics, with the collaboration of technology and a technologically transformed world economy, changed all that.

When purposeful collective action—politics—has altered so much, within the lifetimes of men still alive, what more might it not change? But there is a drastic complication today. The power of collective action is clear to all, but it no longer is possible to believe that this is an inherently progressive power. The old progressivism of the social Darwinists, the social evolutionists, the dialectical materialists—that dominating conviction that society is getting better and going someplace worth going—now is in the most profound *popular* doubt. This is new, and it is very important; indeed, it is not an exaggeration to say that today we have reached the end of an era of common belief. There no longer is any widespread popular confidence that science, technology, and society are on a progressive course.

The popular conviction of social progress in the past rested upon the analogy with scientific progress. The decisive contemporary event is that this analogy has been itself discredited. Quite suddenly—after twenty-five years, one supposes, of internalizing the traumas of technologically conducted genocide and the nuclear bomb—the mass of people are in recoil from what science and technology have done to the earth and to men, and from what they may yet do.

Whether this popular reaction is a just one, a fair or altogether reasonable reaction to the facts and possibilities of our situation, is an argument which changes nothing in the political reality of the present moment. There is in fact no reason to think that popular, or elite, attitudes today are any more discriminating or sophisticated than they were in the nineteenth-century noontime of scientific and historical optimism. But the fact today is that people simply no longer believe that either science or society possesses an inner momentum which is progressive and ultimately beneficial to mankind. This is new.

Thus the structures of value which people had derived from their progressive assumptions are undermined; the confidence they before had possessed in the *intelligibility* both of society and of their individual roles in society is gone. This surely is the explanation for that "crisis of values" which everyone today sees behind our political confusions, contributing to that mass defection from "the system" which characterizes a very wide sector of the American political landscape today.

It is intelligibility which people are searching for in American politics. They complain of powerlessness, a demoralizing inability to change anything of consequence, even to discover the levers of power in our society. They complain about the centralized and massive structures of established power, and the unaccountability of that power. These are ways of saying the same thing, that the structural relationship between individuals and power—our political structure—now seems invalid : distorted, warped, or broken.

This seems an intolerable threat and problem so long as we do not possess, or agree upon, the values upon which a new or reformed structure might be established. Thus the important fact that in our present political situation the center, the area of practical and limited reforms, pragmatic change, a certain confidence in pragmatism and good sense, now is deeply weakened. The people who once occupied the political center in America have fallen away in two directions; towards a revolutionary—or crypto-revolutionary—stance of radical repudiation of the present system combined with radical optimism about the future, and towards a denial of political possibility, a stance of radical despair.

But of course those who are in the first group are actually revealing despair too. Their "revolutionary" position is without serious programs or a plan of action. It is *merely* a stance; for too many it is simply a pose. There is no serious revolutionary party in America. There is not even a serious revolutionary theory; there is simply the revolutionary stance. It rests upon an expectation of cathartic, redemptive change in society to emerge as a post-revolutionary *deus ex machina*. Optimism of this kind amounts to a compensatory formulation of a radical despair of politics. The last of the little band of Americans who took seriously the implications of their revolutionary politics blew up themselves and their movement in the Greenwich Village "bomb factory" explosion of 1970. Even that revealed their dilettante vision : really serious revolutionaries and terrorists take the trouble to learn how to handle explosives.

For a much larger group of Americans the revolutionary

stance is an item of political fashion, reflecting a certain genuine emotion, a perception of contradiction and crisis in the American (and their own) situation, but with no willingness to accept or even admit the terrifying implications of what they so casually are saying. Thus what is sought and talked about in America is most often revolution without tears, and what ensues is closer to a diversion of the bohemian rich—courtiers of "the system" playing dangerous games.

More recently there has been a fashion to seek a revolutionary solution in culture, in the creation of a counterculture of opposition to the established assumptions of society. In practice this too often has meant uneconomic farming communes, unstable collectives and communities of people emotionally and financially parasitic upon the society they purport to despise. The music, drugs, writing, sexual liberation, and styles of life associated with the movement are co-opted by the commercial promoters as rapidly as they emerge. The gypsy kerchiefs, tie-dyes, organic foods, and Yoga and Hindu cults of the counterculture are quickly taken over by the affluent, who would become the movement's fellow travelers without cutting any of their own established ties. The counterculture itself has been without intellectual depth or subtlety. Its moral commitments ordinarily are passionate but provisional, and not without self-indulgence, its most prominent figures firmly in touch with the publishing houses or a university faculty. These people are reclaimable to the system; they have never really left it; they have taken no vows nor burned any bridges. There is no counterculture figure who deserves comparison to a Simone Weil or Kurt Gerstein, with the honorable exception of some jailed war resisters. The commitments of the movement as a whole bear little comparison with those of the revolutionary agents and underground political operatives of the Comintern generation and the wartime Resistance, such fictional figures as Malraux's Kyo or Victor Serge's

Dario, or to the other outlaws and ascetics of the real "counter-cultures" of the past.

What is happening today is that the fashion-setting middle classes together with elements of the intelligentsia, in response to the real crisis and pain of American political life, have adopted a "revolutionary" stance which provides an intelligible critique of our society but demands no real sacrifice. The popularity of Charles Reich's and Jean-Francois Revel's writings confirm this, in that both declare that the revolution is already *inevitably* taking place through the inner dynamics of American society. This makes it unnecessary for anyone to think seriously about what the outcome will be, or how to affect it, or to pay any personal or intellectual costs to bring it about.

We can see in this lack of intellectual and political serious-ness something quite unexpected and perhaps more sobering than all the violence of the late 1960s. America has, in influ-ential sectors of its public and intellectual life, ostentatiously repudiated the political present in favor of changes which no one can, or wishes to attempt to, describe in any but the haziest and most sentimental terms. Why? It was very different in our last time of domestic crisis, the Depression 1930s. Then the intelli-gentsia was largely committed to serious and intelligible socialist or communist programs. They joined Marxist parties and waged a serious political struggle to organize workers and carry out tangible and fundamental alterations in the political and econo-mic institutions of the country. Even the Huey Longs and Father Coughlins and Upton Sinclairs led movements which, whatever else may be said about them, possessed perfectly comprehensible goals which their followers made sacrifices to accomplish. In these circles of both leftist and rightist revolution or reform there was hope, even confidence, in the midst of economic breakdown and national political frustration. And in the established political classes of the country there was work, intellectual seriousness, innovation. The Democratic Party was able to produce the cadres and ideas of the New Deal and carry out a drastic modification of the country's institutions.

Today, by starkest contrast, is a time of hopelessness and intellectual and political default. This way in which the middle classes, the political classes, including much of the political intelligentsia, have taken over the fashions of revolution without its programmatic or organizational content or its moral commitments seems to me a sign of unprecedented despair—behavior which disguises the fact that these people no longer believe in the possibility of deep reform, revolutionary or otherwise, in our society.

II

There is another serious sign of a defection from politics in America. The protest of powerlessness is as keen, if less articulate, among ordinary people as among the elites. There is a strong populist resentment against "the system," except that here the anger is directed against the "liberal establishment," the liberal intelligentsia and press, and to some extent against traditional populist enemies as well : the big corporations and big employers, the international bankers, the "fatcat politicians." It is certainly a protest against experts and technocrats, established academics and intellectuals. It declares that these politicians, bosses, officials, professors, specialists, advisers, and technocrats possess an immense power which they neither justify by competence (or else why are there bad, failed, cruel wars ; economic upheavals ; cars that fall apart?) nor are they accountable to the people for their power—and privilege.

While the populist complaint often takes a rightist form (with respect to war and foreign policy especially), it is by no means a true rightist or conservative phenomenon. And it expresses real grievances. These same people are the ones whose sons man the combat arms—the infantry platoons and artillery batteries—of the Vietnam war in a grotesque and utterly unjust disproportion. These are the people who were laid off their jobs during the recession of 1970, and will be laid off again if economic protectionism and fiscal crisis break down world trade and bring about greater recession, or a world depression. Their resources for surviving economic troubles are slender. Their position—with heavily mortgaged homes, consumer debt, children to be given the schooling their fathers did not have—is very precarious, while their expectations are very high (which sets them off from the hopeless poor, the illiterate, innumerous discards of modern industrial society who populate the ghettos of the secular city—dark camps of disintegrated families, anomic adolescents, blasted lives—and are the potential recruits to quite another kind of populist movement).

But a question must be asked about this defection from politics. Is the political center—the zone of tangible reform, of established liberal and parliamentary politics—any longer a zone of possibility? Is it not possible that the defection from politics in America expresses an inarticulate but perfectly valid intuition of an unpalatable truth : that politics in our day is an illusion? that in all of the advanced industrial states, including Russia and the western democracies as variants of the model, society has become victim of an inadvertent despotism, a "systemic fascism"? that governments are ruled by technocratic imperatives, served by propaganda and police, throwing up a self-serving but not in the least hypocritical fog of liberal platitude or socialist idealism which makes it impossible for a challenge even to be seriously mounted? The implication of this would be that democracy, even in the unsatisfactory terms on which we have known it in this century, no longer is possible under contemporary conditions.

The scale of the modern state and the influence of propaganda and technology upon human life drastically challenge the notion that men can actually control their governments, even in those societies where a liberal political structure exists. Technology admits only specialist decisions—"relevant" knowledge—within those options which technology itself nominates. Its choices all fall within a larger choice which seems to admit no dissent : the perfection and enlargement of the technological structure itself. Bureaucracy, a kind of technology of human rather than material organization, acts and decides by its own criteria, which all serve its own necessities. The formal political structure conducts its debates and elections in an arena of illusory choices and can have no effect upon the matters which really count.

This profoundly pessimistic assessment, best expressed in the writings of Jacques Ellul, constitutes a powerful and logical judgment of our present condition which common experience and impressions would seem to confirm. Certainly in America today, not only do people say and believe that they have little chance to change things which affect their lives in fundamental ways, but their political experience in the last decade provides imposing evidence in support. In 1964 a vast popular majority voted for the peace candidate over a man frankly committed to a military solution in Vietnam. The country got war. Again in 1968 the people chose the Presidential candidate who promised to end the war ("honorably") over a man compromised by his past service in the war administration. The war was then enlarged. The popular experience suggests that great social problems—manifested in the economy, the urban crisis, the depth of racial tension in America, the issue of welfare, the existence of a huge population (non-proletariat) of socially devastated ghetto dwellers—are unremediable by national programs which, under the Johnson and even the Nixon administrations, were conceived by our best academic and political intelligences and given generous funds and imposing popular support.

We find ourselves, then, in a most peculiar situation, and a dangerous one. There are deep and real problems of political structure, competence, accessibility and accountability, and power distribution in American society. These problems are keenly felt at nearly all levels of our national life, affecting the working man and small entrepreueur of the new populism quite as much—if in different ways, providing a different style and character of response—as they affect the ghetto dweller or the middle class intelligentsia.

Yet our response to these problems seems ineffectual, incompetent, even irresponsible. Our liberal elites veer towards a posture of revolutionary repudiation of liberal politics, yet they have been among the chief beneficiaries of the system. Despite their alienation, they, and the other groups in our society which have their own—more tangible, if less articulate—reasons for deep discontent, complain chiefly of their apparent powerlessness, their inability to bring about serious and creative change in our condition. Some of the changes they name are specific and tangible, and are no different from the conventional reform program of liberal parties. But these tangible reforms are not enough. People are unwilling to come to terms with so limited a program of reform. Nor is it clear that these changes alone could bring about any renewal of national confidence. Rather, Americans seem to be looking for a renewal of faith, a re-justification of the near-religious investment of faith which they have placed in politics. And, of course, they are not finding so dramatic a reward. Their quest takes the form of a search for political heroes, charismatic champions able to make some redemptive and symbolic act of political renewal. The search has about it a quality of desperation. There is a distinct note of hysteria in American politics today.

There is, moreover, sound reason to believe that our present situation is unprecedented in certain important respects—in the influence of technology and of a technological-bureaucratic intelligentsia upon political decisions; in the role of propaganda in politics: the centralization, specialization, fragmentation, and manipulation of information; in the centralization of political and economic power at the same time that governmental competence manifestly is in decline. There is doubt that political action of the conventional kind can make a fundamental difference to this apparatus of inadvertent repression.

But if all of this should really be true, then the logical response is not revolution—which cannot undo technology or unmake modern civilization—but (as Ellul argues, and the counterculture attempts) to repudiate politics: to consciously depoliticize society, building up social and institutional barriers against the power of the state, making an unqualified refusal of the gifts of the modern system and of its claims upon the individual.

The trouble with this is that the radical conservatism of an Ellul, like anarchism, and the revolutionary position of a Herbert Marcuse, seem to reflect assumptions that are not political at all, but romantic. All of these present in political language and in the guise of political programs what really are critiques of modern industrial civilization : its anomic conditions of life, its technological imperatives and valuations, its destruction—in a tide of words and mechanized communication—of organic wisdom. And as politics is only a single factor in our civilization, their recommendation that we attempt to cure through revolutionary politics (or "depoliticization") this malformed civilization amounts to an heroic but foredoomed enterprise. Thus what today purport to be political movements nearly always reveal themselves in the end as essentially religious responses : efforts somehow to transform *man himself* through political action in the unspoken and despairing conviction that no less a reform can make a difference.

III

The effects of such an optimism, eloquent of radical despair, upon the poor and inconclusive enterprise of politics is wholly destructive. It betrays an inveterate modern unwillingness to admit that all political action can provide is a decent hope of creative and incremental change in counterbalance to the disintegrative forces of ordinary human passion and disorder. Politics does not cure souls, or—ordinarily—civilizations. Both radical optimism and radical despair amount to a practical denial of the real nature and limitations of politics (things having to do with being a citizen, a *polites*). Radical optimism replaces political hope with something akin to a religious expectation. Radical pessimism, by flatly denying that fundamental change can come about at all, amounts to very much the same thing.

Yet it is a matter of common sense observation that national institutions and policies *are* changed or reversed or dropped under popular pressures, that a technocratic scheme of values *can* be challenged, that the social and economic programs of a government *can* under heavy pressure be changed. It is also a matter of common sense observation that unjustified privilege, exploitation, coercion, are never eliminated from a society, if only because the eliminators much too readily take over those qualities. Nor on any issue does a pure popular will exist (in opposition to elitist power); "the people" in this case are a sentimental invention of ideologues.

The present despair of politics is comprehensible only in terms of illusory and romantic expectations. That traditional politics constitute an impossible—hopeless—enterprise today is simply an assumption which cannot be proved, however attractive that idea may be (and for certain reasons and to certain personalities it may be very attractive). It cannot be proved from evidence because the available data is unlimited : historical experience, common experience, and all the possible perceptions and interpretations thereof ; what is more, the data is not all in, nor will it ever be—in time to do us any good. In the generalized terms of ordinary political argument, it is perfectly clear that for every chronology of contemporary decline a chronicle of progress can be produced. New York, Chicago, Gary undoubtedly are in crucial respects worse places than they were twenty or even thirty years ago at the end of the Depression. It is equally clear that Paris, Barcelona, London are, for the masses of their inhabitants, much better places than before the war, with better housing, good and improving urban services and transport, jobs for the people, cleaned buildings, noble gardens and perspectives.

Both here and abroad, the real anxieties of common life in industrial society must be set against the astounding benefits which the modern system has brought the majority of people : mass education, access to higher education, social insurance, health services, a substantial breakdown of inherited privilege and an opening to talent. All these have been *political* accomplishments. In addition, the economic and industrial system, interlocked with an egalitarian liberal and socialist politics, has also given people an absolutely unprecedented popular prosperity : steady work, the chance for health, holidays, appliances which free the ordinary woman from the brutal labor of kitchen and laundry, good cheap clothes, cheap amusements. It is a matter of common sense that political action and political and economic reform have made tremendous changes in the lives of people, resolved terrible problems, conquered immense threats to human welfare.

If there is a pervasive popular conviction of powerlessness today, this is chiefly a matter of the positive exercise of power, establishing new policies and structures. The negative power which people today possess, even when they are acting in quite small groups, is one of the significant phenomena of recent years, arising from precisely the centralization—and the accompanying vulnerabilities—of the modern state. People have the power to topple presidents, bring down governments, paralyze sectors of the economy, discredit or destroy the authority of established governments. The problem of political power today is as much a matter of powerlessness among the governors as it is powerlessness of the people. As Hannah Arendt has remarked, violence has increased in American society precisely because the power—the popularly conceded and legitimate power—of the state has declined.

It may in fact be that what we see today is an irremediable malfunction of politics within those societies which are so large, and ethnically and ideologically divided, that popular participation tends to make common agreements and consensus unattainable on a large number of issues. Thus however efficient in terms of economic and productive rationality the great continental-scale nations may be—the U.S.A. and the U.S.S.R.—they may also be overextended, inflexible, unresilient, and ultimately ungovernable. Those smaller states which are homogeneous in population and culture, and at the same time possess access to a market large enough to support technological and productive efficiency, may be better suited to survival in the modern world.

The *political* problem today surely is to create structures which are accessible to people, with power decentralized in the matters crucially affecting their lives. This may not be possible where there are internal popular contradictions of belief which arise from essentially non-political (that is, ethnic, communal, racial, or ideological) sources, or worse, where the political center has been deserted. Politics is possible only when the great issues remain party issues, partisan issues within a general agreement on the nature and justice of the national objective. Where there is no agreement on what is just, people think one another wicked or mad, and disagreements become revolutionary issues. The tendency in those cases where there is no natural unity on social goals is for governments to attempt to establish a fraudulent unity on emotional or artificial issues—since governments recognize that people will not and cannot indefinitely endure an anarchical disunity. In America, the proportions of our present malaise, our despair and inner division, provoke pessimism about the future. But pessimism about the United States is not the same thing as pessimism about politics.

Indeed, pessimism—even about the United States—is in fact indispensable to a responsible politics. We must, I think, if we are to be serious about politics, adopt a position which is very difficult for Americans, accustomed to large and idealistic causes, heroic rhetoric, the bandwagon, a politics of personality. It is a stoic position, or even an existential position—if that term can be useful today. It is a position of some detachment about the claims of politics and the results that can be expected from political action and reforms. It requires a commitment to reason and limit, to a conception of politics as *enterprise*, as an intellectually and morally demanding enterprise of provisional constructions and unsatisfactory accomplishments. It requires that those who are the elites of a society, the politically and intellectually privileged, live demanding lives, paying for their privileges.

Freud has of course argued that civilization is built up upon the renunciation of instinct, that it presupposes precisely the non-satisfaction of powerful instincts, and that it constitutes the life struggle of men living in common, imposing the dictates of Eros upon that longing for death which has, in our times, assumed so dramatic and savage a role in political affairs. This is an argument which Americans find hard. Our political classes, our elites, are oddly reluctant to admit how fragile is that membrane of convention, of social structure and institution, of assumption, which encloses the feral reality of human instinct. Just below lies the real culture of unfettered impulse—malice, unchecked ego, casual cruelty, inveterate human exploitation, easy violence—and those even darker and madder depths where Charlie Mansons, satanist cults, George Lincoln Rockwells flourish. Our resistance to this knowledge constitutes a lunatic commitment to optimism.

The matter is quite fundamental. If we expect, through politics, to obtain some "natural" resolution of human conflict and disorder and thereby to redeem our civilization itself, we must assume that the nature of man is peaceful and cooperative. When we encounter evidence that this is not so, it is inevitable that we will despair—or even experience a kind of frenzy of frustration, as is our case today.

The stoic counsel goes against powerful currents in our culture, and against a powerful instinct—the longing for extinction—which is, it seems to me, the real significance of our present-day radical optimism/despair. Let me put it another way : entrophy. We long for rest, resolution, an end to troubles; and that in fact is death. It makes little difference if we disguise this death in some metaphor of life—of a new and radically redeemed social and political order. That merely is another way to describe a condition in which disorder, struggle, restlessness, anxiety, frustration have been ended as conditions of life.

At certain times our unwillingness to submit to life, to admit what we really are, breaks into the open, takes on political form of its own. Then our impulse to die—and to destroy—becomes perfectly open and direct. We do so with a good deal of pleasure. There can be a real joy when revolution breaks out, when people go to war—a splendid sense of relief and decision, of decisions taken out of our hands, a delight in destroying our lives as they are.

In every time of great political unrest we risk an explosion from the caverns of our repressed emotions, instincts, and indescribable fears. Dreams of transcendent change and purification exist there, emerging when the ordinary structures of our common lives, the civil and social structures of society, are weakened or broken. If man cannot have peace, order, and intelligibility in his life through the commonplace arrangements of society, he will look for intelligibility in violent, unreasonable, uncommon ways. There is nothing extraordinary in this observation, but it reminds us that while peace and order are the common desire, war and chaos can provide an intelligibility of another kind, as well as joys which satisfy that other part of us which wants to die, to find rest, to stop.

Today we again see the inveterate effort to define political action as a journey with an end, an enterprise with a terminal, rather than as a process, an adventure without end. The problem with an adventure without end is that it is hardly tolerable when it is also an adventure without intelligibility. The worst thing modern politics has done has been to connive at our need to ascribe an ultimate meaning to secular existence which in the past was understood to lie in the province of religion : an expection of final happiness, order, relief. Before the eighteenth century it was unimaginable that human meaning could be provided by politics, the state. Today, people look to politics for a kind of assurance and fulfillment which before they expected from God, or expected not to receive at all.

The problem is acute in America, where for historical reasons the link between personal and political identity is very close. It is impossible to be an American without that constituting a political affirmation. *I am an American* means that I am committed to a Constitution and a particular form of government; without that commitment there hardly is a meaning in being an American. Historically, Americans have also been committed to a conception of our form of government as superior to others and the form towards which other societies are striving : America as the new political dispensation, successor to the old regimes of autocratic Europe, the secular Jerusalem. The idea seems quaint, repellent, in this political hour in America, yet without this belief Americans are in a moral void. It is significant that many today have adopted the idea's simulacrum : the belief that America is uniquely bad, the worst imperialist, racist, exploitative power in history. What we Americans cannot afford is political detachment, a psychological disengagement from politics. For that would mean attempting to reestablish a secular identity for which we have few national resources. We would be left with this land which we have treated with unsparing ruthlessness, a culture which is thin, limited, largely derivative in its real accomplishments, without masterworks. We have given the world jazz, movies, comics, the electric light, a splendid demotic English, technology and the assembly line, excellent surgery, the Manhattan project. Our only great accomplishment has been political; and that now is in doubt.

It is not enough. Other people can fall back on cultures which are not integrally linked to politics. They can be Frenchmen, Italians, Hungarians, and at the same time practice an essential indifference to the character of a particular political regime, a political identity. They understand what they are by reference to a land, a language, a rooted popular culture. They do not escape the modern conditions of secular solitude, of aloneness with the universe, but they possess wider and more vital cultural resources for establishing and maintaining their balance. We Americans have always sustained ourselves by a political identity, to which we have always assigned much more than a mere political significance. For us to retreat from politics, to abandon these political hopes or have them torn from us, is a vital wound. Despairing of politics, we may be very dangerous, an anomic people looking for trouble, looking for revenge.

America the Perpetual Adolescent

L. John Roos

General reflections on the question of "engagement in or disengagement from the concerns and responsibilities of political life" have been common in the history of our republic. The depth and pervasiveness of such questions at present, however, suggest that the question is being raised in a new way. Before, the question was most often raised in a context of general and unreflective apathy. Citizens who had never really participated asked whether involvement was worth the effort. Now the question appears increasingly to be the climax of long and serious reflection on the character of public life. The events of the 1960s have led many citizens to believe that our regime is so irredeemably corrupt that to extend one's involvement in that regime would be simply immoral, and that our regime is so resolutely established as to doom to sure failure any and all attempts at significant change. Many have come to believe that simple apathy is a more moral alternative than an active political life. Some have gone further and said that given the barrenness of our common life, one can only blast through the impasse with revolutionary speech and deed.

The dilemma that I face in entering a discussion for which the alternatives have already been staked out and espoused is that I wish to take a position and at the same time disagree with many or most others who hold that same position. It may appear (and may be, though I think not) irresponsible to distinguish oneself from those who are seemingly closest to one's own position. Sufficient, it would seem, are the deep scars that divide the hardly silent extremes in American political life. However, nothing is finally served by ignoring differences that divide men's souls if not their votes. Concretely, while I agree with many of the indictments leveled against our republic, I fundamentally disagree with the understanding of moral and political life which is proposed by the New Left, the most frequent and generally articulate spokesman for those indictments. This essay attempts to raise some questions about those indictments and the understandings which appear to underlie them.

Only a fool or worse would fail to notice the most radical flaws in our public life. And only a remarkably soulful or soulless man would have escaped the experience of the 60s without scars of bitterness and despondency. After the tedious 50s, the 60s excited new hopes and longings. John F. Kennedy and Martin Luther King, despite their ultimate shortcomings, spoke of better and nobler things than those before them had known or chosen to speak of. The civil rights movement, the first pitching of the tents of Camelot in the early Kennedy years, promised (yes naïvely and vaguely) a new, deeper, and richer common life. The young especially were touched by words such as they had never heard in their lifetimes. From there the 60s sped towards the destruction of every dream and hope that had been sown, towards a jaded barrenness of spirit that we now live with daily. The greatness to which John Kennedy called America ended in a blind and brutal military adventure (which he helped begin), which has disfigured a great nation and destroyed a proud people. The three men most esteemed by the young were struck down by assassins' bullets. The children's crusade of Eugene McCarthy ended in the streets of Chicago and inherited

Richard Nixon, a curious political heirloom from times that few imagined would ever return. The resistance movement exploded at Kent State, Jackson State, Madison, and in a New York bomb works. Woodstock drained into Manson and Altamont. The counterculture counted heroin deaths and lives wasted through groveling in reality-destroying drugs. The large and noble speech of King and Kennedy was replaced by vulgar and obscene gutter talk from both left and right.

The intensity and the pace of the 60s was perhaps unique; the story, however, which they told was not. Disillusioned youth-fulness is, simply, as characteristic of America as it has been of a particular generation in the 60s. America is forever young. Certainly Kennedy and his circle were young in years and in their dreams of a great renewal to be carried through wit, style, and flourish. Johnson, strangely enough, clung to a desire, conceived in his Texan youth, of being a towering and forceful leader of men. Even Richard Nixon resembles the perpetual American youth when he imagines that tough, cunning corporate lawyers could measure up to the task of "bringing together" a bitterly divided nation, as if such a binding together were just another big deal to be closed. For all his uncomplicated baseness, Nixon, during the Cambodian invasion, looked the sly youth who searched for common ground with demonstrators in small talk about their families and favored football teams.

The bitterness of the losing of the dream in the 60s may be unprecedented, but the basic image and experience is from our past, and it may be that we must return there to understand our own times.

F. Scott Fitzgerald understood something of America's perennial crisis. He understood that there was an almost irresistible exuberance and scale about America that separated her from all other nations. He also understood that the ultimate tragedy of the nation was the failure to ever come to grips with the amorphous ends of the total exuberance, the failure to search

out and articulate ends or objects commensurate with that deep
and unsettling longing in the hearts of America. Others have
pointed to this: James in *The American,* De Tocqueville in
Democracy in America, Hartz in *The Liberal Tradition in
America.* But perhaps better than all, Gatsby shows us America.
Gatsby was always young, for Gatsby always dreamed of some
vast and limitless future in which all the strivings of his heart
would find rest. And Gatsby, like America, never being capable
of the long and painful search for objects commensurate with
that yearning, directed them to an object silly, selfish, and finally
petty. Fitzgerald tells us at the end of Gatsby that it is more
than one man he speaks of :

> Most of the big shore places were closed now and there
> were hardly any lights except the shadowy, moving
> glow of a ferryboat across the Sound. And as the moon
> rose higher the inessential houses began to melt away
> until gradually I became aware of the old island here
> that flowered once for Dutch sailors' eyes—a fresh,
> green breast of the new world. Its vanished trees, the
> trees that had made way for Gatsby's house, had once
> pandered in whispers to the last and greatest of all
> human dreams; for a transitory enchanted moment
> man must have held his breath in the presence of this
> continent, compelled into an aesthetic contemplation
> he neither understood nor desired, face to face for the
> last time in history with something commensurate to
> his capacity for wonder.
> 　　And as I sat there brooding on the old, unknown
> world, I thought of Gatsby's wonder when he first
> picked out the green light at the end of Daisy's dock.
> He had come a long way to this blue lawn, and his
> dream must have seemed so close that he could hardly
> fail to grasp it. He did not know that it was already
> behind him, somewhere back in that vast obscurity
> beyond the city, where the dark fields of the republic
> rolled on under the night.
> 　　Gatsby believed in the green light, the orgiastic

future that year by year recedes before us. It eluded us
then, but that's no matter—tomorrow we will run
faster, stretch out our arms farther. . . . And one fine
morning—
    So we beat on, boats against the current, borne
back ceaselessly into the past.[1]

From the beginning of her life, America has fled from any
moral articulation of her highest hopes or deepest beliefs. Adoles-
cent optimism and smalltime boosterism blown to national
proportions, armed with increasingly diverse and potent technological capacities, have spawned a sprawling affluent nation
which has never admitted defeat and never been compelled to
or attracted by painful, searching reflections upon the appropriate end, character, and responsibilities of public life. Instead,
like Gatsby, the republic has envisioned only a vast, vulgar, and
meretricious beauty.

But there is still another dream, woven from the pervasive
implications of involvement itself, a dream that presents involvement as a conscious option, as if the alternative of withdrawal
were really available, as if it were possible for an individual to
determine the scope and duration of his own involvement in
public life. We began with a question of alternative answers to
the questions of political involvement. Our reflections now begin
to transform our initial question. Is it a question of involvement
or disinvolvement, or rather a question of the character of one's
inevitable involvement? The confusion and tumult of the 60s
call radically into question the character of one's involvement
and make painfully clear the stakes of that involvement; but do
they admit of the possibility of actual, to say nothing of moral,
withdrawal? The obvious and inescapable given appears to be
that we are not alone in the world but together with others. And
men are together not only to the point of sharing a common
space; men clearly share a common fate, a fate plied together
from countless individual lives, whether they are offered wit-

tingly or not for this purpose. Regarding the possibility of moral withdrawal, can one become a good man in any full sense without achieving justice in common with other men?

For there to be a "political" question at all depends upon some prior, fundamental experience of "commonness," some yearning to become and to be which integrally involves other men, some common work or striving. Without such an experience, political questions are groundless and withdrawal or involvement never come to any issue. We seem to imagine that we have altogether transcended, simply left behind, the wonderings of "earlier" men at the mystery of their givenness together, men who told in story and song and ritual the way in which they were together, what it meant to be a people and to be a part of that people.

America seems to have rather characteristically avoided any such experience of substantive in-commonness. We have had only the experience of an oppressive and demagogic unanimity surrounding our efforts to protect the one fundamental common object, the right to individual aggrandizement. No, we would be fools to imagine that we could actually or decently disengage ourselves from others. To step away from others is to leave behind with them that part of ourselves altogether dependent upon their presence. To live in private, were that in fact possible, is to live somehow apart from oneself, to live a lesser life. If, then, withdrawal into privacy is neither acceptable nor available, we might ask what sort of involvement in public life, what speech and what deeds, would be appropriate to men, to ourselves, at this time?

It is against this background of national evasion and disillusionment that we struggle to inquire into the appropriate constitutive concerns of public life. And out of this inquiry emerge the temptations which have mastered us time and again. Those temptations seem to be dual: first, to believe that the pervasive American spirit of compromise and individualism is commensurate with our crises; and second, that all things are ours to control, that some final and irrevocable justice is ours to administer.

What this means is that when confronted with the obvious banality and corruption of our polity and when questioning involvement in that polity, we are directed to two alternatives: first, to claim that involvement is obligatory and means the classical American political art of compromise for beneficent ends, a compromise that manipulates the greedy and base passions ruling our ordinary public speech with a view towards achieving ends which will finally justify the means employed; and second, to reject the art of manipulative compromise and political involvement as equivalent. If, in this second alternative the consequent withdrawal from political life is not immediate and total, there is often a residual effort to force, directly or indirectly, a decisive confrontation which shall mete out once and for all the names of the just and of the unjust.

Both alternatives seem to find their matrix in the dreamlike experiences which Fitzgerald describes. On the one hand, there is the dream that a simple amalgam of politics and baseness can realize truly decent hopes. On the other hand, there is the dream that justice and virtue are simply available commodities wholly at our disposal. There is no sense of an arduous struggle for simple decency which is never wholly one's own and which never wholly delivers one from confusion and complicity with the indecent.

It is not as if involvement on the level of manipulative compromise between interest groups or power blocs were simply a misconception or miscalculation of means towards the end. Rather, it represents a fundamental misunderstanding of the appropriate ends of political activity. For too long, we have believed, like Gatsby, that sentiments of nobility were sufficient guides in political matters. Most efforts at reform today pass over the most festering wound in our public life. Advocates of economic justice decry the drastic misdistribution of America's financial resources, thus further obscuring the roots of this injustice in the pervasive preoccupation with wealth. Such advocates, like those with whom they contend, concur in the all but exclusively economic conception of public concerns, a conception which defines the public good in terms of the equitable distribution of essentially private goods. What the pragmatic liberal in American politics presses for is a peculiar structure to assure equitable distribution of wealth, without inquiring beyond the most base understanding of what wealth is or might be. For all the rhetoric expended on the quality of life and on the great society, we have not witnessed any common, humble, agonizing search for even a minimally adequate understanding of a good human life, what it is and how it might become possible for men. The republic has always depended upon the unlimited pursuit of wealth which gives neither urgency nor even space to more substantive inquiry and pursuits. Fitzgerald was surely right in claiming that America stirred in men's hearts a deep and powerful longing; and he was right too when he pointed to the American failure to find and to formulate a common good or end adequate to that longing.

This much seems clear, that no political action can support and direct our common life unless it is rooted in an altogether honest and searching inquiry into what life together really means or ought to mean. We all but take for granted that being together means, most generally, serving as economic partners and that to speak at all of a "common good" is to speak of stable prices, sound currency, and the G.N.P. Rilke's account of Germany in 1916 reveals that he understood well what his nation had lost and what would be:

> Man-work, as everything has been man-work in the last decades, bad work, work for profit, save for a few painful voices and pictures, save for a few warning figures, a few zealous individuals who clung to their

own hearts, which stood against the stream. Rodin, how often, as always, repeated words of disapprobation, mistrust for the course of things; it was even too much for me that he always did it with the same expressions. I took it for weariness and yet it was judgment. And Cezanne, the old man, when one told him of what was going on, and he could break out in the quiet streets of Aix and shriek at his companion : "Le monde, c'est terrible. . . ." As of a prophet one thinks of him, and longs for one who will cry and howl like that—but they all went away beforehand, those old men who would have had the power to weep now before the peoples.[2]

Rilke understood that nothing short of a turning about, a conversion in some fundamental sense, from the objects of profit and selfishness to objects shining and shareable, were commensurate with the vacuity and emptiness of his times. So with ours.

But Rilke was wiser and truer to his heart's object than those among us who, glimpsing the admitted corruption in our midst, react with apocalyptic frenzy. If, on the one hand, the temptation to mediocrity and compromise is to be rejected, so too must the equally perverse temptation which calls us to believe and act as if a final justice were ours to distribute. Rilke wrote of the revolutionary opposition in Germany in 1918 :

> . . . life itself—in how many instances it simply cannot make itself effective any more, pushed aside as it is by a lot of secondary institutions, grown lazy by their continuance—who would not often wish for a great storm that would tear down everything obstructive and infirm, to make room for the again creative infinitely young, infinitely benevolent forces.[3]

Rilke understood that such longings were illusory, that the character of justice is finally limited and tension-filled, and that to absolutize it is as great a perversion as to deny it simply. Rilke says we can be allied

neither with those who drove ruthlessly ahead nor
with those who met the often criminal outbreaks of this
insanity with old and no less unjust and inhuman
means : the future lay with neither, and to *it* the
intellectual is after all allied and sworn, not in the sense
of the revolutionary, who would presume to create
from one day to the next a humanity freed (what is
freedom?) and happy (what is happiness?), but in that
other patient understanding that he is preparing in
people's hearts those subtle, secret, tremulous transformations out of which alone will proceed the agreements and unities of a more clarified future.[4]

But, one might ask (and perhaps in doing so go to the heart
of things), have you said anything more than that excess is
somehow wrong? In one way yes. That is what has been said,
but implicitly something more is at stake. Americans have
periodically, and perhaps fortuitously, appealed to moderation
as a guiding principle of political life. The problem is that in
such appeals moderation has not been derived from the character of the common life and its objects. It has, in fact, simply
been appealed to, rather than articulated as a consequence of
the nature of political life, and hence in the long run it fails to
serve as a barrier against either rampant venality or the present
apocalyptic fervor.

What unites the seemingly polar temptations elaborated
above is the implicit assumption which they both share. I would
argue that at root the essential object which informs both views
of political life is an individualistic one; the first states that
individual material well-being is the sole criterion of public life
and the second states that the morally good is available only
through one's private conscience and binds one to act individually irregardless of the claims and needs (even for life) of all the
other members of the community.

The alternative proposed here differs fundamentally from
either of these positions in that it begins with a fundamentally

different view of the moral objects and of political life. The experience proposed here as a basis for the living out of our inescapable commonality rests neither in the aggregate of individual calculi which is at the base of modern economic justice, nor in the radically private view of moral absolutes which are valid independent of one's real and shared experiences of community. Rather, the experience proposed here rests on the assumption that public life as common life ultimately rests on something truly common and shareable.

But what might this be? And what would the discovery of such an object mean for our concrete alternatives? One can only appeal to one's experience and try to decide which might serve as a basis for public life. In part, what this object might be is a common bond of justice which transcends our modern notion of contract. What this might be, in part, is a shared general concern that the community honor those virtues which are truly human. What it might mean is that the community be vitally concerned with the question of what, in this community, shall constitute human excellence. What this might mean, in part, is that a substantial share of a community's energies be directed to activities which are essentially uneconomic; for example, speech and symbol which articulate the roots of common life. What this might mean, in part, would be a relationship with nature wherein the community takes cognizance of and is reverent towards the forces which support its common life. In short, what this might mean is that communal life be based not only on those admitted series of mutual dependencies of survival, but also on those experiences of gratefulness which we occasionally glimpse when we together with others celebrate a man who is just, a deed that is noble, or a nature which in some decisive way has succored us.

But, one might ask, have you not secretly opted for one of your own temptations? Is not this talk of justice the beginning of that moralism which threatens not only the community but life itself?

One would be forced to answer this way. The modern liberal state has assumed that the confusing similarity of good and evil dictates that the attempt to instill the good must be abandoned. The modern understanding seems to be that if one eliminates goodness, then one eliminates its opposite, evil, and especially its political form, tyranny. Obviously, a complete answer would involve an investigation into the adequacy of this modern understanding. But cannot this much be said? The very nature of the experiences proposed here would seem to preclude tyranny. For tyranny is defined as the rule of one for private ends. And the experience to which we appealed was one which rested on the conviction that there was something shareable rather than private about our life together. The modern political liberal appears to deny decisively this experience. He appears appalled at corruption, and yet refuses to engage in a search for anything like a common good, because he fears centralization of power in a moral dictatorship. The assumption seems to be that one can only judge a regime externally, according to its degree of decentralization. And yet Aristotle found that the most crucial judgments of regimes were between those with similar degrees of centralization (e.g., oligarchy and aristocracy). Hence his concern with external procedure is slight, and most attention is paid to the decisive difference, that is, the difference in the objects towards which the regimes directed themselves.

There is another dimension to the common experiences mentioned above which speaks to the question of tyranny and also revolution: those joyful moments when some communal celebration might ordain our lives appear to be the most difficult rather than the least difficult thing to attain. Again, if we are true to our experience, which certainly admits the ambiguity of the multiple objects which attract us, we can at least say this: the human virtue of which we speak demands the most painful sacrifices and the most difficult search of anything we have encountered. To those who would invite us to join a final and irrevocable crusade, one would have to reply that the world does not appear to be that way; to be sure, the world offers a hope of some happiness together, but not through chemical ecstasy, sensitivity encounters, or other instantaneous conversions.

The final question we must answer is one which springs from this last experience. One might say that something like this commonality had been experienced in some way, but that for most men it was nothing but a phrase, nothing but a dream which resulted in the maniacal ravings of the revolutionary or the cynical deals of the politicians. Again, one could hardly disagree. And the consequences for public life are severe. For what this may mean is that to affect fundamentally the life of the republic one cannot either manipulate economic totals or appeal to a simply available justice.

What may be involved is a very simple and agonzing task: to reflect on one's life and search out those things which might be commensurate with our deepest longings, to strain with every nerve to live according to those things, and to speak and act with our fellows with them in view. (Which may mean that what we are dealing with here is very objective.) It may be that to achieve a common goal for the republic depends upon a substantial number of its citizens living according to that good. And that may mean the living of long lives by many men dedicated to the creation of a space in which such things can flourish.

Notes

1. F. Scott Fitzgerald, *The Great Gatsby* (New York: Scribner's, 1953), p. 182.
2. Rainer Maria Rilke, *Wartime Letters of Rainer Maria Rilke 1914-1921*, trans., M. D. Herter Norton (New York: Norton, 1940), p. 34–35.
3. Ibid., p. 124.
4. Ibid., p. 125.

The Possibility of a
Political Morality

Aldo Tassi

As another election year approaches we find ourselves, politically speaking, in a house shaken to its foundations. Despair has settled in among a large segment of the electorate who are considering abandoning the political domain entirely. These are not the people we call the "silent majority," for apathy is very different from despair. Rather, we are talking about all those citizens who have been vitally concerned with our political life, especially during the 1960s, but who now feel that it may be necessary to refuse to participate in it any longer. What has happened is that the political crisis we face is so serious that the very necessity of the political order itself has been challenged. The present crisis has forced out into the open the kind of question we do not like to raise, that is, the philosophical question: Is the political order necessary?

It is, of course, precisely such philosophical questions that must be raised when we enter a crisis. When the foundation is threatened, then the presuppositions that constitute the foundation must be examined if the house is ever to stand firm again. Reform or revolt? Continue to participate in politics in hopes of changing the political order or reject politics entirely? The dilemma that faces us today offers no way out unless we decide to examine our conception of the nature of politics, to try to clarify to ourselves what we presuppose the nature of politics to be. This is the philosophical analysis I propose to start here. My concern will be to show that, given our present historical predicament, there is a preconception about what the nature of politics is that has led directly to our despair. Only by understanding this preconception will we be able to distinguish authentic from inauthentic solutions to our present crisis.

The roots of the crisis are clearly to be found in our recent experience. The tremendous resurgence of political involvement during the 1960s meant for many people that the political order had become the locus for a renewal of spirit. Although individual motives for involvement were varied, there did seem to be a common cause, a joining of ranks, a shared understanding of what the political order signified to us. We became involved because of places like Selma, Watts, and Appalachia, and because of leaders like Martin Luther King and John and Robert Kennedy. The charisma of these leaders lay in their ability to rekindle in us a belief that had been dormant in previous years : the belief, in short, that we are all our brother's keeper. It was, above all, by heeding a call to conscience that we became involved in the political order. Political involvement flowed directly from the awareness of having a duty toward those who were victims of injustice. It is important to make clear that more than a sense of moral outrage was entailed ; it was a sense of responsibility. At the core of our commitment was not so much the consciousness that injustice and oppression are wrong, but the acknowledgment that one is obliged to do something. One can, after all, deplore injustice and at the same time maintain that the only remedy is to wait for men's hearts to change. But to use politics as the instrument for remedying injustice is to reject the position of letting nature take its course. The commitment to politics became a refusal to hide from oneself the duty one has toward others.

And yet this very conception of the political order eventually led to our present despair. The instrument which we used to fight against injustice and oppression, and with some successes, was itself an instrument of oppression. Although politics is the means through which the injustices perpetrated by a majority upon a minority can be eliminated, it is also the means through which a minority can further its interests at the expense of a majority. This became all too obvious in the Vietnam issue, in the Chicago Convention of '68, in the response of the government to the ecological crisis, to demands for consumer protection, to fraudulent practices of industries doing business with the government—and the list can be multiplied to infinity. This contradiction at the heart of the political order has caused the present crisis. Despite our good will, we have found ourselves to be "part of the problem."

Although many people of varying political persuasions have been deeply upset by this crisis, only one group has come forward thus far with a philosophical analysis of our situation : the radicals. Let us consider here their appraisal of this crisis and the solution they offer us. According to their thinking, the contradiction at the heart of the political order arises from the incapacity of government to do what it has been created to do. The radical analysis proceeds by way of distinguishing the *political* from the *social* order. A "society" is constituted by the existence of a common set of conditions through which a number of individuals pursue their interests. This set of conditions is expressed in rules governing behavior. What characterizes the interests of human beings is that they require the creation of the conditions for their fulfillment. And every condition that is created, by its nature, is social, that is, capable of fulfilling the interests of more than one. The existence of the social order then is rooted in the nature of man. The interests which are pursued in and through a social order may be homogeneous as in the case of a simple society, or heterogeneous as in the case of a complex society.

A difficulty occurs, however, by virtue of the fact that more than one society exists. Herein lies the possibility (and subsequent actuality) of a conflict between one or more social orders. In other words, the conditions through which one group pursues its interests may conflict with the conditions through which another group pursues its interests. This necessitates a "higher" order whose purpose is to resolve such conflicts. This is the political order. Government is born as the instrument through which conflicting conditions for pursuing interests are resolved. Success is measured by the ability of the political order to establish conditions through which the conflicting societies can harmoniously pursue their interests. This can be understood in two ways.

The political order can be understood to leave the various societies intact. Political rules then are viewed as rules of a higher order whose object is to establish conditions for "inferior" rules. This is more or less the pluralist view of politics in which the political order is understood to be the marketplace where interest groups meet and compromise. Another way of understanding the relationship between the political order and societies is to see the political order as completely superceding the societal order. In this view—which is more or less the socialist idea of politics—the political order is a sort of "higher" society which establishes the conditions through which all individuals pursue their interests.

As a matter of fact, the present American scene operates in both ways. The political order has shown itself to be a compromise not among all the societies embraced by the political order, as it properly should be, but rather a compromise among a small number of interest groups. The conditions established by the political order are those which serve the interests of these small groups, at the expense of all other weaker groups, notwithstanding the advantages such weaker groups may occasionally enjoy. The appeal to national interests has become a virtual travesty : witness the abject failure of all attempts to make those groups whose interests coincide with national interests bear the expense of national policies. At the same time every attempt by the political order to establish conditions through which everyone's interests can be pursued has required the manipulation and dehumanization of interests. Time and again the government reaches individuals by a process of depersonalization—the least common denominator approach. Such a way of relating to individuals systematically ignores precisely those interests with which individuals identify themselves. In attempting to overcome the reluctance of individuals to accept such a depersonalized relationship, the government has manipulated and dominated people's interests—in the name of educating them—to the point of creating artificial interests which can be satisfied through governmental action. On both scores, the radicals maintain, the political order has failed dismally in the very purpose that defines it.

The only solution which the radicals find possible, given this analysis of our crisis, is one of total withdrawal from the political order. Let us turn our attention, they say, to societies instead, and create (or recreate) them in such a manner that the possible clashes which give rise to the political order can be completely eliminated. The beginning of our renewal as people lies in the creation of new societies. Politics will thereby be revealed as unnecessary.

The opponents of the radical position argue that societies by their nature always require a political order because irreconcilable conflicts will inevitably develop. The radicals reply that it is the belief itself that politics is necessary which fosters this dogma. Once we rule out the necessity of politics, then it becomes possible to attend to the task of creating societies which do not generate such conflicts. The advantage which radicals have over their opponents in such a clash is that the radicals can appeal to the political events of the late 1960s as telling evidence that politics will not work.

Although the radical analysis is compelling on one level, it proves nevertheless to be a deficient analysis of the present crisis. While the radicals make full use of the sense of betrayal that characterizes our awareness of the crisis, they would have us forget the very concept of politics which made this sense of betrayal possible. In other words, the radical appraisal achieves its power to persuade us to withdraw from politics by making us forget why we involved ourselves in politics to begin with. The contradiction which the radicals resolve is not *our* contradiction. This reveals itself in the fact that most of us feel that to withdraw from the political order would itself constitute a moral compromise. We would, in effect, have to deny the validity of the call to conscience that led us to politics. To withdraw would mean to abandon those who are victims of injustice and oppression, a position we shrink from taking.

If we find the radical analysis finally deficient insofar as it fails to draw us away from the political order, we still need to find a compelling reason for remaining actively in our political system. What we require is fundamentally an analysis which directs itself to the conception of politics that has been operative in our political behavior during the 1960s. During this period, we considered the political order necessary for the fulfillment of our moral obligations toward others. Quite possibly, this may have been putting politics to a whole new use. Be that as it may, we considered it to be a valid use, and our problem today is whether or not we have any reason to believe that it is no longer a valid use of politics. The radical analysis is directed toward the usual notion of politics. This does not throw any light on our understanding of politics. What we need is a new analysis whose goal is to bring to light the nature and validity of this new use of politics.

As we begin examining this concept of politics, we find first of all that it is based on a different sort of distinction between the political and the social order from that given by the radicals.

If, as we have seen, a social order is characterized by the establishment of conditions for the pursuit of interests, then the political order, in this new sense, establishes the conditions for men fulfilling their duty toward others. The political order here arises not from the clashes between societies, but from the acknowledgment of a duty to work for the elimination of any injustice done to another—whether he be a member of our own or another society. This notion of duty should not be confused with charity or compassion, neither of which call for the acknowledgment of one's responsibility for eliminating injustice. Nor should it be confused with a sense of guilt, for the responsibility is present whether or not one is individually guilty of oppressing others. Quite clearly, then, the political order understood in this manner is a moral instrument, whereas the political order whose purpose is to harmonize conflicts between societies is understood to be a natural instrument. As a moral instrument, the political order is directed toward the elimination of injustice and oppression of others; as a natural instrument, the political order is directed toward satisfying human interests. The necessity of politics as a moral instrument is rooted in the acknowledgment that every man has a duty toward other men; in contrast we find the necessity of politics as a natural instrument to be rooted in the recognition that all men have interests. It may be possible to argue, as the radicals have tried to do, that the political order *as a natural instrument* is not necessary, in which case we understand human interests as capable of being pursued in such a way that politics is not required. But it does not seem possible to argue in the same way that the political order *as a moral instrument* is not necessary, for this would involve the denial that there exists any duty toward others. And although it may be possible to agree with the radicals that the chronic failure of the political order as a natural instrument is due to the very nature of the instrument itself, such is not the case for politics conceived as a moral instrument. Failure in this sphere can only occur when men refuse to acknowledge their duty to others. In the one case, failure can be attributed to the instrument itself; in the other case, failure results from a moral lapse in men.

Our present situation in politics, it seems to me, is somehow parallel to the development of the moral life in an individual person. Initially we live our lives on the principle of pleasure and pain. We espouse values in terms of the pursuit of interests—for example, honesty is the best policy. Then for some reason—God only knows—we find ourselves responding to values for their own sake. Our lives take on a sense of purpose and we are conscious of awakening to the truth about human existence. But very soon a crisis develops when it becomes apparent that our natural life—a life rooted in wants, desires, needs—still has its own claims that must be satisfied. At this point three options appear before us : we can deny the claims of the moral life or we can deny the claims of the natural life or we can transform the natural life. To choose either of the first two courses of action would be disastrous, leading to a life lived without a sense of purpose, in the first case, or to a life lived oblivious to the reality which surrounds it, in the second case. The third choice, that of transforming one's natural life in terms of the moral life, offers a better alternative. The natural claims of our wants and desires remain intact, but the moral claims reveal to the person that, valid as the claims of nature are, he is nevertheless responsible for the conduct of his life. He feels called upon to exercise control over his life according to the moral criterion. In other words, if one acknowledges the claims of morality, one accepts thereby the fact that he is not impotent before the demands of nature.

In a similar way we have discovered a moral use for politics. Our involvement in the political order during the 1960s brought a sense of purpose to our public lives. We acknowledged and acted upon an important truth about ourselves : namely, that we are all our brother's keeper. Our crisis appeared when our moral purposes ran headlong into the intransigence of politics as a natural instrument. The two uses of politics cannot coexist as autonomous and separate instruments. The claims which each use of politics makes on the political order seem at first to be incompatible with the claims of the other use. Certainly this is true with respect to politics as a natural instrument : its claims would destroy the possibility of using politics as a moral instrument. But the reverse case is not true; the claims of politics as a moral instrument do not destroy the possibility of using politics as a natural instrument. Rather, the use of politics as a moral instrument can *transform* its use as a natural instrument, precisely by supplying a criterion according to which the natural instrument can be guided. It appears, then, that our disillusionment has sprung from having insufficiently understood the nature of our political behavior and the meaning of the situation which that behavior has produced. What we face today, in short, is a crisis in the development of political morality. This development ultimately requires that, in the use of politics as a natural instrument, we accept the fact that we are not impotent before the demands made by the nature of the instrument.

The chronic problem with respect to government as a natural instrument has been that public officials, who personally are honest and virtuous, find themselves to be victims of the instrument they use. As public officials they are expected to serve the "national interests"; in other words, they must use the political order as a natural instrument. And therefore "national interests" will dictate the political course of action to be taken. The consequences of the exercise of political power create situations which are viewed as necessary and unavoidable. To impugn the honesty and virtuousness of public officials when these situations involve inequities is to miss the point. As long as political power remains an untransformed political instrument, it must by its nature be guided by "national interests" alone and public officials must accept whatever situations are created in the pursuit of such interests.

This state of affairs will not change merely by insuring that only men of personal honesty and virtuousness become public officials, since public officials are required by their office to use government as a natural instrument. Change will only take place when public officials acknowledge that they are not impotent in the face of the claims of politics as a natural instrument. This acknowledgment must be more than the hope of men who are personally honest and virtuous. It must be *politically* possible. That it *is* politically possible was demonstrated during the 1960s whenever politics was used as a moral instrument. In other words, the political order itself was the instrument through which we exercised control over circumstances. It is because we have used politics as the instrument to remedy injustice that we now are able to refuse—*as a matter of political possibility*—to remain impotent in the face of the legitimate claims of politics as a natural instrument. It is instructive to recall that we entered into politics precisely because we rejected the position that we must wait for men's hearts to change before injustices could be remedied. If we were not prepared to stand impotent before men's hearts, then we are not prepared to resign ourselves to the consequences of the exercise of political power as a natural instrument.

Perhaps it belongs to the nature of the pursuit of "national interests" that some groups of people profit at the expense of others. Let us grant this for the sake of argument. But there are, even so, many ways of pursuing "national interests." Why can we not exercise control *from the beginning* and choose the way of arriving at these goals that leads to the least inequity? And in the face of the inequity which is created, why can we not exercise control over this *at the moment of its creation*—indemnifying those at whose expense "national interests" are pursued and exacting payment from those who profit by it? Surely the human imagination, spurred by a sense of moral duty, can invent more than welfare and taxes, which are in fact testaments to our present impotence in the face of the demands of politics as a natural instrument. Perhaps the 1960s has also given us a rule to be followed in the education of future public officials. Let whoever is to use politics as a natural instrument first use it as a moral instrument. In this way, he will, as a matter of political experience and wisdom, reject any notion of impotence with respect to the political order.

The practitioners of the old politics view politics in terms of a technology. They consider themselves to be technicians who have come to understand the mechanics of the exercise of political power. Their way of understanding themselves as political beings is in terms of politics as a natural instrument. Their political experience and wisdom flow from this initial manner of defining their political behavior. When they speak of the "political facts of life," they mean this technology of politics. But recent experience has introduced a radically new element into the political scene. Great numbers of people were initiated into politics as a moral instrument. The political experience and wisdom of this new group were entirely different from the politicians of the old school. They can reject the so-called "political facts of life" precisely for political reasons. They have learned through experience that something else is possible in politics.

From this discussion we can see more clearly why we reject the radical's invitation to withdraw from the political sphere. His position rests on a fundamental agreement with the present holders of political power. They both agree about the nature of political power and they both accept man's impotence in the face of those situations that he creates through wielding political power. Their opposition is based on this fundamental agreement. The old politics operates according to the belief that the exercise of political power is necessary; the radical believes that it is not necessary. But for each of them politics is only a natural instrument. According to the radical's view, the present political crisis is a clash between politics and morality. But the morality he speaks of is essentially a private morality and, as such, is impotent in the face of the demands made by politics as a natural instrument. For a man of private morality has no option—short of refusing to participate in politics at all—but to accept the rules dictated by politics as a natural instrument. This consideration is the moral basis for the radical's advocacy of withdrawal from the system.

But, as this analysis has shown, this is not the true nature of the clash that characterizes our present political crisis. What we see taking place today is rather a struggle between a moral politics and a natural politics. It is, in short, the kind of crisis wherein a political morality will either develop or die. The concept of a political morality is peculiar.

First of all it must be a morality. And secondly it must be political. For both the "old politics" and the radicals this state of affairs would seem to be a contradiction. And so it would be if all that is possible is politics as a natural instrument. But recent experience has taught us otherwise. The moral use of politics has demonstrated the possibility of a political morality—that is to say, the possibility of a transformed use of politics as a moral instrument.

It is important, however, to understand clearly what political morality does and does not dictate. It dictates the limits under which the pursuit of interests is to take place. It does not dictate what interests are to be pursued. As a matter of fact, it has been the failure to make this distinction that has created the confusion between morality and moralism. Moralism comes about when one group claims to know the authentic needs of the people as a whole and when this claim becomes the justification for dictating what interests are to be pursued. Such assertions are indistinguishable from the claims made by every totalitarian regime. In marked contrast, political morality makes no such claims. It acknowledges that nature and history—rather than morality—are the source of needs and interests. Morality is only the source of limits. In this case, one group claims to know *not* what the authentic needs or interests of the whole people are, but rather that certain situations which result from the pursuit of interests are unjust and oppressive and are for this reason unacceptable.

But how is this claim to know that certain situations are unjust any less dubious than the claim to know what the people's true interests are? Just as there is a pluralism of interests, so too there is operative today a pluralistic morality. Granted that agreement on the level of private morality seems all but impossible, I submit, nevertheless, that this need not be the case in political morality. No such difficulty occurs in agreeing as to whether a given situation in which some men find themselves is intrinsically unacceptable or not. What complicates our assessment of such situations is the insistence that these situations be understood in terms of the requirements of politics as a natural instrument. This means that the necessity of pursuing certain interests conditions the manner in which we see the results created by this pursuit. If we could direct ourselves to a situation pure and simple, there would be virtually no disagreement as to its intrinsic unacceptability. What prevents this shift in attention is our submission to the nature of the political instrument. The distinctive feature of political morality is the possibility of just such a shift in attention. And, accordingly, what characterizes the transformed use of politics as a natural instrument is that it does not prevent us from assessing the intrinsic merits of the situations which politics creates.

This transformed use of politics as a natural instrument, then, will be the exercise of political power with an *internal* limit—the internal limit which morality places on human action. This means that the following maxim should operate in the exercise of political power : *Do not do that which may result in situations for which one does not possess the present means of remedy.* If nothing else, the present ecological crisis has taught us that a politics which proceeds on the principle of trial and error (and the only alternative to this in the practice of natural politics is utopianism) has become a bizarre activity. It has created the very real possibility that we may, in the exercise of political power, create situations that we have no power to remedy. A number of citizens believe that this has already transpired in both the Vietnam issue and the ecological crisis. Be that as it may, the present political crisis reveals to us not just the possibility of political morality, but also its necessity.

Our analysis does not, as the radical might suggest, depend upon our ignoring the internal contradictions of the use of politics as a natural instrument. To say that politics is necessary in order to fulfill our duty toward others does not mean that we must accept the injustices created by the use of politics as a natural instrument. Quite the contrary, the use of politics as a moral instrument ultimately requires us to transform its use as a natural instrument. What this means, in effect, is that on the one hand we are prepared to accept the utter fallibility of the instrument, but on the other hand we are not prepared to resign ourselves to the inequities it may produce. In other words, the refusal to accept injustice is not for us, as it is for the radical, the basis for withdrawal from politics. It is, rather, a mark that we are practicing the "new politics." Our impotence is not rooted in the nature of the instrument we use. It is rooted in the empirical fact that the "old politics" is still dominant. But, as is true of all empirical states of affairs, this situation is changing. The desperation of the "old politics" is a measure of this change. It would be a tragedy—a tragedy that has probably happened all too often in human history—if in ignorance we quit the field precisely at the time when political morality has ceased to be a contradiction in terms and has become a *political* possibility.

III

Privacy, Libertarian Dreams, and Politics

E. A. Goerner

America has come closer to living out the libertarian dreams of modern society than any other country. There have been some nightmares among those dreams. But Americans have generally preferred them, nightmares included, to any other form of consciousness. And so they have never valued politics and public life very highly.

But our recent politics has been such that great numbers of Americans, especially the newly enfranchised young, have come to value politics and public life not at all, have come to think that politics and public life is a realm of degrading lies and murderous actions. The revelations of the Pentagon Papers confirmed for many what was previously only an uneasy suspicion : a wide range of "public servants" and a whole series of administrations, of different parties, consistently conducted (seemingly without shame) a foreign policy in Southeast Asia that recognized no limits to the practice of falsehood or the most hateful acts.

In another society, decent men might think such a spectacle a revelation of monstrous corruption and defigurement of the *res publica* calling them to heroic sacrifices for its reform. But in a society dedicated to libertarian dreams, the *res publica* has always been at best a means, at worst the lesser of necessary evils. Its corruption and defigurement are by no means negligible matters, but its reformation has narrower limits and stands tributary to a consideration of central importance.

In any society organized in terms of the fundamental priority of individual rights, it is important to know what those rights are. For us, no one has improved on the original statement of our public consensus about those constitutive rights: life, liberty, and the pursuit of happiness. That is altogether obvious, but what is not always fully perceived is that they must be understood together, as profoundly interpenetrative. We are not, for example, organized in terms of the absolute priority of the individual right to mere life. Our society makes no sense in such terms. Our public life only makes sense to us and to outsiders in terms of a right to life in liberty.

Liberty is the central element of the triad, but it remains somewhat obscure without the final term, because it is a new kind of liberty. It includes but goes beyond the civic or political liberty of the citizens of the ancient republics. That was the liberty of one who had an active participation in the *res publica* and who was subject to no public rule but that of the *res publica* in which, with the gods, he participated.

But the liberty at the roots of our society goes further. It goes to the very center of human existence in a way the ancients only dreamed of when they dreamt of themselves as tyrants. The freedom the ancients sometimes dreamed the tyrant had was precisely the freedom to do whatever he pleased. And the blazing focus of our libertarian dreams is an unlimited, personal, powerful freedom to accomplish one's heart's desires as they unfold in endless, splendid, kaleidoscopic transformations. More tersely: the pursuit of happiness. And not any sort of pursuit of happiness whatever, but the pursuit of happiness conceived of as an individual right.

No doubt ancient citizens sought happiness as much as we,

but they seem to have been less sure than we are as to what happiness is. That may seem to be a strange thing to say since one often enough hears the opposite maintained. But in fact the moral tension and greatness of the ancient cities grows in great part out of the public debate and life struggle among diverse responses to the question as to what happiness is, as to what it is that the seemingly boundless desire, striving, loving, struggling, leaping of men's lives aims at.

On the surface it seems we surely admit as many, if not more, answers to that question into our "marketplace of ideas" as anyone, ancients included. That is only appearance. In fact we exclude from serious consideration one whole range of possible answers and we base our society, our public institutions, and our public and private discourse on that exclusion. The fundamental significance for the life of the citizen of having structured our life together in terms of the pursuit of happiness as a private right is that happiness is finally *not public* but *private,* that no substantive answer valid for all the citizens can be given to the question : What is happiness? In ancient terms, we have formally excluded from our life together the possibility that happiness has a nature.

We seem, strangely, to be so much surer about what happiness is precisely because we have organized our public life to exclude the possibility that happiness has a nature. We teach one another in an almost infinite variety of modes that one man's happiness may as well be another man's misery, that happiness is, finally, utterly subjective.[1] What that means is that some men may in fact regard participation in public life, and even participation in public life in some particular way, as desirable in itself, as part of happiness for them. But it also means that public life is only a part of *their* peculiar way of pursuing *their* happiness now. It may not be a part of the structure of their desires tomorrow and it is not among the things pursued by other citizens.

Participation in public life, in politics, at least in the form

of a vote in free elections, may very well be viewed by our tradition as essential to our organization of society and certainly one
of the basic institutional tests of libertarian democracy. But that
by no means puts politics at the center of our lives.

Included among the live options for the pursuit of happiness for the ancient citizen was the pursuit and, hopefully, the
attainment of virtue, of manliness in the broadest sense of the
full flowering of great and harmonious human powers and deeds.
That coming to a vigorous maturity of power and deed is only
seriously conceivable in the midst of the testing fire and mirror
of other men. Still, the others in whose midst one strains every
nerve to excel may only be desired as measuring sticks of one's
excellence rather than as companions. (That sort of pursuit of
happiness as excellence is quite conceivable among us, or those
of us who like such things. Indeed, much of business among us
has been organized into a sort of narrow public realm for just
such competition among executives.)

The other sort of possibility within that context, however,
was that the struggling, the testing, the straining every nerve
was finally conceived in terms of a . . . a what? Can I say "a
moral order"? Who would find the savor in that? Those who
shared the life of the Free French in World War II might have
some sense of what is at issue under the term *Compagnon de la
Liberation,* it being important to understand that among the
companions were men already dead before the Liberation. But
for us, what to say? that the struggling, testing, straining every
nerve, though never simply finished except in death, is finally
conceivable in terms of, in reference to, for the sake of living
together with good men? That is not altogether unintelligible to
us, perhaps. But, if intelligible, its references are private, to the
life together of teammates sometimes, of some classmates sometimes, of some small groups.

Struggling, testing, straining every nerve to win through,
even if always insecurely, to the living together, being together,

acting together of good men as the very root of the *res publica,* of public life—that is what our republic and our pursuit of happiness as an individual right and the whole structure of institutions and symbols joined to them are *not* about.

So, even if there is today, especially among the young, a powerful current turning to the sphere of private life and away from politics *even as a means* to secure the world of the intimate, of the private, that turning from public life is only a superficial and curiously temporary manifestation of a deep-running and original turning away from and denial of politics. The American republic, and in this she is the avant-garde of the modern world, is organized for the suppression of public life in the most serious sense. The "new order of the ages" [2] established by the American republic is an order of life within which there is no *res publica* in the most serious sense, that is to say, no public thing simply and in principle preferable to private things, and so no public life simply and in principle preferable to private things.[3]

For two hundred years we have maintained that the pursuit of happiness was a private affair. For two hundred years we have maintained that the public business was to create and maintain a framework of means for those private pursuits, to create and maintain the conditions in which each man could express himself, realize his uniqueness, pursue his own, personal values. The obvious problem posed by such a scheme of things is that one man's values, the happiness pursued by one man, may, in being realized, deprive others of their hearts' desires. The ancients knew that was precisely what was involved in tyranny. We have tried to combine the psychic perspective at the root of the tyrannical spirit—that of unlimited self-assertion, self-expression, self-gratification—with a politico-social machinery designed to prevent that self-assertion from depriving one's neighbor of the like.

The essential genius of our institutions is the mechanical

genius of a vast system of checks and balances at almost every level of our politico-social organization designed to prevent the complete success of any one at the expense of the others. Not only are the governmental organizations structured in terms of that political physics, both among themselves at any level and among levels, but their operation is in relation to a society in which a vast interplay of countervailing and shifting group pressures provides an informal version of the formal checks and balances of the constitutional organs.

That political physics of checks and balances is completed by a social physics that results in the staggering conformism and relative absence of overtly aggressive self-assertion of Americans in comparison with Europeans, who are far less fully inserted into the libertarian world even though, intellectually, that world is a European invention. The conformism and relatively non-aggressive overt behavior produced by the pressures of our social physics have central functional roles to play in our life together. Without them the conflict of individual and group interests could scarcely be kept from being universally seen as the war of all against all. Once that was clearly and generally seen, it would be too much to suppose that interest group politics would indefinitely retain its character of a limited war of border skirmishes, limited gains, and slow movement heavily characterized by defensive moves and accompanied simultaneously by multilateral bargaining. One would have to envisage the possibility, indeed the probability, of the appearance of Napoleons, de Gaulles, Guderians, Pattons of the socio-politico-economic wars. One would have to envisage the possibility of such leaders successfully gaining masses of followers for group struggles in which the blitzkrieg tactics of speed, surprise, risk, breakthrough, and mop-up are directed to the sudden demoralization and then radical defeat of one's opponents.

Such a development would not only involve the definitive collapse of our institutionalized system of checks and balances, but the end of the modern, i.e. mass, version of the libertarian dream in which each seeks the full flowering of his private happiness without destroying his neighbor's chances to do likewise.

The devices of our social physics have molded a conformism in the pursuit of happiness in which the elements of aggressiveness are for the most part socially indirect. By focusing attention on the conquest of nature rather than of men, we have made it possible for our system of checks and balances to continue to work, both institutionally and on the level of group politics. By focusing attention on the conquest of nature rather than of men, a conquest in which the masses participate both as troops and as recipients of the booty, we have produced a society of consumers in an ever expanding economy. That is to say, we have made it possible for each of us to pursue his private dreams in a spiral of ever vaster satisfactions by having lured almost all of us into a kind of vision of happiness not directly and inherently aggressive, in the measure that the conquest of nature seemed to allow for an unlimitedly expanding supply or booty to be divided.[4] We have, in short, taken the advice of Hobbes, who noted that the desire for commodious living inclines men to peace.

Obviously, the devices of our political and social physics have not operated perfectly, i.e., universally. Substantial groups at home and the greater part of the rest of the world have been left out of its regular operation. They are not necessarily exploited or otherwise oppressed. But they are either ignored or, when their interests and ours conflict and when they seem weaker, they are inevitably treated with the most callous brutality, because they are outside the operation of the devices of our political and social physics.

It is at precisely this point that the radical and seemingly revolutionary attacks have been launched on and in America. I say "seemingly" revolutionary because those attacks are in a paradoxical way profoundly conservative, radically conservative. The radical "revolutionary" critiques of contemporary bourgeois society, and of American society as its avant-garde, generally employ Marxist or Freudian terms or a melange of the two. But they operate essentially in the manner of an exposé of the hypocrisy involved in proclaiming the universalistic and rationalistic public dogmas about liberty and equality in the face of the reality of life in those societies. The radical "revolutionary" critiques of bourgeois society point out the infinite variety of socially induced and manipulated enslavements, exploitations, and denials that fill so much of the lives of so many in spite of the formal universalism of the foundational dogmas of modern libertarian societies. The critiques are indeed radical in that they go to the roots of society, but they are radically conservative in that they unquestioningly accept the root dream of bourgeois society : an unlimited liberation of each participant. The "revolutions" in question only involve greater or lesser demolition of the restrictive devices of the current political and social physics. The charge is basically that the bourgeois dream of radical liberation is, in the existing societies, artificially denied *de facto* realization for whole classes of the population and is artificially repressed in whole areas of human activity, most notably in that of sexuality.

The bourgeois view of politics in general is that of the technology of radical liberation. Modern revolutionary politics is the impatient and eschatological version of bourgeois politics in general. Moderate bourgeois politics and modern revolutionary politics both view the politics of human liberation in terms of external artifice, of the technology of restructuring politico-social conditions. The difference between the moderate and the revolutionary views is, in the end, a difference in the estimation of the possibility of a technological breakthrough in the sphere of politico-social physics of such a nature as to establish decisively the definitive liberation of man.

The history of the modern struggle for radical liberation is the history of revolutions conceived in eschatological terms followed by a discovery of limits and, sometimes, by the institutionalization of some particular liberties. There begins again the tension between those who are able to and do choose to pursue happiness in the avenues made available by those liberties and those who are not able or do not choose to pursue happiness there, but engage themselves in the struggle for wider or deeper liberation.

Evidently the mass of the population is not permanently situated in one camp or the other. The majority of the population of modern bourgeois societies of both the moderately and the frenetically revolutionary types is normally relatively apathetic to politics. Yet on occasion vast numbers are swept up into political movements of a "revolutionary" character with a view to restructuring some of the devices of the politico-social physics already in the service, but imperfectly, of radical liberation.

On a less radical level, vast numbers of citizens are from time to time caught up in major movements to change the political personnel of the existing institutions [5] in the belief, not always unfounded, that those currently conducting public affairs are either incompetent or have turned the institutions in directions that are incompatible with the diverse objectives of the rest of the citizenry.

But whether it is a question of "revolutionary" or moderate political engagement, the very nature of the political objective (the creation of a realm of freedom for individual self-realization) is such that the participants quite reasonably tend to oscillate between active engagement in politics and the enjoyment of such spheres of private gratification as may be available in the limited spans of their lives (either an entire life or each major time of life).

The shift by so many to relative political apathy after the diverse and intense engagements of 1968-70 is thus wholly within the tradition. Both those who had hoped only to stop the war in Indochina and those who hoped for wider political changes found the established order and the established politicians and the established majority (and, in the case of the assassination of Robert Kennedy, even the fates) infinitely tougher than had been hoped. And since even revolutionary politics is but a means to the liberation of individuals for self-realization, it is only reasonable and quite within our customary rationalism to calculate the costs against the gains. The outcome of the calculation for many has been the search for what happiness can still be had within our several private worlds.

But what is new in the present apathy is that the withdrawal from politics is vastly more profound and has become vastly more troubled and quietly more explosive than before. The current withdrawal is the product of a more terrifying clarity about the nature of our life together in the world of libertarian isolation than most of us have ever had before. For the first time, the full range of political consequences implicit in the pursuit of happiness as an individual right has come into view.

Americans have never thought much of public men. We have always, and logically enough, been quite ready to suppose that politics and hypocrisy were essentially the same : the politician pursuing his private advantages, material and psychic, behind a conventional rhetorical cloud of slogans about the public good, the common interest, and the like. The genius of our system (and the foundation of that rhetorical convention) was recognized by all in that system of competitive checks and balances conferring success on those politicians whose private interests seemed best to conduce to the private interests of those holding the majority of the votes.

But what many have just come to see is that for more than a decade, all our ingenious politico-social technology of competing checks and balances notwithstanding, successive administrations have managed to sacrifice the lives, limbs, hopes, and innocence of a generation for the sake of a politico-military project so essentially private that its mere revelation would have destroyed it. What many have just come to realize is the abyssal depth that can separate the private visions and projects of public officers and the world of seeming they manage to construct.

That puts the mass of us on the verge of another discovery that, in its terror-striking integrality, has been so far the private possession of some seers and poets of the modern world and of some of their readers. The mass of Americans are on the verge of discovering that the war in Indochina and the manner of its perpetration are perfectly normal expressions of a human reality in which each man necessarily follows his private aims, because there is, in the end, no shared happiness, no communion in the splendor of the good. We are on the verge of discovering that the universe of the pursuit of happiness as the final right, i.e., the universe of radical personal liberation, is the universe of absolute loneliness. We are on the verge of discovering that the universe of absolute loneliness, the psychic manifestations of which are all around us, is the world in which we have already conditionally murdered everyone in principle; what remains to be done being only the materialization of that spiritual attitude by actually killing when the appropriate conditions of the cost-benefit calculus are present. We are on the verge of discovering that to be radically free to do and be one's personal vision means to be in a position to prevent others from realizing theirs when they are incompatible with ours. We are on the verge of discovering that our public discourse has no central terms available with which to deal with the failure of the American engagement in Indochina except those of miscalculation.

We are on the verge of discovering that our universe of discourse is such that our public officers can scarcely be expected to perceive their dealings with foreign peoples in terms other than calculations of weight, force, position, and direction, those being the central terms in which our public life is constituted and understood from its beginning, as the Federalist Papers attest. In foreign affairs that manifests itself today in the language of politico-strategic calculus of escalation and de-escalation, of megatonnage, and, final obscenity, the calculus of relative body counts. Everyone who has steady eyes has always known that matters of weight, force, position, and direction, of battle casualties and of firepower are important matters in international relations. What we are on the verge of realizing is that such terms are the only terms we really know and that they are absolutely inadequate. We and our leaders do not move in a universe of discourse in which it is possible to say what we have been about except in terms of miscalculation.

Obviously, cynicism and calculation are not new in politics, domestic or international. But a politics can only be called cynical if there is some alternative way of conducting public affairs. We are on the verge of discovering that our politics cannot be called cynical within our universe of discourse because it is a universe that only admits of calculation. Oh, there is, of course, the universe of raw emotional reactions, of disgust and outrage in this case, but that is a chaos rather than a universe. To that mass of howls and value judgments we deny either rational validity or counterpart. But rational validity and counterpart are the conditions of universality. And so our raw emotional reactions correspond to nothing but our private world, a world to which public officers engaged in a struggle to bring off their private schemes will scarcely feel bound. So we can howl our disgust and outrage at their projects and at the price to be paid for them. And if we, in our turn, can get a majority of the available political power on our side, we can impose our alternative projects. But educated Americans have no reasonable grounds to condemn the war's perpetrators, except perhaps for their failure to carry it off quickly at as low a cost as they thought they could at first.[6] That is manifested in the fact that the leading participants in that fantastic project, even those who

became disenchanted with its continuance and chose to withdraw or even to begin resisting it, are not overcome with shame
and chagrin. And they are not alone in their shamelessness. We
do not expect of former Presidents and Cabinet members con-
fessions rather than memoirs, nor do we even hope for them
against expectation, because we do not expect them or even
hope for them from ourselves. To be overcome with shame and
chagrin [Can I hope to be understood not to be referring to dis-
appointment and despite at having failed?], to articulate it, to
be understood, and to set out on a penitential pilgrimage [I am
not talking about going back to one's ranch or law practice to
lick one's wounds] would require a universe of public experience and of corresponding symbols richer than ours now are.
That would require an experience of and religio-philosophic
symbols for a sacred communion, for a sacred being-together
beyond the level of similar emotions, and an experience and
symbols for the breaking of that communion, and an experience
of and symbols for penance, the healing of the breaks and the
living with the scar.

To sense the depth of our divorce from such a world, read
Lincoln's Second Inaugural Address. Ask yourself whether our
discourse about public things, your discourse about public things,
has any place for an analogous (obviously not equivalent) perception and articulation of our situation. Were the humor not
too bitter, one could imagine the unfolding of an analysis of
Lincoln's speech in terms of our social or political "sciences."

Evidently, we and modern rationalistic societies in general
are not in possession of any such symbols in common nor shall
we be for the Presidential elections of 1972. In this context, the
flight from politics is profoundly ambiguous. Part of that flight
is simply another expression of our accustomed individualistic
and, therefore, mass pursuit of new private pleasures. Having had
a fling at political ferment, one gets bored and turns to something
else. But part of the flight has a quite different significance.

Part of the disenchantment with politics is a reflex of the discovery that the world of politics *against* the war was, in spite of the righteous slogans, also a world of illusion and lies, of self-delusion, of false hopefulness and real despair, of proclaimed unity and community, and of real isolation, division, maneuvers, and abysmal loneliness amid the shallow and easy fraternity of protest marches. Most seriously, part of the disenchantment with politics seems to be a reflex of a discovery only on the verge of articulation, a discovery very hard to take after so many years of education in rationalistic optimism and belief in progress, evolutionary or revolutionary but progress, a discovery on the verge of articulation but not yet named and faced, about the awesome depth, variousness, universality, and tenacity of our evil in spite of our never-ending cries for justice and love, for communion and the truth. Not a few have noticed that the anti-war movement drew not only the best, the most generous souls, but also the worst, as self-righteous as any bourgeois, the haters, the vengeance seekers for a thousand personal hurts getting their fill under cover of slogans about justice and peace.

In sum, many of those who have become disenchanted with politics after tasting both the enormous power of the perpetrators of the war and the less than holy righteousness and the illusory realities of the political protest movements, have hoped to find a refuge from the power of evil in the privacy of small communities, of mystical experience, and of the revolt against reason.

The shift from public to private life is both supported by and supports the contemporary interest in mysticism (religious and philosophical, eastern and western) and in small communities and in the revolt against rationalism and reason. That set of relationships is both a sign of health and a force retarding the development and expression of mystical experience and community in the whole gamut of life, including politics. Those new interests retard the transfiguration of ordinary life, including politics, insofar as they are articulated in radical, Manichean opposition to the rest of our ordinary, rational experience rather than being developed as its transcendent culminations. But the concern with mystery and mysticism, with community, and the revolt against reason and rationalism (and so against scientism and technologism) are signs of health insofar as they manifest a permanent thirst for the universal, for the reality of communion, for the splendor and gratuitousness that sometimes blazes out at us in things and in great-hearted deeds. They are signs of health insofar as that side of our being searches to realize itself and searches for the symbolic articulation whereby to be shared even in a cultural climate that has no place for it.

It is not, therefore, inconceivable that a candidate find, however haltingly, awkwardly, and without the support of an appropriate universe of public discourse, the words to interpret our experience in Indochina as more than a collossal miscalculation (as to how much the Indochinese opponents of our project could bear, as to how many lies could be successfully carried off at home, as to how much Americans could be induced to suffer for the vague patriotic objectives that shrouded our Indochinese venture). It is not altogether inconceivable that a Presidential candidate find words wherewith to lead his fellow citizens to a perception of their agony in Vietnam as the divine retribution—as fitting, as necessary, as inexorable as in a classic tragedy—of our staggering self-satisfaction, self-righteousness, and self-confidence in and because of our enormous technico-military power, the external proof of the superiority, not of our virtue, but of social institutions that are so smartly conceived as to make authentic human excellence irrelevant. It is not altogether inconceivable that a Presidential candidate find the words to lead his fellow citizens to the first, hesitant, penitential steps toward binding up the wounds. It is not altogether inconceivable that a Presidential candidate find the words to lead his fellow citizens on some modest first steps toward a new spirit from which might develop a community over the scars not only of the war but of our centuries-old racism and the centuries-old rape of nature and of the economically weak.

It is not altogether inconceivable. It is not very likely either. And if the unlikely does not come to pass? Two things are to be feared. On the one hand, some gravely unsettling event may very well precipitate a mass return to political engagement, but in a politics of eschatologically revolutionary illusions at fever pitch, fed by our damned up hopes so long denied. We cannot pretend not to know where that leads. We have seen, more than once this century, the sharply whetted thirst for liberation find its archetypal expressions in concentration camps and death factories. On the other hand, for fear of stirring up that madness, out of despair of finding a middle way, men of balanced intelligence and courage may hunt for what happiness and virtue they can find in privacy alone. Then in the world of public action we will lose even the occasional sight of even-handed and great-hearted deeds without the experience of which the very concept of authentic community loses its most visible referent and substance. And in the world of reflection we will have no hope of untangling the epistemological web that isolates us all, denying ultimate foundation and counterpart to the experience of community in even-handed and great-hearted deeds.

Notes

1. Happiness as subjective does not necessarily mean that each man chooses freely (one view has it that there is no free choice at all), but only that there is no way to specify the limits to what may be regarded as desirable nor to specify any common order among desirable things.
2. The *novus ordo seclorum* begins in 1776, according to the great seal of the United States, as can be seen on the back of a dollar bill.
3. It must be repeated that this does not prevent individuals, whose personal fancy so inclines them, from making public life their private pursuit of happiness.
4. We are only recently beginning to wonder whether we really can rape nature forever without one day reducing her to some haggard old whore, an object of horror from whom no technological Ovid can wrest yet one more delight.
5. Note the frequency with which such movements bear "revolutionary" slogans such as "New Deal," "New Frontier," "Great Society," "New Society."
6. The Marxist version of that judgment only adds the self-satisfaction that Marxists are on the winning side, since, knowing the laws of historical development, they know in advance who will win in the long run in such a struggle.

In Defense of Political Liberalism

David Little

In the light of all that has happened over the past decade, it is bewildering to recall the attitudes one held in the early 1960s. Given current sentiment in this country, I can now hardly believe that, as an innocent American student visiting West Germany in 1961, I could have been astonished at the pervasive political apathy and cynicism among German young people. To one who was inspired, as I was, with the promise of American politics as articulated and represented by John F. Kennedy, the prevailing political spirit captured in the phrase *ohne mich*— "without me"—was incomprehensible. In America of 1971, neither the spirit nor the phrase is any longer incomprehensible. It fits the attitude of cynicism and indifference many Americans feel toward politics, an attitude that is partly born of a growing hostility to some of the traditional ideals and patterns of American political life.

This hostility seems to take one of three general forms: withdrawal from typical political concern and activity; disparagement of accepted patterns of thought and action and pro-

I am indebted to my colleague, James F. Childress, for some very helpful suggestions.

posals for far-reaching changes; total rejection of existing political institutions and advocacy of violent revolution. I limit myself here to consideration of only the first two forms—withdrawal and disparagement. (A response to the advocates of violent revolution involves very complex questions and long discussion. I do, however, sketch my general reaction in a note, No. 27.)

Withdrawal from typical political concern and activity is of several types. There is "hedonistic" withdrawal from politics, which is, I suspect, more dominant than one would like to think.

> [Alienation] means that the only things which can move me to action are immediate pleasures—eating when I'm hungry, sleeping when I'm sleepy, listening to beautiful music, or reading a light novel. The old routine things just can't motivate me. I need something that will give me immediate pleasure. That's all I'm interested in.[1]

There is also "spiritualistic" withdrawal, according to which individuals may forsake public involvement for a quest after meaning, usually with mystical or religious overtones, that is private or restricted to small groups. In its more extreme occult forms, spiritualism may represent a magical substitute for political action, as when a group chanted "Om" and "Hari Krishna" in an effort to levitate the Pentagon and thereby purify its inhabitants of their fascination with war and weaponry.[2] Less extremely, there appears a widespread interest in religious circles to develop new forms of religious awareness by focusing upon the nonrational, upon things like "feelings" and "experience," and on activities like "celebration" and "play," a focus that is apolitical, at least as politics has customarily been understood. Still another variation of the rejection of politics is the "cultural revolutionary" who proposes a total mental and social reorientation on the order of the "Woodstock Nation."

Disparagement of accepted patterns of American political thought and action centers particularly in the disenchantment with "liberalism." Books like Michael Harrington's *Toward a Democratic Left*, Marvin E. Gettleman and David Mermelstein's *The Great Society Reader: The Failure of American Liberalism*, Robert Paul Wolff's *The Poverty of Liberalism* and *In Defense of Anarchism*, and Theodore J. Lowi's *The End of Liberalism* and *The Politics of Disorder*,[3] reflect this disenchantment. Each book, in its own way, attests to the inability of traditional American liberalism to meet the current "crisis of public authority." Each book, in its own way, attempts to provide a set of philosophical and/or institutional prescriptions to heal the ailing body politic. Different in many respects, these books are one in their harsh denunciation of the spirit of politics I carried with me to Germany in 1961.

We need not belabor the point that many things have happened between 1961 and 1971 to warrant a negative reaction to American politics. As a result of the obvious deficiencies of several major domestic and foreign policies, there is plenty of room for disenchantment and for an "agonizing reappraisal." But surely the time for solemn reminders that the American political system is in trouble is past. That is a cliché. The interesting subject is what that trouble is, and what we intend to do about it. Accordingly, we should turn to a specific examination of the various diagnoses of our political ills and the various recommended courses of action such as were introduced above.

In doing that, I shall contend that while the arguments for withdrawal and for disparagement have made certain telling and appropriate points, they do *not* succeed, at least as we have them so far, either in convincing us to abandon politics or in demonstrating the end of American liberalism. After working our way through some of the arguments, I hope it will be clear that both politics and liberalism, when the terms are properly understood, are still with us.

II

In a perceptive essay, "The Liberal Crisis," [4] William V. Shannon begins to specify the particular sorts of criticism against the going American political system that are advanced by the advocates both of withdrawal and of disparagement. "Many groups for varying reasons have come to doubt the moral legitimacy and the competence of liberal government. They distrust the liberal political values—rationality, pragmatism, compromise, piecemeal reform—which make self-government possible." Altering the order of Shannon's checklist a bit, let us elaborate the charges.

First, nothing quite arouses the critics of the American political system like the liberal claim that the system is pragmatic or experimental or nonideological. President Kennedy's famous remarks at Yale on the economy are typical of that claim :

> What is at stake is not some grand warfare of rival ideologies which will sweep the country with passion but the practical management of a modern economy. What we need is not labels and clichés but more basic discussion of the sophisticated and technical issues involved in keeping a great economic machinery moving ahead.[5]

During the early 60s, the spirit of these remarks was reflected in the writings of many "liberal" social scientists who spoke of the "end of ideology." [6]

Characteristic of the reaction to this "endless talk of the need to be pragmatic, flexible, open," is C. Wright Mills' rebuke :

> The end-of-ideology is of course itself an ideology. . . . It is a weary know-it-all justification, by tone of voice, rather than by explicit argument. . . . The end-of-ideology is a slogan of complacency, circulating among the prematurely middle-aged, centered in the present, and in the rich Western societies.[7]

The charge is that the commitment to a pragmatic, "non-ideological" approach is itself a commitment to a specific set of values, institutional arrangements, and social prescriptions that are by no means self-evidently right. On the contrary, from the point of view of the critics, such as Mills and Robert Paul Wolff, this unavowed and undefended set of liberal values has produced "the moral disaster of American politics." [8]

The second criticism, levelled against the liberal emphasis upon compromise or bargaining or "public contestation" [9] among competing groups, is closely related to the first. The contention is that whereas older laissez faire liberalism presupposed a beneficent invisible hand that harmonized the competing interests of a free marketplace for the greater benefit of all, so "interest-group liberalism" presupposes an analogous self-regulating, beneficent mechanism that harmonizes group differences through the process of compromise and bargaining. "The hidden hand of capitalist ideology could clasp the hidden hand of pluralism, and the two could shake affirmatively on the new public philosophy, interest-group liberalism. . . . Pluralist equilibrium is really the public interest." [10] The point is made again that contemporary liberalism assumes a very definite ideology.

The problem with the ideology is that it is conservative. It reflects the status quo. It legitimates established groups—farm organizations, business groups, labor unions—which have, through one means or another, made their way into the arena of public contestation. But once there they naturally resist relinquishing their place. They work out an accommodation satisfactory to themselves and other established groups, but the accommodation excludes disadvantaged people and unarticulated interests. While the system creates conditions of rough justice for its own, its restricted processes of bargaining and contestation unjustly stack conditions against those outside the system. Insofar as government legitimates the established configuration of interests, it authorizes injustice.

Moreover, according to Wolff, the best pluralism can do is to make a stab at balancing some of the interests of certain groups within the community. But that leaves pressing issues, such as public order, beautification, cultivation of the arts, and, undoubtedly, environmental and population control, which cannot be solved by the pushing and hauling of pluralist compromise.

> To deal with such problems, there must be some way of constituting the whole society a genuine group with a group purpose and a conception of the common good. Pluralism rules this out in theory by portraying society as an aggregate of human communities rather than as itself a human community; and it equally rules out a concern for the general good in practice by encouraging a politics of interest-group pressures in which there is no mechanism for the discovery and expression of the common good.[11]

Thirdly, attacks against liberal confidence in rationality come from many sides. The diversity of criticism is the result, no doubt, of the open-textured character of the word "rationality" : it means many things to many people, though most of the meanings, one gathers, are bad. To the proponents of withdrawal, rationality represents the tendency of the liberal to view man as a thinking machine, an abstracting, organizing being without the human emotions and passions that distinguish what is really "human" about man. Since politics is preeminently the realm of organizing, of planning, of seeking technical solutions for complex problems, it is a realm to be avoided in favor of a small, intimate *Gemeinschaft* where feeling and immediate experience can prevail. Or, from the same analysis, a more revolutionary conclusion is occasionally drawn. A Harvard student wrote, within the context of the Harvard "liberation" in 1969 :

> Action is its own reason for existing. Rebellion can only

be understood by a rebel, who knows that the only "reason" for rebellion is the pleasure (or whatever feeling) of rebellion itself. Revolution for the hell of it, because there is no other reason big enough for rebellion.[12]

The assault on liberal rationality comes also from those who disparage and seek to reform the present state of American politics. Political scientist Carey McWilliams broadens a critique of the American military establishment to include the entire society. The Army, argues McWilliams, has traditionally justified its existence in terms of bureaucratic expertise and technical rationality.

> But even that justification reveals the debatable character of American political morality and theory. Underlying it is the liberal creed that officialdom should be a "government of laws and not of men" where human character is reduced to the least possible importance in favor of skill in the "mastery of nature" by science, confident that such success and progress were equivalent with human liberty and fulfillment. . . . All of the bureaucratic tendencies visible in the Army are characteristic of all organized power in America. . . . The very tendency of bureaucracy—and an aim of liberal theory—is to produce men with a desire to *avoid* responsibility and authority, who will fly to the safety of laws, rules and technique rather than imposing judgments of their own.[13]

Though he comes to somewhat different conclusions from those of McWilliams, Theodore Lowi concurs in the general attack on bureaucratic or organizational rationality. Lowi admits that industrial societies, with their characteristics of division of labor and specialization of function, inevitably generate complex business, labor, and political organizations. These bureaucracies are sometimes effective means of articulating the interests of the society, but they also exact substantial costs to the society. "Among the costs the greatest is the 'iron law of decadence,' that tendency of all organizations to maintain themselves at the expense of needed change and innovation." [14] That is, bureaucracies rigidify and become more interested in self-preservation than in advancing the general needs of society. This charge is obviously related to the attack on compromise and pluralism mentioned above. Rationality, like compromise, winds up acting in the service of vested interests.

These criticisms are reminiscent of the claim, now especially popular in the light of the Pentagon Papers, that policies such as those concerning Vietnam are the product of a technical, bureaucratic, or rational bent of mind that reviews only the means and never reconsiders the basic objectives and moral justifications of policy. This bent of mind encourages, it is argued, the sort of "value-free" attitude reflected by a Rand Corporation official: "Rand just does not consider moral inputs . . . they don't even bring up the questions." [15] In the eyes of many critics, such assertions echo Max Weber's famous description of modern bureaucrats as "specialists without spirit, sensualists without heart." [16]

Fourthly, there is a widespread disenchantment with the typical liberal emphasis upon piecemeal reform or "incrementalism" or "reform within the system." For Lowi, Harrington, and Wolff, the problem with piecemeal reform is related to the other difficulties with liberalism we have reviewed, namely its restricted vision of what needs doing. To try to effect change "within the system" is to accept the prevailing norms and rules which define what may count as "improvement." There, of course, is the rub. For "improvement," according to the critics, must be defined by *new* norms and *new* rules.

> Last generation's reforms will not solve this generation's crises. . . . For all the official figures prove that it is now necessary to go far beyond Franklin Roosevelt. And this, as Washington has so magnificently documented, cannot be done by trusting in the incremental zigs and

zags of utopian pragmatism somehow to come out right. The country has no choice but to have some larger ideas and to take them seriously.[17]

Finally, there is pervasive doubt regarding the general legitimacy or authority of traditional liberal democratic institutions. Wolff's short book, *In Defense of Anarchism,* focuses this critique. Briefly, his argument is as follows. Traditionally, liberals have attempted to justify the right of representative governments to expect obedience to their laws and directives on the grounds that representative institutions most effectively protect the autonomy or freedom of individual citizens. But, Wolff continues, this claim is inherently contradictory. "Autonomy" means the "refusal to be ruled" or the sovereign right of the individual to pass judgment on those laws and directives that shall govern his life. To retain his autonomy, an individual must consistently reserve the right to pass judgment over every governmental directive and determination that affects his life. Consequently, he may never properly accord legitimacy to those particular laws which he has not himself, on deliberation, authorized. That is, an individual "will deny that he has a duty to obey the laws of the state *simply because they are the laws.* In that sense, it would seem that anarchism is the only political doctrine consistent with the virtue of autonomy." [18] Wolff admits that there may well be reasons of expediency for complying with the laws of the state, but in the interests of protecting his moral autonomy, an individual "will never view the commands of the state as *legitimate,* as having a binding moral force." Wolff spends the remainder of the book trying to show that the arguments of classical liberals, like Locke, in favor of the moral legitimacy of majoritarian democratic procedures, must be rejected.

Wolff's reasoning provides more or less sophisticated support for a claim that is prevalent in our society. As empirically constituted, government, including liberal democratic government, stands in unalterable conflict with the autonomy or freedom of the individual to shape his own destiny. If we understand "morality" to consist in the self-direction of free individuals, then government is only legitimate to the extent that each of its laws and directives concurs with the private judgment of each citizen. To the extent such concurrence does not exist, no government, apparently, has the moral right to expect obedience. Nor may it, with any moral justification, punish a citizen for non-compliance.

Given this sort of argument, it is not surprising why Wolff, along with many others, asserts that a "myth of legitimacy" or "superstitious beliefs in the legitimacy of authority" are operative in our society. According to Wolff, government has now been demythologized, and the speciousness of liberal political justifications revealed. Thus liberated from such myths, no citizen need feel the slightest moral compunction about resisting laws or directives that appear at odds with his private moral judgment. In Wolff's hands, more than doubt about the moral legitimacy of liberal government has been encouraged. Government has, in moral terms, been radically devalued.

III

We have specified some of the major charges against American liberalism—that it wrongly perpetuates confidence in pragmatism, compromise, rationality, piecemeal reform, and the moral legitimacy of democratic institutions. We must now assess these charges and along with them some of the alternatives offered in place of liberalism.

First of all, we need to respond to those who advocate either some form or another of cultural revolution or withdrawal from politics altogether. Steven Kelman, a recent Harvard student who is wise beyond his years, provides an eloquent rejoinder:

The problem with the "liberation" proposed by the cultural radicals is that it forgets that the old routines developed for a purpose. Helpfulness and love were the order of the day during the "revolution" of the great power failure, but if the power had stayed out much longer you would have seen street fighting and dog-eat-dog. No electricity is "liberating" for a while but enslaving if it lasts. Dancing in the streets is fine, but soon you begin to get hungry and thirsty.[19]

Whether one is motivated by a drive for immediate gratification, as is the advocate of hedonistic withdrawal, or for some rarefied religious or cultural liberation, there are the inevitable political problems of organization and allocation of the services and resources that bring gratification or make liberation possible. Had Woodstock actually formed a "new nation," it would have been interesting to observe the emerging patterns of authority and delegation, the routines for rearing children, for settling disputes, for collecting garbage. Nor do the communes or religious communities seem free of these inevitable political requirements. It is, of course, possible to take an "experimental" attitude toward the withdrawing groups and the cultural radicals. Perhaps they can make a contribution to problems of child-rearing, education, cooperative patterns of living, and the like. But to take such an attitude presupposes the importance of the political conditions of the wider society to which the groups may make some contribution. Any way you slice it, the basic requirements of political organization seem unavoidable. Withdrawal and cultural liberation offer no escape at all. The only serious question is *how* we propose to meet the requirements of political organization in particular cases.

The claim of the critics we have mentioned is that at least the "liberal" proposals for meeting the requirements are not satisfactory and must be strenuously revised. But their criticisms are not entirely successful. To begin with, the critics are extremely imprecise in their use of the word "liberal." This is peculiar, because by now it is customary in discussions of political theory to acknowledge the complexity, if not ambiguity, of such words. One suspects, therefore, that part of what the critics disparage constitutes but one aspect of the liberal tradition. Before we can decide whether liberalism has ended, or is poverty-stricken, we must identify what we are talking about.

For example, from the very beginning of his discussion in *The End of Liberalism,* Lowi fails to distinguish between *political* and *economic* liberalism. He accuses contemporary interest-group liberalism of perpetuating the fallacy of auomatic adjustment contained in economic and, as Lowi believes, classical liberalism. But Giovanni Sartori is certainly right when he states :

> Locke, Blackstone, Montesquieu, Constant—to mention a few of the real founding fathers of classical liberalism—were not the theorists of a laissez faire economy. To them liberalism meant the rule of law and the constitutional state, and liberty was political freedom, not the economic principle of free trade or the law of survival of the fittest. . . . Very simply [classical] liberalism is the theory and practice of individual liberty, juridical defense and the constitutional State.[20]

If it is true that, historically, political and economic liberalism have at times been allied, there is nothing logically necessary nor sociologically inevitable about that alliance. As we shall see, it is perfectly acceptable to espouse the basic tenets of political liberalism—individual liberty, juridical defense, and the constitutional state—and still leave open the question as to which set of economic conditions most satisfactorily brings those tenets to realization.

What is most striking about Lowi's general argument is that having called for "the end" of liberalism, he proceeds to advocate a solution which conforms exactly to the tenets of political liberalism ! Lowi contends that interest-group liberalism stands convicted for inhibiting the extension of justice and fair treat-

ment to all members of society. "Liberal practices reveal a basic
disrespect for democracy." [21] His solution is to institute what he
calls "juridical democracy," which amounts to the elaboration of
legal procedures, of "juridical defense," for assuring that all
groups in the society, and not just the established, "decadent"
ones, get a fair hearing. Lowi advocates, in short, a return to the
constitutional state.

Despite what he implies, Lowi does not succeed in repudiat-
ing the basic tenets of classical political liberalism, nor in
demonstrating that they are at an end. His singular inability to
refute the basic concerns and commitments of liberalism provides
a paradigm of the plight of many a critic.

With respect to undermining the legitimacy of liberal democratic institutions, Wolff is no more successful a critic than Lowi.
It is unfortunate that though Wolff deals with Locke's treatment
of majoritarianism, he does not first attend to Locke's way of
arguing for the moral legitimacy of democratic institutions. It
is unfortunate because the argument shows why Wolff's attack
will not work.

Locke assumes that control of one human being by another
is a fundamental fact of social life. But equally a fact is the
tendency of human beings to ask why they are being controlled,
to ask for reasons to justify (or legitimate) the restriction placed
upon them. To ask the question "Why?" in this context, to call
for reasons, presupposes at least two conditions: first, that a
restriction of one person's liberty of action by another requires
defense and that the burden of proof for the defense rests with
the one doing the restricting; second, that the defense, if it is to
be rational, must be in the form of an appeal—it must invite
and allow for the consent of the one under restriction. In other
words, an adequate defense must be subject to the review and
agreement of *both* parties. For Locke, the law of reason (or
nature), implanted in all men, was a shorthand phrase for these
two conditions. It expressed the equal right of autonomy or

liberty of all men, and it provided a norm for distinguishing legitimate from arbitrary control.

So far, Locke and Wolff appear in agreement. But Locke introduces a further consideration in his discussion of the grounds for political and legal authority of which Wolff seems dimly aware.

> For though the law of nature be plain and intelligible to all rational creatures; yet men, *being biased by their interests, as well as ignorant for want of study of it,* are not apt to allow it as a law binding to them. . . . For every one in [the state of nature], being both judge and executioner of the law of nature, *men being partial to themselves,* passion and revenge is very apt to carry them too far, and with too much heat in their own cases, as well as negligence and unconcernedness, to make them too remiss in other men's.[22]

We may call Locke's description of the human situation the *condition of defective competence,* due to perversity (Christians would call it "sin") and finitude.

It is hard to understand how Wolff could slight this condition. To men with any awareness of themselves, it should appear self-evident. Clearly, the condition affects the question of political legitimacy. Locke contends that it is rational for men to agree to the restrictions governments place upon them, by means of the functions of making, applying, and adjudicating laws, because, given the condition of defective competence, ordinary men are incapable of regulating their lives with complete success according to the law of reason. In the heat of disputes, men do not invariably respect the autonomy of others or their right to full review and consent. Therefore, it seems justifiable, *precisely in order to increase the effectiveness of the rule of autonomy,* to support a legal system that may, in particular cases, come to decisions with which at least one party disagrees. Or, considering the complexity of issues and the limitations of time which prevent citizens from becoming experts on all legal and policy questions, it seems rational to bequeath to the government the right to make policy determinations without each citizen's day-by-day participation, even in the knowledge that individuals may at times be out of sorts with specific determinations.[23]

There is support here for a *limited* notion of legitimacy. According to Locke, a democratic government is legitimate because it is needed to fill in the gaps created by the condition of defective competence. But its legitimacy is strictly limited by the law of reason. A government is legitimate only to the degree it embodies and protects the rule of autonomy. Locke even contends that every man, according to the law of reason, has a right, in the last resort, to judge for himself whether a government has exceeded the bounds of legitimacy, and whether, therefore, he shall revolt against it. But here Locke is contending that rebellion is justifiable because in a particular instance a government has forfeited the legitimacy it might otherwise possess.

Though Wolff, then, speaks disparagingly about the "poverty of liberalism," his assumptions about the rule of autonomy are very close to the moral position of Locke. Where the two differ, Locke retains the upper hand, as I have suggested.

It ought to be clear from the foregoing that when C. Wright Mills, Wolff, and others castigate contemporary liberals for pretending they need not engage in "ideological" controversy in order to support their value-free, "pragmatic," or "rational" approach to politics, the critics are in this instance on sound ground. Whatever the reasons by which contemporary liberals try to excuse themselves from the requirement of providing an explicit justification for their position, that attempt is a marked, and, I believe, indefensible, departure from classical liberalism.[24] John Locke wrote: "True Politicks I looke on as a Part of Moral Philosophie." [25] And his discussions of government bear this claim out.

What is more, the emergence of American liberalism, around the time of the Revolution, also bears this claim out. From our beginnings as a nation, matters of government have been moral matters of a distinctive kind. The Revolution itself and the creation of a new constitutional democracy were seen as actions authorized by the law of reason as conceived by John Locke and his intellectual forebears of the English Civil War. "We hold these Truths to be self-evident, that all Men are created equal, that they are endowed by their Creator with certain unalienable Rights, that among these are Life, Liberty, and the Pursuit of Happiness—That to secure these Rights, Governments are instituted among Men, deriving their just Powers from the Consent of the Governed. . . ." The founding of America was understood as an event of universal moral significance : here, at long last, government was being defined and limited by the rule of autonomy, by the right of consent. This is as it should be everywhere. Political power in general ought to be framed by and harnessed to the inalienable rights of man. This was a declaration not just about the United States of America, but about the universal relation of "true Politicks" and "Moral Philosophie." [26]

I do not believe that either contemporary liberals or their critics have begun to grasp how deep-seated are these convictions in the minds of Americans, nor how operative they are in the minds of both liberals and critics alike. How else can one explain the curious phenomenon of people like Lowi and countless others, who day-in-and-day-out proclaim the end of liberalism and the need for a "new morality" to direct American politics, while all the time holding America accountable for "arbitrary" or "illegitimate" use of power at home and abroad, accountable, that is, according to the rule of autonomy and the right of consent, as the classical liberals understood those terms.

It may be, as so many state these days, that America needs

a totally new "value system" by which to guide her affairs. We
will need to examine and assess the proposals. But obviously it
will not do to argue, as do so many critics of liberalism, that we
need a completely new morality because under our present one
we do not sufficiently respect the rights and sovereignty of other
peoples or extend to the disadvantaged of our own society the
rights that are due them. That argument assumes the very thing
it proposes to replace. This is a common fallacy in political discourse.[27]

It is my observation that, in general, the highest-level
values of the American Creed, partly embodied, for example, in
the Bill of Rights, are not the subject of attack. The real controversy comes more at the level of implementation and institutionalization. The critical debate surrounds the matter of *necessary conditions* for actualizing the rule of autonomy.

Again, with the possible exception of Wolff and his assertions about the "common good," there seems widespread agreement, despite the rhetoric, that in principle a system of pluralism
or "polyarchy" or "public contestation" is most likely to guaran-
tee the rule of autonomy, the right of consent. The real problem,
one infers from the writings of Lowi and others, is that the conventional patterns of interest-group liberalism have, in reality,
worked against the principle of pluralism. The patterns have
not been pluralistic enough, and Lowi recommends opening the
system to mobile, vibrant social movements so as to grant wider
access to more interests in the society. We shall thereby overcome the rigidification and "decadence" of established collec-
tivities. Among the critics of liberalism, Lowi is hardly alone in
attacking pluralism in the interests of greater pluralism.

The principle of pluralism requires toleration of diversity
and, concomitantly, a willingness on the part of participants to
settle differences by bargaining and compromise. This method of
"working out" disputes and conflicts is appropriate and defensible so long as the basic conditions of the pluralist system them-

selves are not "compromised." That is, the method is defensible so long as the bargainers are in a roughly equal position and the agreement they reach does not in turn "compromise" the interests of an affected party without his having a chance at review and consent.

IV

This much seems to follow acceptably from the tenets of liberal philosophy. But when it comes to describing the necessary socioeconomic conditions under which to implement a truly inclusive pluralistic system, the classical liberals, it is true, need revision. No doubt one of the greatest shortcomings of Locke's position is his set of unquestioned and ill-considered assumptions about wealth and property. While Locke's support for "the dictatorship of the bourgeoisie" has been exaggerated,[28] he is completely complacent about the existing economic inequities, and he does not reveal the slightest awareness of the connection between economic and political equality. Unfortunately, Locke's obvious, but by no means necessary, insensitivity has been mindlessly perpetuated by many American liberals.

As a helpful corrective, Robert Dahl has suggested :

> The chances that a country will develop and maintain a competitive political regime (and, even more so, a polyarchy) depend on the extent to which the country's society and economy, (a) provide literacy, education and communication, (b) create a pluralistic rather than a centrally dominated social order, (c) and prevent extreme inequalities among the politically relevant strata of the country.[29]

Dahl's list of necessary conditions could be expanded to include other considerations, such as a relatively dependable system of public order and security, population and environmental control, adequate health and safety provisions, etc.

The point is that given the liberal commitment to pluralism, attention to such necessary conditions becomes unavoidable. That pluralism is difficult to maintain in face of severe inequities in wealth, education, health, and the like is empirically certain. Contrary, then, to Wolff's claim that pluralism "rules out in theory" attention to all concerns that citizens share in common, it is clear that supporters of pluralism must address such concerns, on the logic of their own position.[30]

If we look closely, then, at many of the criticisms by the opponents of liberalism, we will see that they are actually aimed at the patterns by which pluralism has been historically implemented and institutionalized. It is the particular arrangement of political and legal institutions, the specific provisions made for the necessary conditions of pluralism, that are often the real target. This is certainly the case with Lowi. By means of a sometimes trenchant analysis of the inequities of American political and economic life, he has demonstrated the need to address, in the spirit of the classical liberals, the *organizational* aspect of political life, namely the matter of the *rules and regulations* according to which authority and power in the society are constituted and arranged. Consequently, Lowi recommends the widespread overhauling of the federal regulatory system in keeping with clearly articulated laws and administrative procedures. Among other things, he prescribes certain Congressional limitations on the power of the executive, and he comments at length on the general need for legal control of political leadership in this country.

In this respect, Lowi's concern, like the concern of Harrington and others, is nothing if it is not "rational." He himself remarks: "Democracy is not safe for the world so long as it is not organized for consistently rational action. Without a capacity for real planning, allies cannot trust the system and enemies can too easily miscalculate." [31] The concern to limit, to systematize, to plan, to produce consistency and accountability in organizational life, political or otherwise, is preeminently a rational activity, the sort of rationality Weber properly associated with the development of bureaucratization. For all Lowi's distress at the rigidification and decadence of bureaucracies, it is evident that he is proposing a bureaucratic solution for these problems. That is not necessarily as self-contradictory as it sounds. Michael Harrington wisely accuses all who rail constantly against governmental bureaucracy of failing to understand "one of the most important paradoxes of the time: that bureaucracy is itself a weapon to be used against bureaucracy." [32]

In any event, to concentrate on "rationalizing" the organization of political life in keeping with clearly defined rules and regulations, as Lowi does, is a further manifestation that political liberalism is very much alive and well in our midst. Moreover, it is alive and well in the activities of people such as Ralph Nader, who, like Lowi, seek the strengthening of regulatory procedures, the institutionalization of control in behalf of disadvantaged groups like the consumer. Indeed, it is my intuition that individuals like Nader provide an image of effective action that already has much greater influence among those who favor social change than the image of Che Guevara or Abbie Hoffmann. If that is so, liberals may take heart.

The recurring concern among critics of liberalism to propose organizational and bureaucratic reforms in government, business, universities, etc., is not accidental. It does not appear that there exist any serious alternatives to the rational organization of modern social life. [33] Obviously, the socialistic recommendations of Gettleman and Mermelstein [34] necessarily entail extensive bureaucratic regulation by the government, as do all socialistic proposals. The only puzzling thing is that criticism of American life should take the form, as for example in the words of Carey McWilliams cited above, of a wholesale attack on bureaucracy. If it is difficult to live with bureaucracy, it appears equally difficult to live without it.

Does this mean, then, that there is also no alternative to a procedure of piecemeal reform, of tinkering with the system? As was suggested above, the answer to this question depends on determining, to begin with, the standards for what constitutes "reform." Some contemporary liberals have muddled this matter by failing to explicate and defend the values by which to measure "reform." But more importantly in this context, they have failed to defend the assumption, implied in the phrase "piecemeal reform," that liberal values can always best be realized (and "reform" achieved) by incremental political and social adjustments, by adjustments, that is, that do not unduly disturb the established system. This assumption is unwarranted on empirical grounds. One must decide from case to case whether piecemeal adjustments or radical alterations will best accomplish liberal or any other kind of reform. Certainly, the classical liberal position, as articulated by Locke, did not rule out legitimate rebellion.

It is this problem of careful and sophisticated determination of *the means of reform* that has unquestionably been slighted by liberals and which demands their attention. How are the necessary conditions of polyarchy promoted and how are polyarchic institutions sustained? Liberals have undoubtedly oversimplified and overgeneralized their answers to these questions in reflecting on both foreign and domestic policy matters.

Whatever the reasons for their failure, liberals will find themselves more and more called upon to speak intelligently and discriminatingly to the issue of realistic reform. Now that the glow of pragmatic optimism, so prevalent in the early 60s, has passed, there is need to identify afresh the obstacles to social progress and to experiment with effective ways of coping with them. Whether the ways turn out to be "piecemeal" remains to be seen.

Alice M. Rivlin has made a helpful start in three articles in the *Washington Post*.[35] Taking the issues of health care, the attack on poverty, and population control (all of which would fall under our category of the necessary conditions of pluralism), she argues that the reason it is difficult for us as a society to do what we ought to do is not only that we lack the will or that there is a group of villains standing in the way or that we are all powerless in a faceless system, a la Charles Reich. In place of these theories, she offers a "conflicting objectives theory," which holds that "we are failing to solve social problems because we do not know how to do it—the problems are genuinely hard."

It is downright difficult to find the means to reconcile in one program the objectives that most members of our society hold dear—for example, in the medical field, universal care, good quality care, and care that does not waste scarce medical resources. After examining in detail the perplexities of harmonizing these objectives in specific programs, she concludes :

> The point is not that no solutions can be found— indeed some other countries seem to do better than we do—but that the problem is complex and no solutions are obvious. . . . But uncertainty should not be an excuse for inaction. At the very least the government should act to reduce the uncertainty. If a vigorous program of experimentation with new forms of medical care and new types of reimbursement had been under- taken 10 years ago there would now be a body of experience to answer [hard] questions.[36]

Miss Rivlin points out that until the 1930s national political figures were saved from the tough job of detailing programs that could reconcile conflicting objectives. And during the 30s, solu- tions to problems such as education, welfare, health, etc., were couched in either/or terms—you were for them or against them.

> Now we are running out of "yes" or "no" issues. National health insurance may be the last one avail- able. Moreover, the liberals have lost their innocence. By the end of the 1960s it was evident that just spend- ing more federal money was not necessarily going to

produce results. Money for education would not automatically teach children to read. It would be necessary
to find out what was preventing children from learning, perhaps to redesign the whole education system;
to attract different sorts of people to teaching and to
give them different incentives, not just more pay and
better buildings. More money for health might just
escalate the price of health care, or put more people in
hospitals who need not be there. To improve health
care it would be necessary to redesign the whole health
system, to introduce new incentives and new ways of
reimbursing doctors and hospitals. More money for
welfare would just perpetuate a badly constructed
system. It would be necessary to set up a new system
which did a better job of reconciling the objectives as
to adequacy, incentives and equal treatment.

All these design problems are hard to think about
and even harder to explain to the public. They are un-
suitable for campaign oratory which almost of necessity must deal with simple questions of "yes" and "no"
and more or less. *This is why being a liberal leader in
the 1970s is so much harder a job than it used to be.
It may be why we seem to have so few real leaders.*[37]

Though there is a hint of the "end-of-ideology" thesis here,
there are important differences. For proponents of the "end-of-
ideology," there was a confidence, an optimism that the existing institutional arrangements would be able to work out
incrementally the technical details of a liberal democratic
system. The spirit of Miss Rivlin's articles could hardly be more
opposed to such confidence. She suggests the possibility of much
more than piecemeal, incremental change. She entertains the
prospect of redesigning the entire educational or health care,
system. Moreover, she does not exude the optimism of the early
60s. The fact that people share many values and objectives may
not necessarily simplify the political task of implementing them;
for many of the values and objectives may themselves conflict.
It is with a recognition of *that* fact that Miss Rivlin identifies

the "loss of innocence" of the liberal.

In a way, the optimism of the early 60s presupposed that though values and objectives were plural, they would, through the mechanisms of existing American society, more or less automatically harmonize themselves. Miss Rivlin also sees the "pluralism" of values and objectives in modern society, but she sees the task of reconciling them as anything but automatic. Reconciliation is a difficult matter of choices and compromises. What is more, those compromises do not necessarily take place between discrete individuals, or even groups, but among values and objectives all of which may be shared by certain individuals and groups. This makes the notion of a "pluralistic" society a good deal more complex than conventional formulations do.

Miss Rivlin's "conflicting objectives theory" will naturally have to be tested for adequacy in particular cases. But its apparent plausibility suggests once again the relevance of the classical liberal approach to politics. When Miss Rivlin calls upon the modern liberal to address without flinching the complexity of a pluralistic society, and to persist in designing, proposing, and organizing novel institutional programs that will account for this pluralism, she recalls the image of a seventeenth-century Locke and his predecessors of the English Civil War. When she calls upon liberals to approach politics "experimentally," rather than dogmatically, she recalls the genius of eighteenth-century American experiments in government. So understood, the terms "compromise," "pragmatism," and "reform" take on their proper liberal meaning.

In defending political liberalism, my strategy has been to contend that the alternatives of withdrawal and cultural revolution are not really alternatives at all, and to show that most of the assaults on liberalism either presuppose what they are attacking or fail to mount an effective attack. Certain criticisms we considered were telling, but mostly as reminders of the points at which classical liberalism needlessly went astray.

In a time of much ill-considered political argument, this enterprise has been intended to clear the air. If it causes a few people to reflect on the word "liberal," it will not have been in vain. However, it is at best a preliminary enterprise. We have not attempted a thorough justification against all possible criticisms, nor have we confronted all possible deficiencies. That is another chapter.

Notes

1. Comment by a Harvard student in Steven Kelman's *Push Comes to Shove: The Escalation of Student Protest* (Boston: Houghton Mifflin, 1970), p. 86.
2. See, for example, John Charles Cooper, *Religion in the Age of Aquarius* (Philadelphia: Westminster, 1971), pp. 92–93.
3. (New York: Macmillan, 1968); (New York: Random House, 1967); (Boston: Beacon, 1968); (New York: Harper & Row, 1970); (New York: Norton, 1969); (New York: Basic Books, 1971).
4. *New York Times*, July 25, 1971, p. E11.
5. Cited in Arthur M. Schlesinger, Jr., *A Thousand Days* (New York: Fawcett, 1967), pp. 593–94.
6. See, for example, Seymour Martin Lipset, "End of Ideology?", chapter 13 in *Political Man* (New York: Doubleday, 1960); Daniel Bell, *The End of Ideology: On the Exhaustion of Political Ideas in the Fifties* (Glencoe: Free Press, 1960).
7. C. Wright Mills, "On the New Left," reprinted in Paul Jacobs and Saul Landau, *The New Radicals* (New York: Random House, 1966), p. 104.
8. Wolff, *Poverty of Liberalism*, p. 118.
9. See Robert A. Dahl, *Polyarchy: Participation and Opposition* (New Haven: Yale University Press, 1971), for a useful elaboration of this term in relation to pluralistic or polyarchic political development.
10. Lowi, *End of Liberalism*, p. 47.
11. Wolff, *Poverty of Liberalism*, p. 159.
12. Kelman, pp. 209–10.
13. From a paper entitled "Vietnam and My Lai: Moral Responsibility and Military Honor," delivered at a Council on Religion and International Affairs consultation in Washington, D.C., May 1971. Subsequently published: Carey McWilliams and Henry Plotkin, "Military Honor After My Lai," *Worldview* (January 1972), p. 45.
14. Lowi, *Politics of Disorder*, p. 5.
15. *Washington Post* (July 18, 1971), p. A15.
16. Max Weber, *The Protestant Ethic and the Spirit of Capitalism* (New York: Scribner's, 1958), p. 182.

17. Harrington, *Toward a Democratic Left*, p. 15.
18. Wolff, *In Defense of Anarchism*, p. 18.
19. Kelman, p. 171.
20. Giovanni Sartori, *Democratic Theory* (New York: Praeger, 1965), pp. 362, 364. Sartori continues: "But if the liberal State was born as an expression of distrust of power, and therefore with the purpose of reducing rather than augmenting the functions of the State, one must not for this reason put the size of the liberal State ahead of its structure, that is, a contingent characteristic ahead of the essential. However much the constitutional State may have been conceived of as a small State, and also as a do-nothing State, this does not prevent its becoming, if need be, a large State which does something, and even a great deal— on this essential condition: the more it ceases to be a minimal State, the more important it is that it remain a constitutional State."
21. Lowi, *End of Liberalism*, p. 288.
22. John Locke, *Of Civil Government, Second Essay* (Chicago, 1948), p. 74, paras. 124–25 (emphasis added).
23. In *After the Revolution? Authority in a Good Society* (New Haven: Yale, 1970), Robert A. Dahl provides a useful discussion of the way the "criterion of competence" and the "criterion of economy" figure in the question of political legitimacy (see ch. 1). A striking feature of Dahl's discussion of the "criterion of competence" is his neglect of what we have called the "condition of defective competence," though there are hints of it later in the book. Because of the prominence of this condition in the argument of Locke, as well as of his predecessors in the English Civil War (such as John Milton), more attention needs to be given to it.
24. One recent and particularly painful example of the recurring attempt to reduce the role of moral evaluation in political reflection is an essay by Arthur Schlesinger, Jr., entitled, "The Necessary Amorality of Foreign Affairs," in *Harper's Magazine* (August, 1971), pp. 72–7. As in the case of George Kennan and Hans Morgenthau before him, Schlesinger's use of the word "moral" is confused and unsophisticated. If Schlesinger's sort of argument is all we can expect in the way of a liberal approach to political ethics, then contemporary liberalism is indeed poverty-stricken.
25. In a 1697 letter to Lady Peterborough. Cited by Esmond S. De Beer, "Locke and English liberalism: the *Second Treatise of Government* in its contemporary setting," in *John Locke: Problems and Perspectives*, ed. by John W. Yolton (Cambridge: Cambridge University Press, 1969), p. 40.
26. See Bernard Bailyn, *The Ideological Origins of the American Revolution* (Cambridge: Harvard University Press, 1968), esp. chapter 5, for an exceptionally good account of the centrality of moral language in the thinking of the participants in the American Revolution. In describing his own reactions to the literature of the Revolution, Bailyn makes a comment worth remembering: "I began to see a new meaning in phrases that I, like most historians, had readily dismissed as mere rhetoric and propaganda: 'slavery,' 'corruption,' 'conspiracy.' These inflammatory words were used so forcefully by writers of so great a variety of social statuses, political positions, and religious persuasions;

they fitted so logically into the pattern of radical and opposition thought; and they reflected so clearly the realities of life in an age in which monarchical autocracy flourished, . . . that I began to suspect that they meant something very real to both the writers and their readers; that there were real fears, real anxieties, a sense of real danger behind these phrases, and not merely the desire to influence by rhetoric and propaganda the inert minds of an otherwise passive populace." (p. ix).

27. The proponents of revolutionary violence against the established American system often presuppose, without realizing it, the "liberal values" of the constitutional state in order to justify the right of revolution against a "corrupt" government. When radicals speak of the "illegitimate" exercise of power on the part of the U.S. government at home and abroad, they normally determine "illegitimacy" according to those liberal forms of government generated to protect the individual against arbitrary power. As we mentioned, Locke was far from opposing "legitimate rebellion." If revolutionaries argue in this way, then the only difference between them and more conservative liberals is in the *factual assessment:* first, whether the liberal norms have been violated to the degree the revolutionaries claim; second, whether the violent proposals of the revolutionaries promise more good than harm, according to the liberal norms, that is, whether the result of revolutionary action will insure the exercise of less rather than more arbitrary power. This is, then, an "in-house" debate among basically liberally oriented people.

There can be other defenses of violent revolution that do not presuppose liberal values at all. Facist proposals, of the National Socialist sort, were perhaps the clearest example we have of a total and explicit repudiation of the liberal tradition. Certain Marxist positions are probably also examples, though one would want to analyze specific arguments very carefully. When the liberal is confronted with such positions, he is pushed back to the "final vindication" of his liberalism, a level of discussion that I do not get into in this essay, though one that must obviously be dealt with.

Part of the complexity of dealing with revolutionary arguments is this distinction between arguments over violence that presuppose basic liberal norms and those that do not.

28. Crawford B. Macpherson's famous argument, in *The Political Theory of Possessive Individualism* (Oxford: Clarendon Press, 1962), that Locke's primary concern was to bolster the bourgeoisie and their acquisitive predispositions has been effectively repudiated by Alan Ryan in "Locke and the Dictatorship of the Bourgeoisie," reprinted in *Locke and Berkeley,* ed. by Charles B. Martin and D. M. Armstrong (Garden City: Doubleday, 1967).

29. Dahl, *Polyarchy*, p. 74.

30. It may be that my argument does not take care of all Wolff's examples of common concerns, such as cultivation of the arts and beautification of the landscape. They may be of a different order from the necessary conditions I mentioned. But be that as it may, all I need to show, for purposes of the present argument, is that a pluralist approach does not

"rule out in theory" *all* concern for the "common good" or the "public interest."

31. Lowi, *End of Liberalism*, p. 186.
32. Harrington, *op. cit.*, p. 150.
33. See Zbigniew Brzezinski, *Between Two Ages: America's Role in the Technetronic Era*, (New York: Viking, 1970), for a provocative statement of the unavoidability of rational organization in the future.
34. Gettleman and Mermelstein, *The Great Society Reader;* see their running introductory comments.
35. "Obstacles to Social Progress," I, II, III, *Washington Post* (July 23, 25, 31, 1971).
36. "Obstacles to Social Progress," II (July 25, 1971).
37. "Obstacles to Social Progress," III (July 31, 1971). (emphasis added).

Creativity and Fatigue in Public Life

Robert Neville

Fatigue

We have all been taught the importance of civic responsibility and of participation in public life. In a democratic society the rationale for individual participation is unassailable. From voting booths through ward politics to high elected office, representative governmental structures provide legitimate sanctions and roles for participation. Our society supports universal education, the chief institutional resource for democratic participation. Election campaigns are still enthralling forms of spectator sports. Every reason seems present to expect vital and near universal participation in public life. Even the eighteen-year-olds have been given the vote.

But it seems too many Americans are tired of public life. That statement is more profound than intended by most who make it. The usual implication is that with a little rest things will be all right again. But fatigue is a profound condition of society. It results from a dissolution of the social environment supportive of vitality and creativity. And whereas an organic body has built-in recuperative mechanisms, a political body may not. For an organic body, fatigue is a natural periodic condition, and the environment for organic life supports rest periods. But fatigue is a deadly condition for a social body because its environment requires constant attention.

Of course, fatigue of the body politic cannot be inferred just from the fatigue of many citizens for public life. The frustration might be something characteristic only of isolated social classes. For instance, many of the people who talk about dropping out of society are young, and young people are supposed to have little patience for slow political processes and the even slower forces of change. Remember how the springtime student anger about Cambodia and Kent State seethed with threats of a wholly new Congress come fall? But the elections in the fall of 1970 were not especially distinguished either by student participation or by left-wing victories. Sociologists say that lower-class "white ethnics" are supposed to exhibit a feeling of helplessness when it comes to influencing the political process, or even when it comes to demanding promised municipal services.[1] The hard-hats are sometimes noisy and violent, but they seem less to exert their own political power than to hand it over to those claiming spokesmanship.

It is not really so clear, however, that young people and ethnics have a disproportionately large share of political disillusionment. Perception is always of what contrasts with its background, and news-media perception focuses on the violent and bizarre contrasts. Not many young people have escaped to communes and hard drugs, and even among those who have, many consider their actions to be *political* acts, not escapism, albeit outside the sphere of calculated effectiveness. Nor is the feeling of ethnic helplessness much reinforced by a study of the names in municipal government.

But suppose there *is* a disproportion of disillusionment regarding the efficacy of public life among some social groups. What does it prove? Not that apathy is idiosyncratic and therefore insignificant. It proves rather that the larger social structure from which the apathetic groups derive their special characteristics is productive of fatigue. This goes a long way to justifying the claim that, because many people are fatigued, the social body itself is fatigued. A body, organic or social, is fatigued when it fails to provide a proper environment for vitality and creativity. If a social body inhibits the public vitality of some of its constituent groups, it is a tired society.

In reality, if a social order is a soporific for some people, that effect probably extends to nearly all social groups. After all, as the old American rhetoric put it, the vitality of American life stems from the "creative competition" of the interacting social groups. If some essential components are tranquillized, the others will get soft too. And is this not what has happened?

Parents lament they cannot reach their children. It used to be the kids fought back in active rebellion. Now they quietly slip into their own culture.

Businessmen, except perhaps in the very top positions of the most powerful industries, feel themselves drawn by economic conditions they cannot control.

Educators run through a new theory of education at least once a year, but are depressed because none slows the trend toward less literacy and more misology.

Even the conservatives, long wont to decry attempts at social engineering, seem to defend their old values less because they are worthy now than because they bloomed with vitality once, in the days before they withered.

Political Philosophies

The ubiquity of fatigue in public life is illustrated by our elected political philosophy. Three political philosophies, in a most general sense of that phrase, seem to be competing for majority allegiance in America.

First is the faith in participatory democracy advocated by the far left. The heart of this belief is that each citizen keeps his political power and authority to himself, lending it out to representatives only on conditions of quick recall.

Second is the traditional belief in representative democracy, the baseline of moderates and the moderate left. The orientation in this philosophy is toward handing over one's political power, authority, and responsibility to elected representatives, receiving them back only at election time. Between elections the representatives are trusted to use their judgment.

Third is the managerial philosophy of much of the political right. According to this conception, the important things in life are private matters, and are better left in private hands. To the extent the body politic must be publically ordered, it is better to have an expert do it than trust the ordering to the whims of the whole people or to the arbitrariness of power politics.

All three political philosophies have played roles in American history. The first inspired the young Jefferson in the Declaration of Independence. The second is embodied in the move from the Articles of Confederation to the present Constitution. The third was urged by Alexander Hamilton and is embodied in Richard M. Nixon.

The election of Nixon in 1968 has been interpreted to mean many things, and it is hazardous to suggest one more. But he seems to project the image of the manager more than he does that of the political reactionary or the defender of the little man or the proponent of rural middle class values (although he certainly embodies the last, it seems). Perhaps most successful national Republicans project the managerial image. It certainly was Dwight Eisenhower's philosophy.

Affinity to the managerial image must surely be felt by businessmen, a managerial class by its own genesis; this explains why business is pro-Republican, despite the fact that it tends to prosper more under Democrats. But why did the various "middle

Americans," many of whom had voted for Truman against managerial Dewey, support Nixon? If the managerial thesis is correct, the reason is that the various wars of the 1960s—on racism, on poverty, and on the Vietnamese—were believed to have been bungled. The failure was not that the aims were wrong; it was that the programs were badly managed. (Remember that Nixon, like Eisenhower in 1952, campaigned on the promise of getting the country out of a messy war.) Middle Americans were fed up with liberal enthusiasms that so often failed to produce. Even the liberal's gripe that Nixon is better called "Tricky Dick" is to be explained by his managerial philosophy, not any especially conservative positions on particular issues. The problem with Nixon from the liberal standpoint is that his political philosophy does not have any ideals, that is, no moral ideology for the direction of political policy; he sees his job rather as that of finding efficient means for attaining ends that either are obvious or given by someone else. He, in part, seems genuinely to support goals he privately disagrees with, for instance the Supreme Court's declarations on school integration or perhaps even the public outcry for disengagement from battle with the communists in Vietnam.

The popular support for the managerial approach to political office bespeaks the fatigue of American public life. If public life were more vital, the managerial approach, though having its essential point, would be submerged in debate over more particular substantive issues in which individuals find themselves invested.

Power and the Spirit for Change

The emphasis on general apathy should not be overdrawn, however. The 1960s witnessed attempts at radical social change and political control equalled only a few times in American history. The social sciences have provided hope for new effective means for change. The general social trends separating students from their parents and uniting them as a social class of their own have created a new force for change; the civil rights movement, the anti-war movement, and even the Peace Corps lived off the students' willingness to see and commit themselves as a social class with a power of its own. Furthermore, minority groups, especially blacks and chicanos, and to a lesser degree the Indians, have put their problems near the top of national priorities.

But so often the hopes for change have been dashed, and this has contributed to the desire for managerial government. The point is that whereas hopes have been high, the energy to fulfill them has come in short bursts and has had insufficiently lasting effect. It is probably true that the hopes have changed the *minds* of people, and this will be effective in the long run. But in the short run, the exertion of great energy has produced little results.

Is this not another sign of fatigue? When we are tired and there is still much to do, our exertions become greater and yet less effective. Fatigue means a breakdown in efficiency of action. Our society is fatigued because its energy, the devotion and commitment of people even to the extreme of martyrdom, and the most informed prudence the world has seen have failed to add up to what they should. Like flashbulbs popping in the darkness, they entertain and illuminate vignettes, but they do not cast enough continuous light for us to move around as we would intend.

It would be nice to think that if our public life were fatigued, at least our private lives ought to be flourishing. But this seems not to be the case. Our private lives, in which we should be creative and fulfill ourselves as individuals, seem to have become routinized. Too much we use time off for mere recovery instead of self-creative leisure. Television has become a narcotic instead of a stimulant. We escape to summer houses and camping trips more because they lack the problems of city living than because of the resources they provide for handling urban life. Critiques of American private life, no doubt overstated themselves, must surely add up to a core of truth.[2]

Public and Private

The connection between public life and private life is not hard to discern. The individual vitality and creativity prized for so many thousand years as the virtue of human life requires not only the biological resources of the human organism but also the social resources of the environment. To make the best of themselves, men must be able to appropriate a heritage, a sense of appreciation and values, and a life style unique to their own choosing. They must be able to interact with each other in the basic educational, economic, political, religious, and geographic institutions of society. And they must be able to participate in the institutions of their society without giving up their heritage, their culture, or their individual life styles.[3] The organization of society provides the resources for all these things, which in turn are the environment and resources for creative self-determination. Public life has to do with the establishment and preservation of those essential social conditions. Private life is the exercise of the free, creative life to fulfill the individual. (Although most affairs of life are neither public nor private according to this definition, most affairs are insignificant unless they do have effects either on the environment for private life or on the creative fulfillment prized by the public for its citizens.)

There is an important sense in which private life is defined by convention rather than by creative imagination. Whatever forms of creativity a society prizes it will support by its institutions, at least in a minimal way. Those forms, therefore, must be defined conventionally for the environing social institutions.

There is a parallel sense in which creativity is required for public life. Plato said that, lacking a demi-divine statesman whose wisdom is above the laws, governments should be conservative because they are intent on maintaining conditions supporting a certain level of creative life. But Plato also noted that conditions beyond men's control undermine the best of constitutions so that they no longer support the vital life they once did. His pessimism stands in contrast to the democratic optimism that, by encouraging individual participation, a society brings individual creativity to its own reconstruction, albeit in small increments.

In a democratic society, participation must be creative as well as conservative. But the function of the public creativity is essentially that of providing an environment for other creativity justified on its own. And since creativity cannot be commanded, public life requires (but cannot be sure of) private devotion. Public life is merely conservative to the extent it can be routinized. But to the extent public life must be creative, it requires what otherwise would be private activity to be dedicated to public ends. Creative public heroes are those whose creativity would ordinarily be private if it were not for the special dedication.

Social and Organic Bodies

The distinction between public life and private life reflects that analogy of society with organic bodies in terms of which society can be called "fatigued." The analogy is contrary to what is usually thought, however. An organic body is more like a society than a society like the common-sense notion of an organic body. A person's body is a kind of society of little happenings—chemical, electrical, symbolic, intentional, reminiscent, causal, etc. Some happenings are environments for others. The rather ordinary animal body men have is an environment for the quite unique human brain. In ways little understood, the chemistry of the brain is the environment for their precious few conscious thoughts. Of all the thoughts men have, only a minute fraction are creative. Of all his creative thoughts, only the most carefully environed can trigger the causal processes that do something new in the world. When a person is tired, his little train of creative efforts loses its supportive environments. One of the most important adaptive features of man is the capacity of lower-level organic features to regenerate the environment for creativity.

A society of men is also an arrangement of happenings, some of which are structured as environments for others. The happenings are mainly the activities of men to arrange the physical environment economically, to provide food, shelter, and the pleasures of the fruits of the earth. But the arrangements are intended to provide desirable environments for the people in the society. So part of the social environment is the culture—the symbol systems—for directing activities in non-random ways. And of course there must be social structures for communicating the culture. The ideal, as mankind sees it now, is to structure the physical, social, and psychological environment so as to provide two kinds of *conduits*. On the one hand, there should be *afferent* conduits to present the world to those precious creative human happenings as a set of resources for creative patterning. On the other hand, there should be *efferent* conduits to convey the creative intentions out to physical effects in the world. The conduits, afferent and efferent, must move through many levels of the psychological, biological, social, and physical environments.

Public civic life, on this model, is aimed to structure the *social environment* to do its part in providing people resources for their creativity and media to express it in. Men are also concerned for the *psychological, biological,* and external *physical* parts of their overall environment. These are spiritual, medical, and labor concerns respectively, and are closely connected to political concerns of public life. But they are often private matters, whereas concern for the social structure is public, affecting all citizens necessarily.

That our society suffers from fatigue means in the long run that its structures block some essential conduits to the vitality of human creativity. This is especially apparent when creativity is called for to restructure the society itself. Those who would reform society lack access to the necessary and *apparently* available resources. And the social structures prevent their best efforts from bearing fruit. So people withdraw their contributions to the public.

Practical Conclusions

These rather metaphysical reflections give rise to several very practical conclusions regarding participation in public life.

First, public life will not be restored to vigor by appeals to greater effort or by moral exhortation. The problem is not with the spirit but with the structures in which men's intentions must dwell. This is true despite the insecurity, venality, and depravity of the criminals of our society. No amount of rehabilitation, in the penologist's sense, will correct the structures inhibiting the conduction of resources and intentions to and from creative life.

Second, the structures relevant for attention and effort are those especially important as conduits from resources to creativity and back to public expression. This is an important, though general, conclusion, because in a time of cultural turnover such as ours every institution is changing and seems to beckon as the decisive structure to control. So there needs to be some sorting principle for directing public-oriented efforts.

Third, if public life is fatigued, its structural reformation cannot be accomplished by those people or classes who suffer from structural blockages of resources and actions. This means the "revolutionary classes," to use the Marxist phrase, will be either those so profiting from the present structure of society as not to be fatigued, or those so alienated from organized society as to be equally free of fatigue. And this seems to mean the rich (or their children) and the disenfranchised—the students and minority groups denied access to the economy. This is a surprisingly elitist conclusion, emphasizing as it does the rich and the students. But it makes sense of the experience of Marxism, in contrast to its theory.[4] The mention of minority groups requires a special qualification. Not all blacks, for instance, are interested in changing the structure of society. But the most alienated ones are. At least from the standpoint of rhetoric, the greatest dedication to public life comes from the prisons! Some people say this is because the most alienated have nothing left to lose (a Weatherman definition of freedom). But this does not explain why the loss of hope, after everything else, is not a further freedom. Rather, the situation is that in some particular cases the alienated lack the structural *impediments* to appropriating the resources of creativity and acting on them. With free education and easy mobility a black revolutionary or a student has more vitality and power in public life than his labor union counterpart.

Fourth, the structures to attend to are the conduits accessible to the groups capable of vital public life. Although this is a matter for scientific determination and not mere philosophical speculation, the afferent conduits seem to be primarily of three sorts: educational institutions, communications media, and cultural elements giving a sense of identity or location in the world. The first and third of these have already been singled out for attention by people engaged in public reconstruction. From Head Start to Continuing Education, from Open Admissions to Non-Western Curricula, educational institutions are being restructured. The sense of identity and location in the world is the lure behind Black Studies programs, behind the studies of Asian cultures, and behind the travel odysseys characteristic of the education of so many college students and drop-outs. Access to the communications media is more difficult for poor people. But more and more of the educated elite are heading in that direction. The efferent conduits are more difficult to identify. Legal political channels are the traditional means of getting one's public will accomplished, and the vital groups in our public life flirt with them from time to time. The Democratic Convention in 1968 seems typical, however, of the frustrations of organized political conduits in a society otherwise sunk in fatigue. The conduits of power more effective for the vital groups seem to be outside the political channels, blocking the business-as-usual of the tired system and forcing views and interests to be taken account of by non-political means. Demonstrations, the organization of community groups parallel to the political wards, the formation of coalitions among groups who see themselves as unrepresented by traditional political channels—these seem to be the most effective conduits of action. They have the effect in the long run of forcing the more traditional political conduits to come around. The only traditional channel of public action still effective for vital groups seems the judicial and legal system.

Fifth, the ideal of opening both the conduits conveying resources to the creative moments of people's private lives and those conveying their intentions out into public expression is a condition leading to *participatory democracy*. The ideal has been interpreted in public terms, that is, in terms of individuals inheriting their physical and spiritual environments, and contributing an inheritance for the future. An alternative expression would be, in private terms, to say that an individual attains freedom when he can appropriate the environment, constitute himself a novel agent by patterning what he receives in an especially valuable way, and then stamp this pattern on the social medium as a resource for others and for his later actions.

This more private expression would need a model of creativity. The public and private models are combined, however, in a conception of participatory democracy in terms of which each person contributes his patterns to the media in which the decisions affecting his own life are made. In a participatory democracy a person determines the conditions under which decisions are made affecting him, to the degree and in the respects he is affected. It is, to be sure, unclear how power can be distributed so as to accomplish this. But the ideal of open conduits, provisioning all men with available resources and making their creative moves effective, is an essential ingredient.

Sixth, there is a close association, apparent from the last few paragraphs, between public vitality in a democracy and the notion of participatory democracy sought by the new left. In a managerial state, only the managers are politically active, and they can hardly be said to be politically vital! In a representative democracy where the electorate believes it delegates its political authority to its representatives, vitality lives only at election time, and that may not be the time the important decisions are made.

Seventh, the energy for revitalization need not be created from nothing; it lies in the American tradition. For those groups whose conduits to the tradition are not blocked by ideologies justifying their own class advantage, the heritages of political self-determination, of inalienable public responsibility, and of the subordination of self-interest to the interest of open social structures are as American as apple pie. Of course, the American tradition carries anti-participatory elements. Perhaps most disastrous is the mistaken interpretation of representative government as an *ideal* of democracy rather than as a *vehicle* of democracy. There are reasons enough in the history of political thought to explain why the mistaken interpretation was made. But the time has come to make the distinction. The vehicle has already been taken to the repair shop, and some advise junking it completely!

Summary

Fatigue has set into American public life because too many of the conduits conveying the resources and products of creativity are blocked. Public life has become routine, hence fatigued. The remedy for this lies in structural change opening the conduits for inheriting from and contributing to the environment. Vitality for this structural change can be found only in those groups of people so far unfatigued, i.e., those at the top of the social ladder and those not in it in any significant way. What those groups should do is to open those social structures that are the afferent and efferent connections of the world to private creativity.

The opposite of fatigue is vitality. Vitality exists in a society of events in which the great structured mass of happenings allows for a continuous series of creative inventions, small but effective through the whole mass, each novel but inheriting the creative moments of the past as well as the routine substructure. It is no exaggeration to say that the present problem of Western civilization is to discern how much and what kinds of stability are necessary to sustain a continuity of creative life. Too much stability snuffs the creative spark. Too much change forces private energy to the conservative public task of maintaining a minimal environment. Public and private vitality require a providential blend of stability and spontaneity.

Notes

1. See, for example, "Culture, Territoriality, and the Elastic Mile," by Melvin M. Webber and Carolyn G. Webber, in *Taming Megalopolis*, by H. Wentworth Eldredge (Garden City: Doubleday, 1967), vol. 1, pp. 35–53.
2. Critics as diverse as Lewis Mumford, Gunnar Myrdal, Vance Packard, and Charles Reich cannot be all wrong!
3. These points about cultural inheritance and social participation summarize a lengthy and more theoretical discussion in this author's forthcoming book, *Freedom: Personal, Social, Religious.*
4. Robert C. Tucker has pointed out that the Communist revolutions have come more from a coalition of disaffected sons of the rich with impoverished peasants than from an uprising of the industrial proletariat. See his *The Marxian Revolutionary Idea* (New York: Norton, 1969).

On Public Consciousness and the Revisioning of Political Life

Douglas E. Sturm

Charles Reich made a valiant effort to convince us that a new form of consciousness was sweeping the land and that the result would be not only a cultural revolution but also a radical transformation in institutional structures. Some of us suspected that his prediction could be viewed as an attempt at self-fulfilling prophecy. However, whether the "greening of America" is or is not the most determinative process in our midst, Reich has performed the valuable service of reminding us of a point too easily and too often overlooked in political analysis: what is possible within the political realm is contingent in large part upon the expectations, perceptions, aspirations, understandings, values, orientations of people—leaders, followers, and nondescripts. In the jargon of political scientists, political culture is among the significant data determining what policies and actions are within the limits of possibility.

There may be, indeed there are, many other factors that bear on the formation and substance of political policies—economic, demographic, military, geographic. But *how* these factors influence policy depends in no small degree upon the manner in which people perceive them, evaluate them, react to them, and feel about them. In Walter Lippmann's words, "an important part of human behavior is reactions to the pictures in their heads." [1] It has even been argued that whole times change as human ideas change. Generative ideas and seminal notions introduce the possibility of new epochs. By itself, this is too simple an understanding of social and political change. Marx, Malthus, and Freud have properly cautioned us against over idealizing human action. But on the other hand, one cannot witness the modern political drama without discerning the profound significance of images, symbols, myths, and modes of consciousness. Moreover, one cannot witness the modern political drama without sensing that willy-nilly all of us are among the dramatis personae. This means that how the drama unfolds depends in part upon the pictures we have in our heads, powerless as we may feel. The possibilities of the next scene are contingent upon the form and content of our consciousness.

My thesis is that there is a profound need in our time for a new type of political consciousness that I shall call public consciousness. I would even suggest that whether one is genuinely a citizen, or indeed a representative of the public, depends upon whether one's mind is imbued with public consciousness. The notion of public consciousness is very similar to concepts of public interest, common good, and public philosophy, and I am acutely aware that sophisticates among us are wary of such terms because of their definitional difficulties. They have an elegant enough ring about them, but they are too often used merely as rhetorical devices, without substantial meaning. Granting that problem, I propose that the resolution of the multiple crises that pervade the modern world is contingent in large part upon the emergence of public consciousness among both leaders and led, officials and citizens of the political realm.

Parochials, Subjects, Participants

Public consciousness is a type of political awareness. It stands in contrast to three other types of political awareness— the parochial, the subject, and the participant—distinguished by Gabriel Almond and Sidney Verba in a recent study of political attitudes.[2] The modern world is filled with parochials, subjects, and participants, but I would contend that none of these forms of political awareness is adequate to solve the difficult problems of our period of history.

The prototype of the parochial is the primitive, although we find him now and then in our suburbs. He has virtually no awareness of relations, conditions, events that are beyond his immediate surroundings. He is concerned exclusively with his day-to-day existence. His understanding is limited to his natural environment, traditional customs, and the mythologies of his clan. He has some sense of communal identity. But he has little or no sense of communal decision making. Procedures for deliberate social planning and legislated political and economic change are beyond his ken. In his modern form he knows nothing and cares less about the larger human world about him. He wants simply to be left alone.

Subjects are distinguished from parochials by their awareness of persons who exercise authority over them. The subject knows that there are officials whose function is to make decisions about the future and to issue commands to implement those decisions. He knows furthermore that he is expected to conform to those commands when they are directed to him, and he is quite aware that non-conformity will result in punishment. In some instances the subject is the beneficiary of official action. In other instances he may be deprived and may suffer as a result of political decision. But in all instances he is acted upon, he is himself politically passive, he is a pawn of the political process. Whether he takes pride in or denounces, commends or condemns the political structure, he remains a subject. He does not conceive himself able or competent to participate actively in the actual determination of political policies.

This is the point on which participants differ from subjects. The participant conceives himself as an activist. He is aware of institutions and procedures of social and political change. He knows how the conditions of human life have been and can be transformed. He has sensed the impact of change on his own life and feels able, even eager, to participate in the processes through which future change will be effected. He may be self-centered and defensive in the sense that his desire to participate derives from an effort to assure that his personal interests and sensibilities are not ignored. He may be community-directed in the sense that he feels he knows what is best for all who might be affected by a proposed policy. But in any case he conceives himself as properly a participant in the political process.

One is tempted to correlate these three types of political awareness with three distinct types of society. The parochial is found in traditional society. The subject is the typical denizen of an authoritarian, hierarchically organized social order. The participant is the characteristic citizen of democratic society. But life is not that simple. Within any given political society, one can find all three types in varying proportions. Indeed, any one of us may at different times and on different issues manifest a different form of political awareness. One may be a parochial on issues of industrial safety, a subject in relation to the laws of taxation, but a vigorous participant on matters touching civil liberties, particularly when one's own interests are at stake.

Public Consciousness: Who is a Public?

The political awareness of the participant comes close to public consciousness, certainly closer than the political awareness of the parochial and the subject. Yet, at the same time, public consciousness has its own distinctive qualities. It is the type of political awareness that has always been required for dealing with *res publica,* but is critically needed today at the very least for the sake of sheer survival and at the most for the humanization of political processes.

Vigorous participation in politics, whether out of self-interest or in the pursuit of ideological concerns, is not in itself an expression of public consciousness. To get out the vote, to support the candidate of one's choice, to press for specific legislation, to organize a campaign to kill a bill, or to transform an administrative or military policy are manifestations of the political awareness of a participant. But whether they are acts of public consciousness depends on other qualities, qualities which are needed to orient the political process toward the fuller actualization of human community and human creativity.

The key word is the word "public," a word that recurs constantly in the rhetoric of politicians and jurists, but whose definition is the bane of the serious political thinker. It is easy enough to assert that the public interest ought to supersede all private interests, and it is self-gratifying to identify one's own cause with that of the public. But who exactly is the public? How can the public interest be distinguished? What demarcates the line between public and private?

Some years ago John Dewey made an effort to draw this line by attending to the fact that human acts have consequences. He distinguished two types of consequences: those affecting only the agents directly engaged in the action and those affecting others.[3] This is, in effect, the distinction between a private action and a public action. A private action affects only the principals involved. A public action involves a third party. Thus, setting aside for the moment possible complications, two persons playing chess, several families planning a neighborhood picnic, a group of string players meeting to play chamber music are engaged in private action. But raising (or lowering) the price of a staple commodity, constructing (or refusing to construct) low cost housing in the inner city, starting (or stopping) a war—these are actions that have an impact far surpassing the principals who made the decision. These actions affect third parties, and in Dewey's usage, the third parties who are actually or potentially affected constitute the public with respect to that action.

Within this framework, there is no single public. There are many publics. Publics shift and change depending upon the character of the issue, its relative importance, and its relative duration. When the consequences of an action are extensive, enduring, and serious, persons affected may become aware of their common interest in the action and consequently they may organize and may designate someone to act on their behalf—an advocate, a representative, an official. The function of the advocate is, negatively, to seek ways and means of assuring that his public is not manipulated, exploited, misused, or affected unjustly. His function is, positively, to press for action that will result in the welfare of his public.

The presumption is that persons whom we call public officials are in truth acting on behalf of the many and various publics that are affected by decisions of individuals, groups, corporation, industries, and even governmental agencies. But one of the perverse curiosities of the modern political scene is that many officials and representatives serve the principals of action more effectively than they serve the public. It is a truism of modern politics that regulative agencies established to control an industry rather quickly become an extension of the industry rather than an advocate for the public.

Even more seriously, the most fundamental issues of a public character of our period are of such an extent and character that they transcend completely the ken and control of any public. Dewey observed the problem almost half a century ago :

> The machine age has so enormously expanded, multi-
> plied, intensified, and complicated the scope of the
> indirect consequences, [has] formed such immense and
> consolidated unions in action . . . that the resultant
> public cannot identify itself and distinguish itself. And
> this discovery is obviously an antecedent condition of
> any effective organization on its part.[4]

Since Dewey's writing, this "eclipse of the public" has become
even more serious. The public, in the sense of those persons and
societies whose lives are affected, indeed determined, by policies
and decisions beyond their immediate control, is even more
helpless than five decades ago.

This helplessness stems in part from the fact that prevailing
modes of political consciousness are not oriented to comprehend
the new publics that are being formed and affected in the modern world. Styles of political thought that may have been apt for
a previous period are no longer adequate. For a political consciousness to be publicly oriented in the modern age it must
incorporate the radical shift that has occurred in some circles of
recent philosophical and theological thought, but that was
already present in Dewey's thought. There are two aspects to
this shift: from substantive to relational thinking and from
static to dynamic thinking. The old style of political thought
tends to focus on separate political substances: nation-states,
legal jurisdictions, sovereign powers, and corporate entities, each
with its set of alleged rights, privileges, prerogatives, and interests. Further, the old style of political thought tends to think in
static terms. This is manifest in efforts to attain stability, balance
of power, consensus, order and in efforts to pursue long-range
objectives without modification. In contrast, the new style of
political thought, public consciousness, is relational and dynamic.
As such, it (a) is world conscious, (b) has a sense of corporate
responsibility, (c) accepts dissent as politically functional, and
(d) is open-ended and flexible.

World Consciousness Versus the Nation-State

A public consciousness that is adequate for our time must be a form of world consciousness. It must extend beyond the boundaries and territorial limitations of the nation-state. It must embrace, by intention, all peoples of the world.

The blunt fact is that many major decisions made by economic and political institutions have a global effect. It is impossible to localize the effects of all the policies of the United States government or of the management of General Motors Corporation. This has been a fact for some time and has been recognized in a number of ways. "When America sneezes, the world gets pneumonia" is a well-known twentieth-century aphorism (though we are witnessing the waning of its one-way truth). In any case, in the realm of political responsibility, the full import of the fact of global and reciprocal effect has not impressed itself upon the minds of men.

The import is that the entire world of mankind, including mankind yet unborn, is in a significant sense the public to whom statesmen are responsible in the instance of major policy decisions. To be sure, the public may be only nascent. Clearly not all persons are, or even can be, aware of the effects of long-range decisions upon them. The consequences may be indirect even when they are not remote. Further, persons affected, and affected profoundly by such decisions, may not be effectively organized. Thus, by dint of lack of knowledge and organization, they may not be fully a public. But they are a public so far as they suffer consequences of decisions made by persons other than themselves.

A statesman with public consciousness must thus become a spokesman for and representative of these peoples. His frame of reference cannot be the nation-state. His responsibility extends beyond the nation-state to embrace all peoples in the world.

This is no easy task, for the nation-state is strongly embedded in our political mentality and symbolism. It has fulfilled and continues to fulfill a number of crucial psychological functions. Nationalism, as the ideology of the nation-state, provides a sense of identity, a sense of belonging to a people, a sense of group security. A nation-state is not just a system of power. It is a group with interests, character, and a self-defined mission. This dimension of the nation-state gives the individual a mode of understanding and identifying himself. He is American, Russian, Chinese, Peruvian, Ghanian. He is proud of this identity. His cultural expectations, his language, his memories, his physical and psychological orientation are all tied in with his nation which is defined and controlled and defended by a state system. Even when he rebels against the state system, he often does so on behalf of the nation.

On the other side, the nation-state system is a means of canalizing aggressive tendencies. The nation is defined in part by its separateness, its distinction from other nation-states. Because I am American I am not Russian, Albanian, Indian, Japanese. Furthermore, by virtue of this division and of my identity with my nation, I am led to judge, to assess, and to compare those groups that I am not. They vary in their degree and quality of similarity to my nation. We have, we say, more in common with the English than with the Cambodian. The English are more "our kind." The Cambodian, on the other hand, is (relative to us) odder, queerer, more eccentric. Moreover, other nation-states vary in their degree and quality of support of our nation. We are led to classify the other nations into at least three categories : friends, enemies, and neutrals. Of course, the basis for assessment, comparison, and classification is one's own national identity which is, we are wont to say, always the best. This is why the appeal to national interest, national defense, national emergency is so effective in commanding allegiance and mobilizing a population. The entire nation-state system, fulfilling as it does a profound psychological identity-function, provides all the conditions needed for directing aggression to the "outer" world.

But despite the functions that the nation-state has filled and continues to fill, it is now basically dysfunctional from the standpoint of a genuinely public consciousness. Even on the narrowest possible grounds of concern for the future welfare of the peoples of one's own nation, the nation-state system is dysfunctional. The development of military technology, for instance, has totally destroyed the customary raison d'etre of the nation-state, namely, defense. There is, in the final analysis, no defense against nuclear attack. In the sphere of economics, national boundaries make little sense. For decades, corporations have ignored lines of political demarcation and discovered ways and means of overcoming the constraints of national interest. Cultural communities, intellectuals, artists, scientists have long found the jurisdictional walls of the nation-state artificial obstructions to their work. Thus, even if a statesman were to serve only the interests of defense, economic welfare, and cultural development of his own people, his consciousness must transcend the nation-state.

More broadly, many political issues are of such a character and scope that the actual public includes the peoples of the world. Issues of population growth, pollution, monetary balance have an impact beyond the confines of any particular nation-state. In relation to such issues, the number and the complexity of which are increasing, we are in desperate need of a new type of statesman and a new type of citizen. We need the type of statesman and citizen whose mind will not be fixed on separate and distinct political substances—nation-states, jurisdictional areas, confined political units. We need rather the type of statesman and citizen whose mind will think relationally, who will understand that political responsibility means responsibility for all peoples and groups and individuals affected by given actions.

Thus, the proper political consciousness for our time can no longer be a national consciousness. It must be a world consciousness.

Sense of Corporate Responsibility Versus Private Enterprise

Secondly, a public consciousness that is in keeping with current times must be sensitive to the need for radical change in the economic realm. Business is in truth a "system of power." The fusion of economic enterprises and the concentration of economic activity that Adolf A. Berle and Gardiner Means documented in their dramatic study four decades ago [5] is still a basic datum of our social order, but even more so. Large corporations continue to grow. Even though the rate of growth may have slowed somewhat, it is common knowledge that a relatively few super corporations or conglomerates command a dominating position within the American economy.

There are several million business enterprises in the country if one counts the corner family grocer together with I.B.M. But of those several million one can isolate a few hundred that account for the lion's share of economic assets or sales. In an imaginative conjecture, Robert Heilbroner observes that if the 150 firms that own at least a billion dollars' worth of assets or have annual sales of at least a billion dollars' worth of goods and services were to be obliterated, the American economy would be effectively destroyed, given concentrations in transportation, steel, chemical production, electrical and agricultural machinery, defense industry, banks, insurance companies, and retail sales.[6]

It seems clear that the modern corporation, perhaps the inevitable result of the industrial revolution, has a dramatic impact on the lives and fortunes of persons and associations who are not in positions to participate in the decision-making processes of those corporations. There are far-reaching and systemic consequences that result from decisions made within corpora-tions—wage settlements, pricing policies, levels of investment, directions in research, advertising in mass media, efforts to influence public policy, even internal reorganization which may involve geographical shifts in personnel and factories. In every instance there are not just a few third parties to these actions. The actions have an impact on the entire national community and indeed upon peoples in other countries throughout the world. It is, incidentally, significant that many of the super cor-porations have extended themselves throughout many countries and that the assets and sales of the largest corporations surpass the budgets of many nation-states.

In effect, the modern corporation is not a "private" enter-prise. Because of the extent, the seriousness, the importance of its influence, it has created a vast public in the sense of the indi-viduals, groups of persons, whole societies that benefit from but also suffer the consequences of corporate action. The questions are : How can these publics attain some control over their fate? How can they attain sufficient knowledge of the dynamics of economic corporations and conglomerates even to understand the degree to which and the ways in which they are affected? Who will be their spokesman? How can they get some degree of effective control over these enterprises?

It should be stressed that these questions pertain as much to the internal organization of the corporations as they do to groups of persons outside the enterprise. One of the seldom acknow-ledged incongruities in modern organizational ideology lies in the fact that those who are strongly devoted to democratic prin-ciples in the political order at the same time tolerate and support the most tightly controlled oligarchy in economic structures. Even "stockholder democracy," were it to become a reality, would not provide a channel of effective control for the junior executives, employees, and workers within a corporation. Union organizations and the collective bargaining system have provided such a channel to some degree and for some purposes. But the laws, language, customs, and expectations of business organizations by and large perpetuate the notion that the enterprise is owned and controlled by the few whose proper and primary concern is to maximize profits and whose responsibility to employees extends only as far as is required by law. There is an enormous effort, to be sure, through various forms of highly sophisticated public relations, to promote the belief that the multitudes own the businesses and industries of the country through their investments in stocks and bonds and that, even if that were not the case, the managers and directors of these corporations are motivated by a keen sense of social responsibility. There is, however, a tragic gulf between this propaganda and the actual operation of corporate existence. The language of advertisements and glossy flyers is not the intramural language of managers and directors; the style that is assumed for popular consumption does not conform to the structure that is maintained for corporate efficiency. When management is challenged, when there is indeed some attempt at genuine public control or an involvement of employees in policy formulation, the more deeply held notions of private enterprise, free market, and noninterference (which in effect means control of the corporation by the economic elite) are instantly invoked. Ownership of stocks and bonds has no direct bearing on effective control. The notion that would be more in keeping with the concept of public consciousness is that all participants in the process are bona fide members of the enterprise and have a rightful voice in the formulation of the policies and in the conduct of the enterprise, for all are affected by what the enterprise is and does. They are all part of its public.

But the public of corporate enterprise extends to other people as well. When steel companies effect a wage settlement, raise prices, increase productive capacity, when automobile manufacturers establish assembly plants in other countries, when insurance companies shift their investments, when for purposes of diversification a major conglomerate moves into land speculation or housing development, when oil companies determine to ship by pipeline instead of truck to increase efficiency and decrease costs, when shipping concerns increase the carrying capacity of their tankers, when financial institutions raise or lower interest rates or alter their policies—the impact is felt directly or indirectly, sooner or later on many peoples. These peoples constitute publics in relation to those decisions. But who speaks for them? Who is there to assist in assuring that their welfare is taken into account in the making of these decisions? To be sure, there are efforts, some of them effective efforts at regulating economic enterprises on behalf of the publics. But in consciousness we are led to think of these enterprises as "privately" owned, as self-contained, as separate substances to be managed and controlled largely for the benefit of the owners. Regulation is exceptional, to be imposed only when the enterprise gets "out of hand."

But economic corporations are now of such a size, character, and impact that the idea of their status as property must be reconsidered. As Walter Lippmann wrote over fifteen years ago:

> Absolute private property inevitably produced intolerable evils. Absolute owners did grave damage to their neighbors and to their descendents: they ruined the fertility of the land, they exploited destructively the minerals under the surface, they burned and cut forests, they destroyed the wild life, they polluted streams, they cornered supplies and formed monopolies, they held land and resources out of use, they exploited the feeble bargaining power of wage earners.[7]

Major economic enterprises are at the present time willy-nilly public. They must be viewed not as separate and privately owned substances. They must be viewed within their relational context, as having various effects on various publics. Public consciousness must incorporate them as part and parcel of the common life of mankind and subject to open, detailed, and public scrutiny, criticism, and control. Statesmen and citizens alike with public consciousness must look on corporate entities as an integral part of their responsibility. The economic system must be directed not toward the interests and ideas of management and directors nor toward the benefit of stockholders alone, but toward the welfare of the various publics that are affected by its working.

Acceptance of Dissent Versus Consensus Politics

Thirdly, a genuinely public consciousness will be receptive to dissent and opposition. American governments have been notoriously security conscious over the past several decades. Of the many factors that have led to this development, the Cold War in particular has been cited as a dominant reason for supporting not only an inordinately expensive defense establishment, but also a highly organized system for identifying and neutralizing the work of presumably subversive organizations, movements, and individuals. The Joseph McCarthy syndrome has persisted in many groups and institutions such that any criticism of the values of middle class America is considered dangerous if not treasonable. Intolerance of opposition has become virtually a national characteristic.

Thirty years ago, David Riesman wrote :

Many, if not most, American groups, as they admit or as can be inferred from their behavior or ultimate beliefs, would if they could deny certain civil liberties to some of their political opponents. . . . Where reactionary Catholics are in control, they seek to deny freedom of expression to "Reds" (as defined by them), to atheists, to advocates of non-rhythmic birth control. Protestant fundamentalists have sought to silence evolutionists, and some from the same background would silence Catholics or Jews, and of course Negroes. Business groups, such as the National Association of Manufacturers, veterans' organizations, the Hearst opinion empire, have sought to curb civil liberties for critics of capitalism, as well as for critics of "democracy" (as defined by them). The list is as endless as it is familiar.[8]

The pattern remains unchanged. But the clash has become more widespread, dissonant, and fearsome. In particular, the encounter between official agencies and dissident groups has intensified, given the black revolution, the peace movement, women's liberation associations, welfare rights organizations, counterculture, and the variety of groups formed on behalf of deprived segments of the population. Through the use of conspiracy trials, antiriot squads, intelligence agencies, dossier collections, and organization infiltration, governments on all levels have acted to stifle dissent and to blunt criticism. Indeed, more or less covertly through the C.I.A., but openly through military aid and provision of troops, the federal government has cooperated with other governments to subdue opposition movements on the supposition that such movements constitute a threat to the security of the United States.

Some degree of common-mindedness would of course seem to be a requisite for society to exist. As Plato and Augustine both observed, even the members of an outlaw group must have a meeting of minds and be able to trust each other, else they could not engage effectively in their common endeavor. However, the extent and the character of the drive against dissent and toward uniformity in American society at the present time constitute a virtual repudiation of one of the simple but profound truths that should be impressed upon the minds of all of us, namely, that men err, that they are fallible, that their vision is limited and their knowledge incomplete. Furthermore, perspectives vary. There are different ways of looking at, interpreting, and drawing practical conclusions from the same data. In the face of this condition of mankind, the most appropriate form of political communication is the dialectic. In the dialectic there is agreement, but the agreement is to struggle over meanings, ideas, definitions, goals, policies, and projections. The agreement is to raise questions of each other, to criticize and to be criticized, to challenge and to be challenged and not to let up until all parties are satisfied that they have arrived, for the moment, at as close to mutual understanding as possible. Only through such dialectic within the social and political realm can the possibility of error be decreased and the probability of justice be increased.

Unfortunately, the art of genuine political dialectic has given way to that form of political rhetoric where words and symbols are used to deceive, to manipulate, to convince, and to soothe. The interest of the political rhetorician is to establish a sufficiently widespread and strong consensus that he can do whatever he thinks is best for the nation or his constituency without opposition and without criticism.

From the standpoint of public consciousness, however, political dissent fulfills an indispensable function. It is one of the primary means of identifying the neglected areas, the inequities, the injustices within society. The voice of dissent is often the voice of the injured or the voice of despair. By listening to the voice of dissent, one increases the possibility of constructive social change. This is not to conclude that the dissenting voice is always right. It is, however, to agree with John Stuart Mill that :

> Truth, in the great practical concerns of life, is so much
> a question of reconciling and combining of opposites
> that very few have minds sufficiently capacious and
> impartial to make the adjustment with an approach
> to correctness, and it has to be made by the rough pro-

cess of a struggle between combatants fighting under hostile banner [and that, on any of the most critical questions of social life], if either of . . . two opinions has a better claim than the other, not merely to be tolerated, but to be encouraged and countenanced, it is the one which happens at the particular time and place to be in a minority. That is the opinion which, for the time being, represents the neglected interests, the side of human well-being which is in danger of obtaining less than its share.[9]

It is through the free expression of opposition to prevailing social policies and the established social system that new publics can be discovered. One must grant the possibility of pathological politics, but it is improper to identify all political dissent as extremism, and all extremism as ipso facto pathological. In general, groups do not dissent unless in some fashion and to some degree they are suffering from the consequences of the actions of others. In that sense they constitute a public, and public consciousness requires not merely the toleration of dissent. It requires the reception and encouragement of dissent. It even requires providing the facilities needed for effective dissent.

Open-ended Orientation Versus Means-end Orientation

Fourthly, public consciousness is characterized by an open-ended, flexible orientation. This orientation is required by the fundamental nature of the modern age as a time of pervasive, continuous, and profound change. Orders of human relationship that were once thought secure are under attack. Systems of association upon which men had relied are breaking apart. Traditions and authorities that in the past were an integral part of historical expectations are now questioned or ignored. The forces that are provocative of radical change are many and diverse—demographic and technological as well as political and cultural. The modern period is considered transitory, revolutionary, transformative, and either creative or destructive depending on one's perspective.

Whether we are simply moving historically from one relatively stable epoch to another or instead moving into a new type of epoch in which, paradoxically, change will be the order of the day is an open question. But in either case the inadequacy of the prevailing political orientation seems clear.

The prevailing orientation involves the projection of a set of objectives and the definition of ways and means of obtaining them. The preoccupation of the political group is first of all with interest and power, and, where necessary, with compromise. That is, the primary concerns of the political group, whether special interest group or governmental organization, are survival, growth, and the attainment of its objectives. Its secondary concern is power, for it is only by means of various forms of power that a group can satisfy its interests, insure its survival, secure its growth, and attain its objectives. Lacking sufficient power, the group may be forced reluctantly to resort to the art of compromise which has so long been identified as the heart of the political game.

Nations, states, political parties, special interest groups acting out of this orientation tend to engage in three forms of politics: a politics of defense, a politics of attack, and a politics of conquest. These forms of politics dominate both the domestic and the international scene. All three forms involve the traditional supposition of political sovereignty. That is, any given political entity is understood by its members to have its own definite and specifiable identity. It is clearly distinguishable from other political entities. It has an absolute right to exist, to defend itself against any threats to its existence, to extend its boundaries where that appears necessary for its survival, and to pursue its own self-defined ends without interference. The political world is thus divided into "we" and "they." "We" must look out for ourselves for no one else will look out for us. "They" may be either friends or foes, allies or enemies. Thus, in all political action "we" must be cautious and be certain to maintain sufficient power to defend ourselves and to fulfill our objectives whatever they are. The mode of thinking expressed in the politics of defense, attack, and conquest underlies the armaments race and constitutes the basis of whatever is plausible in the doctrine of the balance of terror. The tragedy is that the defensiveness involved in this form of politics may have a reverse effect. It may result in world destruction. The additional tragedy is that an avowedly free society is led to justify the most blatant forms of secrecy, manipulation, deception, and oppression in the name of national security.

But revolutionary changes are occurring and will perforce continue to occur. The important political question is not how to defend pre-established political boundaries or to secure the pre-established ends and interests of given political groups. The important political question is how to participate constructively and creatively in the transformative processes that every culture is experiencing. The crucial question is how to assure the humane quality of these processes.

In the midst of rapid cultural, social, technological, economic changes, new publics are being formed because the results of such changes are not wholly predictable. Different classes and groups of persons are affected in different ways. A public consciousness will be receptive to the concrete consequences of such change. A public consciousness cannot be satisfied with the form of politics that plans the movement of men, mountains, and matériel to attain predetermined objectives; for that too often results in ignoring the consequences of the process on human lives and thus neglecting the public, that is, those persons whose lives are affected by such logistics. Furthermore, public consciousness will always remain wary of secrecy, private deliberation, and deceptive communication, because these methods too often prevent the articulation of a potential public.

This means that public consciousness is more concerned with processes and procedures than with strategies and tactics. It is more concerned with patterns of interaction and consequences of action than it is with set goals. It concentrates more on the quality of communal living than it does on the achievement of ends or the protection of boundaries or the accumulation of power. It considers the question of procedures in political decision making as of at least equal importance to the question of the substance of the decision.

Public consciousness is open to the transformation, even the radical and continuous transformation, of the political and social order with all of the risks and uncertainty that involves, only seeking to assure that the quality of the process is of a humane character, which means to assure that every emerging public has some effective means of participating in the process. A genuinely public consciousness will thus be experimental, exploratory, open-ended, tolerant of uncertainty, ready and willing to reexamine and to reconsider the policies of the polis.

In sum, public consciousness is a form of political awareness that is relational and dynamic. It is not concerned first and foremost with the maintenance of national or state or city boundaries, the pursuit of national interests, the preservation of the rights of corporate bodies, gaining support through consensus, or the manipulation of power to attain predetermined goals. Instead, it is concerned primarily with the various and many publics that are formed by the major decisions of man's common life. As such, public consciousness in the modern age must be world conscious. It must include a sense of corporate responsibility. It must be receptive to dissent as politically functional. It must be open-ended and prepared to consider transformative changes in political structure and procedure.

From this perspective, the political realm is conceived not

as a struggle for power nor as a battlefield of nation-states and interest groups. It is revisioned as the arena in which the world of mankind is confronted with the task of deciding from moment to moment how to live, to play, and to work together. Indeed it is only with public consciousness that one can begin to conceive of a mankind and of a politics that is fit for a mankind. Other forms of political awareness arise from narrower bases—tribal, national, class, special interest group. Public consciousness does not and cannot overlook differences among groups and societies; for publics are made up of differences. But at the same time, public consciousness is concerned with the welfare of all possible publics and thus provides the basis for a specifically human form of political thinking.

Whether public consciousness is a live possibility at the present juncture of human history is a serious question. Most persons in America yearn for the mentality of the parochial. They want to be left alone. They do not want to know or to be bothered with public issues. But they cannot be left alone. They are forced by dint of laws and taxes, wars and unemployment to suffer the mentality of the subject. Some even are provoked into becoming participants in political consciousness. But, with some sterling exceptions, most participants possess a constricted understanding of politics; they fail to grasp the full context of the issues that concern them.

However, the future remains future and is by its nature open, uncertain, indeterminate. Further, the mere articulation of an idea is itself the projection of a possibility. Thus, the formation of the image of public consciousness in the minds of some citizens is a beginning. How the political drama unfolds tomorrow depends in part upon the images we form in our heads today. One's hopes and expectations should not be determined by past structures or present trends. In that sense, public consciousness is a live possibility and the political realm open to creative re-visioning.

Notes

1. Walter Lippmann, *The Public Philosophy* (New York: Mentor Books, The New American Library, 1955), p. 73.
2. Gabriel A. Almond and Sidney Verba, *The Civic Culture* (Boston: Little, Brown, 1965).
3. John Dewey, *The Public and Its Problems* (Chicago: The Swallow Press, 1927), pp. 12–13 and passim.
4. Ibid., p. 126.
5. Adolf A. Berle, Jr. and Gardiner C. Means, *The Modern Corporation and Private Property* (New York: Macmillan, 1932).
6. Robert Heilbroner, *The Limits of American Capitalism* (New York: Harper & Row, 1966), pp. 11ff.
7. Walter Lippmann, p. 93.
8. David Riesman, "Civil Liberties in a Period of Transition," chapter III in *Public Policy*, C. J. Friedrich and Edward S. Mason, eds. (Cambridge: Harvard University Graduate School of Public Administration, 1942), pp. 56, 57.
9. John Stuart Mill, *On Liberty* (Indianapolis: Bobbs Merrill, Library of Liberal Arts, 1956), p. 58.

Obscenity and Common Sense: Toward a Definition of "Community" and "Individuality"

George Anastaplo

Prologue

"How like a man who's reluctant to speak you are,"
[Glaucon] said. "You'll think my reluctance quite
appropriate, too," [Socrates] said, "when I do speak."
"Speak," [Glaucon] said, "and don't be afraid." . . .

PLATO, *The Republic* 414c

Is a volatile decadence inevitable in our community because of what our prosperity and our numbers both permit and reflect?

To speak of prosperity today (for a people spared as ours has been war's devastation and instructive austerity) is to speak of a successful pursuit of material happiness by countless millions, the repeated satisfaction of the multitude of desires that flesh is heir to. To speak of community is to imply restraints upon self-expression—to imply discipline and limitation upon what one might want to do or to say. But the very prosperity the community cherishes has been made possible among us by the energy and ingenuity which have come with the unleashing of private desire.

A respectable everyday image of the secure self-indulgence we have earned may be seen in the airconditioned automobile, in which rides a family or a couple or even a lone potentate sealed off from nature and the rest of mankind, as it cruises the highways maintained and policed by the community. Contact between men is fragmentary. Each is legitimately on his own.

And since each man *is* on his own, what can he do but explore the potentialities of his psyche? The requirements of the community can be kept to a minimum (one even hears of the government as merely an "umpire"), and private adventures are called for. Only the timid or the crippled refrain from experiments in the arts, in narcotics (both physical and spiritual), in "experience."

But when each is thus on his own, it is the rare man who can escape the futility and ultimately the despair which await the self-indulgent. And even the rare man—as witnessed in Martin Heidegger's political experiment of the 1930s—can go basely wrong in discerning an escape route for himself and for the anxiety-ridden community he would redeem. That is, even the rare man can forget what every decent man is aware of, that there are cures worse than mortal afflictions. (See Aristotle, *Nicomachean Ethics,* III, ix. Cf. the beginning of Plutarch's *Pelopidas.*) At what seems to be the other end of the contemporary political spectrum, we have the observation by Joseph Stalin's daughter. "For twenty-seven years I was witness to the spiritual deterioration of my own father, watching day after day how everything human in him left him and how gradually he turned into a grim monument to himself." (See, on tyranny, Averroes's commentary on Plato's *Republic.*)

The thoughtful man realizes that there is necessarily a tension, in a healthy community, between the demands of the public and the charms of the private. To sacrifice either one to the other is to deprive mankind of something essential to the full flowering of the human being or to the competent dedication of citizens. (See Homer, *Odyssey,* XII, 41-54, 153-200. Cf. Plutarch's *Antony.*) Yet to balance properly the contending claims of the public and the private is, indeed, difficult : men who are not restrained and guided by institutions and traditions tend to vacillate between rigidity and abandon, between anarchical selfishness and tyrannical selflessness.

The thoughtful man also realizes that communities, like the men who make them up, are mortal : contending forces cannot be held in balance forever. He realizes, that is, that there is nothing to wonder at in the discovery that the community in which he happens to find himself is in process of disintegration. Such disintegration, which may even have its interesting facets, can come after impressive successes in realizing some of the goals which have been long aspired for by mankind. (Indeed, it is no mean achievement to have so harnessed the resources of nature that men are now able, for the first time in the history of the race, both to walk on distant planets and to destroy overnight all of their own kind.)

Citizens, as such, care about the community. They not only take it seriously, but *they* regard it as potentially immortal—and hence they can always be expected to "keep on trying." Citizens may resent, therefore, the detached (even amused) curiosity of the thoughtful man : they cannot help but make an effort (even when things seem desperate) to purge their community of its grossness and decay and thereby to attempt to restore it to a healthier condition. Of course, they are likely to mistake symptoms for underlying causes and thus to leave the causes untouched, but that *is* the way of citizens : appearances are for them quite important. Citizens are not wise men; they may, in the best of times, be informed men. They do not go to the root of things—*that* is left to founders and to the teacher of founders.

Consider, as an example of what dedication to the community can mean, how articulate citizens may speak about the contemporary problem of obscenity. The subject is in some respects rather pedestrian, but it nevertheless raises in a practical manner enduring questions about the relation of community interests and individual self-expression. The allure of the prurient can thus be put to good use : for when one talks intelligently about obscenity one is obliged to talk (or at least to think) about the role of the community in shaping and preserving the character of citizens and hence of the regime itself.

The *logos* of citizens who have been influenced (in the Periclean tradition) by both poetry and philosophy—a speech which may be aware of but cannot be expected to repudiate the presuppositions of their community, including the attraction for the community of the economic fruits of relatively unencumbered individuality—may, it seems to me, go something like this :

Logos

"But," [Socrates] said, "I once heard something which I trust. Leontius, the son of Aglaion, was going up from the Piraeus under the outside of the North Wall when he noticed corpses lying by the public executioner. He desired to look, but at the same time he was disgusted and made himself turn away; and for a while he struggled and covered his face. But finally overpowered by the desire, he opened his eyes wide, ran toward the corpses and said: 'Look, you damned wretches, take your fill of the fair sight'."   PLATO, *The Republic* 439e

I

There is so much uncertainty in the accounts which our more articulate fellow citizens have left us as to the significance of obscenity today that scarcely anything is asserted by one of them which is not called into question or contradicted by the rest. Still another account is justified only if it can escape from the present confusion by going back to old and, in some instances, perhaps even first principles.

Politics, Aristotle reminds us, is the master art : something must recognize what is highest in the community and must order the activities of the community in accordance with that which is highest.[2] Even a political order which, in the name of liberty, refuses so to arrange matters is itself based on an opinion of what is highest : that is, the invocation of liberty reflects an opinion of how the best may be secured.[3]

We are obliged to ask what the end of government is. A Supreme Court justice provided, in 1890, an old-fashioned American answer to this question :

> The protection of the safety, the health, the morals, the good order and the general welfare of the people is the chief end of government. *Salus populi supreme lex.* The police power is inherent in the States, reserved to them by the Constitution, and necessary to their existence as organized governments. The Constitution of the United States and the laws made in pursuance thereof being the supreme law of the land, all statutes of a State must, of course, give way, so far as they are repugnant to the national Constitution and laws. But an intention is not lightly to be imputed to the framers of the Constitution, or to the Congress of the United States, to subordinate the protection of the safety, health and morals of the people to the promotion of trade and commerce.[4]

A century earlier, James Wilson, one of the principal draftsmen of the American Constitution, had observed in the Constitutional Convention :

> [I cannot] agree that [the protection of] property [is] the sole or the primary object of Government and society. The cultivation and improvement of the human mind [is] the most noble object.[5]

We observe in turn that it may be imprudent to talk of any important activity of man as strictly or altogether "private" : much of what is cherished as private depends upon, and at least indirectly affects, civilization which is "publicly" established and maintained.

II

Thus we are obliged to confront the question : What makes men as they are? This question presupposes that there is no effect without a cause, a proposition which seems as valid here as in the other affairs of men, as well as in nature generally. What then can obscenity (whatever it is) be expected to do to the shaping of men's character and conduct?

The evidence, we are told again and again, is inconclusive. But this conclusion is pronounced from the perspective of modern social science, which often seems determined to disregard what common sense tells us. Is not longstanding and virtually universal community opinion as to what makes people behave, and misbehave, worth something? There are, in any event, many matters about which social science is at least equally inconclusive—as, for instance, about the effects of various economic measures, of diplomatic and military measures, of desegregation measures, and of welfare measures—and yet we appreciate that lawmakers should be permitted if not obliged to regulate conduct with respect to these matters, even to the extent of life-and-death decisions. If, that is, the same degree of certainty were generally required that is demanded with respect to obscenity, there would be (for better or worse) far less legislation than we now deem necessary.

Furthermore, if it cannot be shown that there are no bad effects from obscenity, it cannot be shown either that there are good effects. In fact, it would seem to follow that there can be little harm in attempting to suppress something which is so inconsequential in the life of the community. Certainly, the community may (because of its "prejudices") find obscenity highly offensive, whatever the causes of or justification for such an attitude. Why not permit the community, then, to control or discourage that which happens to be so offensive to it? Why should not the community's "taste" be permitted to prevail over

that of individual producers and consumers of what the community considers "obscenity"? Thus, one can see that the argument from lack of knowledge about the effects of obscenity—
which would, by the way, seem to suggest that good literature
has no determinable effects worth encouraging either!—can be
employed to support suppression as well as permissiveness.

But is the case as inconclusive as it is said to be? What *do*
we think education does for men? [6] Must we not grant that there
is a place for restraint and even for a sense of reverence in a
community, that without these the noblest life, perhaps even a
simple decent life, is unlikely if not impossible? Plutarch tells of
Thales, the poet,

> whom Lycurgus, by importunities and assurances of
> friendship, persuaded to go over to Sparta; where,
> though by his outward appearance and his own profes-
> sion he seemed to be no other than a lyric poet, in
> reality he performed the part of one of the ablest law-
> givers in the world. The very songs which he composed
> were exhortations to obedience and control, and the very
> measure and cadence of the verse, conveying impres-
> sions of order and tranquillity, had so great an
> influence on the minds of the listeners, that they were
> insensibly softened and civilized, insomuch that they
> renounced their private feuds and animosities, and
> were reunited in a common admiration of virtue. So
> that it may truly be said that Thales prepared the way
> for the discipline introduced by Lycurgus.[7]

There are ages, that is, when the artist is taken seriously.

III

We return to a consideration of the possible effects of
public obscenity. One legal scholar has collected from the literature "four possible evils" against which obscenity legislation is
directed:

(1) the incitement of antisocial conduct;
(2) a psychological excitement resulting from sexual imagery;
(3) the arousing of feelings of disgust and revulsion; and
(4) the advocacy of improper sexual values.[8]

He adds in a footnote at this point:

It is possible to assert a fifth evil: the impact of obscenity on character and hence, slowly and remotely, on conduct.

He then appraises the possible evils in this manner:

It is hard to see why the advocacy of improper sexual values [No. 4] shall fare differently, as a constitutional matter, from any other exposition in the realm of ideas. Arousing disgust and revulsion in a voluntary audience [No. 3] seems an impossibly trivial base for making speech a crime. The incitement of antisocial conduct [No. 1] . . . evaporates in light of the absence of any evidence to show a connection between the written word and overt sexual behavior. There remains the evil of arousing sexual thoughts short of action [No. 2]. What puzzled Judge Bok and amused Judge Frank was the idea that the law could be so solemnly concerned with the sexual fantasies of the adult population.[9]

Is the first possibility ("the incitement of antisocial conduct") to be dismissed as easily as is here assumed? We should recall our comments on the degree of certainty and on the kind of evidence usually required for legislative purposes. Are we so materialistic as to believe that the striking changes in behavior we have witnessed in recent decades have not been preceded by *any* changes in ideas? It should be noticed that the third possibility ("the arousing of feelings of disgust and revulsion") has had added to it in this appraisal the fact that the disgust and revulsion are created among a voluntary audience. Even so, do we as a community want, or want to permit, activities in a voluntary audience (made up of strangers, not of relatives and intimate friends) which are likely to arouse disgust and revulsion?

The answer to this question depends, in part, on how seriously we should regard the fifth possible evil, the one that most sophisticated intellectuals today would tend to overlook (or, at least, relegate to a footnote): "the impact of obscenity on character and hence, slowly and remotely, on conduct." Suppose the worst obscene materials became generally available and, for some (perhaps accidental) cause, even generally attractive or at least generally tolerated. Should we not expect in such circumstances a vitally different spirit in the community? Would there not be here an "educational" influence that schools and families and churches would be expected to make desperate efforts to counteract? Would it matter to the community which of the contending opinions prevailed? If it would matter, what could legitimately be done by the community to support decisively the opinion it favored? Is it not naïve to assume that obscenity can never prevail in the marketplace if the community acts merely as "umpire"?

Still another, related, evil has been staring us in the face all along. One does not have to read much of ordinary obscene writing to realize that the people who develop and distribute this stuff are, for the most part, corrupt or, at least, very low if not sick people. And they, in effect, attempt to make others like themselves, evidently succeeding in some cases. That is, one does not need to determine whether bad *actions* result from such materials: for even worse than bad actions is that one should think or talk like the authors of these books and magazines. There is no problem about "cause and effect" *here*. Is not this an evil that a self-respecting community has a right to be concerned about? We recall James Wilson's insistence in 1787 that "the cultivation and improvement of the human mind [is] the most noble object" of government. And we are reminded as well of Aristotle's observation (in the concluding pages of the *Nicomachean Ethics*) that sensible political effort is necessary for the general realization of human goodness in a community.[10]

We venture to suggest a seventh (also related) evil about which the community may legitimately be concerned, and that is the evil cf ugliness and of things that make for ugliness. Do we not have the right and perhaps even the duty to establish and preserve what we consider beautiful? Certainly, it will be granted, when the concern is directed to keeping billboards off our highways or to protecting our forests, our waterways, and our cities from depredations. Why not when we deal with the moral beauty (that is, the character) of our people as well?

All this presupposes, of course, that we *do* have some idea of what a good man looks like and that we also have some idea of how to make and keep him that way. Perhaps even more important for our immediate purposes, all this presupposes that it matters very much, in defining and reinforcing a community, that it be shown to one and all that there are things which will be ardently (even, to some degree, blindly) defended. Do not both the morality and the morale of a community depend on such dedication?

IV

And yet there is the cause of liberty and of intellectual curiosity, even the cause of truth itself.[11] For this is the elevated ground on which the better champions of obscenity stand, not in the low swamps of the unprincipled, self-serving purveyor.

We are obliged, that is, to look even more closely at the obscene. Is there not here essentially the perennial question of the attitude men should take toward intimate things, toward peculiarly private things? The consumer of obscenities tries to have his cake and to eat it too : he takes pleasure in looking at private things, but in such a way that they are not treated by the voyeur as private. If he should succeed completely in exposing everything to public view, then his special pleasure would disappear. What would he "have" to try next?

But, one might ask, why preserve what some regard as merely a conventional distinction between the private and the public? Because, it can be answered, of the nature of things. We are reminded of Sophocles's *Antigone,* with its deadly recognition of an ultimate irreconcilable conflict (as well as intimate tie) between the public and the private, between the city and the family. We are reminded also of the reticence exhibited by Plato in his account, in the *Phaedo,* of Socrates's last day. We are given much of the conversation between Socrates and his companions that day. We are shown something of the death of Socrates late that afternoon. But we are not given the final exchanges between Socrates and his wife and children. Nor are we shown Socrates's final bath in preparation for death : he retires into another room to wash himself. An old friend covers Socrates's face as he dies. Not everything is open to public display.

And yet, it might be asked, does not such reticence keep us from the truth? This depends on how much one needs to see in order to understand certain things. Delicate matters have to be handled delicately, if they are to be properly understood. Indeed, mere exposure may impede understanding, if only because it manhandles what is delicately made. One learns more of human nature, and of the nuances of human character, in the novels of Jane Austen than in the plays of an Edward Albee : in the former, the subject is ministered to by the artist ; in the latter, the personality and hence the deficiencies of the author who insists on saying everything intrude and block the view.[12]

V

The "quarrel between the ancients and the moderns," it has been noticed, "concerns eventually, and perhaps even from the beginning, the status of 'individuality.' " [13] It is in its excessive effort to serve the cult of "individuality" that we see a critical deficiency of obscene writing.

Such writing (whether or not adapted to the stage or to film) must, if it is to continue to titillate the consumer, deal in novelties.[14] But there is something self-defeating about this: practices of a more and more bizarre character must be conjured up. Where this sort of thing is the dominant concern of an author (or of his public), the off-color songs, stories, and jokes which satisfied earlier generations are replaced by a series of fantastic inventions. One need only look through a few contemporary works of this character to detect an intrinsic despair, a despair reflecting the groping of people broken loose from their moorings.

These moorings, which law attempts to discern so as to reinforce, are the dictates of nature. They are perversely acknowledged by the pathetic efforts of the professional obscenity producer to present the antics of his characters as the truly *natural* way. They must assure themselves and their customers that they practice what nature preaches, an assurance which would be more persuasive if the practices described remained somewhat more constant than they are. This instinctive concern to show themselves in conformity with nature should move us to wonder what *is* truly natural. But to investigate this properly, one needs a seriousness of purpose and a self-restraint which cannot coexist with the restlessness of the seeker after mere pleasure.

The lure of the obscene may draw at its roots upon the desire of the young to learn and upon the desire of the ageing to be again young. But, ultimately, must not the obscene be rejected because it is neither true nor useful? [15]

VI

Let us now make explicit a definition of the obscene which has been assumed in what we have been saying.

The obscene is, as a concerned man has written, "that which should be enacted off-stage because it is unfit for public exhibition." [16] A decent community senses that there are things which, although perfectly proper behind closed doors,[17] it is better not to probe publicly without very good reason, and then only with tact and great care. This "off-stage" formulation, which does depend to some extent on contemporary standards and practices, is useful for understanding the phenomena with which we have been dealing. Although it may not be immediately useful for legal purposes, it should underlie, inform, and guide the community's approach (legal and otherwise) to these problems.

The courts often have recourse today to a definition which, although somewhat circular, gives a fair indication both of the community's concern and (to put that concern in practical legal terms) of what a jury can be expected to find. That is, it is said that obscene productions are those which "appeal to the prurient interests," and hence minister to "shameful or morbid interest" in bodily functions, particularly the sexual—functions which are customarily kept private. The emphasis of the community *is* on the sexual, but this emphasis need not be seen as a depreciation or resentment of the sexual life of man. Rather, it may be seen as an effort to protect human sexuality and the joyfulness of love and of lovemaking from the demeaning exploitation of them by the purveyor of obscenities.

When the community thus acknowledges the importance of the sexual, it may not reveal its own obsessions but only its instinctive appreciation of the facts of life and of love. For it is essentially acknowledging the virtue of temperance as fundamental (at least in time of peace) to the other moral virtues which citizens should develop. And when we consider the virtue of temperance—the proper attitude toward bodily pleasure—it is to be expected that our primary concern should be with that most intense (and hence most diverting) of bodily pleasures, especially since it is critical as well to the proper ordering of the family and to the procreation and nurture of children.

We all know, or know of, people who are warped in their attitude toward sexual activities, either their own or those of others. Some of these people "express themselves" as producers and consumers of obscenities. Others of them "express themselves" in efforts to police what everyone says about sexuality. But it is only fair to recognize that those seeking to police others do deal with matters in which the community has some legitimate interest. It is against the *exploitation* of sexual activity, then, that obscenity sanctions may be said to be primarily directed. Such exploitation includes the building up of expectations which cannot help but be thwarted, to the detriment both of the defrauded consumer who is frustrated and of the community which must minister to his frustration.

There is an 1868 legal formulation by Lord Cockburn which (although somewhat eclipsed in this country in recent years) seems to have merit:

> . . . I think the test of obscenity is this, whether the tendency of the matter charged as obscenity is to deprave and corrupt those whose minds are open to such immoral influences, and into whose hands a publication of this sort may fall.[18]

This formulation could, when used as a basis for prosecutions, be modified in one respect, by providing explicitly for what may have been implied, "into whose hands a publication of this sort *is intended* to fall." This permits, in the interest of an efficient fairness, a common-sense distinction between material written for and distributed among adults and materials destined for children. This test of "deprave and corrupt," which may be limited to materials dealing with specified bodily functions or perhaps even extended to certain portrayals of violence, is one which draws upon contemporary standards. It has as one advantage that it takes character for granted as a vital concern of the community.

Can it be honestly maintained that the normal writer or bookseller does not really know what his community desires in a particular case? Is it not significant that purveyors of obscenities almost invariably know what is being referred to when customers make requests of them? This suggests that the problem of definition for legal purposes may not be, in the ordinary case, as serious as it is sometimes made out to be. Consider how adept the typical politician is, even when most impassioned during heated election campaigns, in shying clear of public obscenity.

We all have, and have had from childhood, a fairly good idea of what the community expects in public—as good an idea as we have of what is expected in the way of due care on the highway, in the way of due care on the part of the physician, in the way of due care on the part of the cook or of the innkeeper in serving his guests, to say nothing of the standard of good faith in commercial transactions. And when the self-confidence and authority of a community are stable, what it expects in public it is very likely to get. In such circumstances the law, which serves primarily to ratify explicitly what the community does expect, has to be invoked but rarely. That is, there may be something seriously wrong when, as among us today, frequent recourse to obscenity prosecutions has been thought necessary by the community. (Perhaps such recourse is a crude way of reassuring ourselves that there *is* a community.)

There are, of course, borderline cases in any attempt by the community to establish what it means by obscenity. That should always be expected when the law draws lines. But we should not, in the name of realism, be unrealistic about what we understand each other to mean. Few reasonable men, and for good reasons as well as because of long established opinion, would permanently condemn such works as the Bible or Shakespeare or even the delightfully bawdy Chaucer—and it simply avoids the problem we confront to pretend otherwise by singling out (as is sometimes done in debate and in litigation) certain passages in such books. There is no reason why a healthy community, aware of what it is doing, cannot treat borderline cases sensibly.

Certainly, it is not sensible for a community to allow itself to be persuaded that it does not or that it should not care deeply about its sensibilities. The following exchange from the trial transcript of the prosecution of a Los Angeles dealer for selling what, from every indication (in both the state's and the defendant's briefs), is a miserable piece of trash exploiting (and thus promoting?) a variety of sexual fantasies, is illuminating : [19]

> *The Court:* . . . Would you read it?
> *Defense Counsel:* I have read it as part of my job, your Honor.
> *The Court:* Thank you, sir, for saying as part of your job. I read it because it was my duty.
> *Defense Counsel:* And I say to your Honor with as much honesty as I can, and I think your Honor knows I have always tried to be at least as straight as I can—
> *The Court:* There is no question about it.
> *Defense Counsel:* I do not believe that book is obscene. I do not believe that book has a substantial tendency to corrupt or deprave persons by arousing lustful thoughts or lascivious desires. Now, I think there is much that can be said about the book that it is not good. I think that as a literary work it has much to go before it qualifies. But, your Honor, that book should be killed by the Saturday Review or the New York Times Book Section, not by law. And this is the point I would like to make, your Honor : That there is a lot of merchandise put out every day, a lot of books, which form the same classification that your Honor would place this in terms of not by good

standards, by good judgment, reaching out and saying that this has sufficient value to warrant our time and reading. But that doesn't make it criminal, your Honor.

The Court: If you have read the book, sir, you discovered the young woman in that case was a perfectly normal woman and after the experience [described in the book] became a perfectly abnormal woman. Now, if that isn't acting upon a normal mind, that kind of a plot, I don't know anything that is. And we do know, sir, we unfortunately have had many years of contact from time to time with this and we do know that a perfectly normal person, that on certain occasions, being subjected to certain things, becomes changed and altered. Now, I have heard this story—I have heard it so many times when I have been in a position as a Public Defender and I have represented them and I asked "How did you get that way?" and had the same story repeated time after time, being subjected to it. It is like intoxicating liquor. It affects some that are otherwise perfectly normal until the experience. And that book there, I thought, was a perfect illustration of a normal person, one whose thoughts were entirely different, had never entered upon that field, upon being subjected to it forcibly became an entirely altered person. The book, I thought, carried its own proof. And I cannot contemplate you or anyone else or myself reading beyond a certain portion of it if we didn't have to do it because of some duty to perform.

Defense Counsel: But I would say this, your Honor, I would say this, that having read this, and I really don't consider myself to be different than the average, normal person, that I could sit on the jury here too, that after having read that book I don't believe that I was either a better or a worse person. I don't think I was corrupted. I don't think I was depraved, and this is the point, your Honor, that I want to hammer home.

The Court: I was depressed, sir. I was depressed, very
   depressed.
Defense Counsel: Your Honor, I thought I was wast-
   ing my time.
The Court: I know your point. You think I would
   reject it so quickly—I would. But remember, sir, I
   am not a young man.
Defense Counsel: I am not talking about you, your
   Honor. I am talking about myself. I am a young
   man and I am saying I wasn't corrupted. I wasn't
   depraved. And I don't believe [the prosecuting
   attorney] was corrupted or that he was depraved or
   that any other normal person would become corrupted or depraved.
The Court: Yes, but we are in the position of physicians. Physicians are not expected to catch the disease in order to treat it.
Defense Counsel: I think in this area, your Honor, we
   are all subject to the same whims of fate. We are not
   special people, your Honor.
The Court: We try to keep ourselves from getting
   affected, don't we?

Defense counsel (a specialist in obscenity cases) made essentially the arguments of the sophisticated intellectual in the service
of the arts; the judge, on the other hand, expressed the sometimes confused opinions of the concerned community. The
exchange recorded here warrants careful examination. Is the
judge (shaped by the conventions of the community) so clearly
wrong that his experience and impressions should be dis-
regarded? "I was depressed, very depressed," is the lament of
one who believes he sees his fellow man led astray. To rely, on
the other hand, upon the denunciations of the *New York Times
Book Review* or of the *Saturday Review* to "kill" such books as
this is rather unrealistic : the clients of this particular bookseller
would no more be influenced by what those august journals said
than those journals would even notice the existence of such books
as these.[20]

It may be true that we cannot be certain about the effects of such books. But, to return to what we have already said, is not a healthy community one in which it is known that both citizens and their governments *care* about influences which may deprave or corrupt, care enough to *try* to do something about them? [21]

VII

When we look again at "deprave and corrupt," we may see something that is basic to contemporary opinion. There can be little doubt that the position taken here is not one which would recommend itself to most intellectuals today. May not the underlying difficulty be that they are skeptical of anything being truly depravity or corruption? That is, does not the intellectual who, although ahead of his time, does have his effect in time—does not the intellectual see such judgments as mere matters of taste?

To be able to speak objectively of depravity and corruption, there must be some reliable opinion among us of what a decent man, a good man, and perhaps even a good community look like. Again, we are obliged to turn to the guides nature provides us and to take seriously any inquiry about them that we may come upon.

It is well to notice also that we have been speaking about the more obvious cases of obscenity; the less obvious, and in some ways more pervasive and perhaps even more critical, cases are obviously much more difficult to police. Consider, for instance, the photographs in respectable journals and on television portraying the intense grief of men and women who have just lost a loved one. Or consider the stories which reporters have pried out of a family which has just suffered great misfortune. Such things as this, to say nothing of much of the advertising and the exploitation of violence even in the magazines and newspapers most self-righteous about obscenity, cannot but contribute to the corruption of the moral spirit of the community.[22] If we keep in mind what the obscene really means—that which should be enacted off-stage—we are better able to judge and influence what is done all around us. This is clearly an aspect of the problem about which legislation can do little and an enlightened, confident public opinion can do much.

The potential gravity of the situation today is suggested by what has happened to, and because of, influential intellectuals: they with their denial of the reality of goodness as anything other than mere taste, do affect the spirit of the community. It is evident that lawyers prosecuting obscenity cases are remarkably defensive about what they are doing. They are, at heart, converted to the cause of their opponents who proclaim themselves in the service of truth and liberty. We have attempted to show what the truth may be in such matters. We question whether men subjected to the intellectuals' prejudices in these matters are truly free.

We return to the question: What is a good man? We should not forget that we do have an answer, if only a tentative answer, in the light of which we have shaped and continually revise our educational and political institutions. We should, in short, not insist on ignoring what we do know.

VIII

Nor should we ignore what we know to be on the other side of the coin. Certain public and private actions can, despite the best of intentions, only make matters worse. In fact, it is possible that much of the distrust today of the official challenge to obscenity has been caused by serious abuses by censors of their power in recent centuries. Of course, the possibility of abuse of a power is no argument against its use. But, one must wonder, is abuse inevitable in the exercise of this particular power?

Have the legions of decency learned how to restrain themselves in their crusade? There is no doubt a tendency among them to want to go beyond what is strictly necessary or even defensible, despite the fact that one best teaches restraint by exercising it oneself and explaining how and why one *is* exercising it. But, as we have noticed, the censorious often do have (with all their faults) what the typical purveyor of obscenities rarely has: the interest of the community at heart. In addition, they usually work out in the open and are thus subject to public scrutiny and control—at least, much more so than the self-serving purveyor. Is not puritanism (with all its disagreeableness) less destructive of virtue and beauty than licentiousness (with all its attractions)?

It should be acknowledged that any serious effort to police obscenity will, almost inevitably, sweep out (at least temporarily) some serious books as well. We cannot expect juries to be as perceptive in this respect as trained book reviewers and students of literature. We can expect here what is true of all legislation, that a few good things may be caught up with the massive bad. But, on the other hand, may not certain good books seem to the undiscerning public so much like bad books as to make it difficult to distinguish them? If certain good books are permitted to circulate freely, will the trash which crudely resembles them follow in their trail? Is this what has happened since World War II?

The proper training of lawyers, especially those who prosecute and who sit as judges, should provide a substantial safeguard against indiscriminate indictments. But there are no foolproof programs. Each of the alternative courses of action available to us today has undesirable effects. Presumably, the serious book will have more to be said for it, even before a jury, and can probably be depended upon to win a place for itself in time. In any event, we should take care lest our insistence upon always having only the best leads to the subversion among us of simple goodness.

Once we see the problem for what it is—once we again recognize that there are good books and bad, virtue and depravity, wholesome influences and pernicious—we can do something about the problem in the ways that only an informed, self-confident public can. That is, we can try to do even more than we do with our educational institutions, not only by providing the proper medical and moral training for our children but also by reviving an informed dedication to liberal education.[23] And we can make even more use than we do of intelligent private action. Perhaps most important, we can let it be known that we regard as contemptible—and in this there may occasionally have to be some hypocrisy—those who traffic in such materials that even a child can recognize to be obscene.

But, unfortunately, a reformed public opinion may not suffice. The problem has become what it is today—and, indeed, has become a problem at all—partly because of technological developments which, with respect to production and distribution of printed matter and film, permit businessmen to have their effects in communities far removed from those in which they live (where, presumably, the opinions of their neighbors would be more apt to shame or intimidate and hence restrain them). And, it should be recognized, some men simply do not care what others think of them, especially if callousness serves either financial gain or simple rebelliousness or an illness in the psyche. That is, the law may be of some use in such matters, even if not rigorously enforced. Indeed, it may suffice, in making clear the opinion of the community and in setting the tone of public discourse, to compel the distribution of obscene wares to return to its former tolerated "under the counter" status.

The principal cause of excessive—even obscenely excessive—and hence self-defeating suppression is indignation that runs away with would-be ministers of justice. Still, the just man—the man who cares primarily for the welfare of the community—must nevertheless be prepared to say (*or to tolerate,* if not to support, *those who say*), as did Lear after his betrayal by Goneril and Regan, "Touch me with noble anger."

IX

But what of the Constitution? That is not a critical concern for us on this occasion. One is not induced to examine seriously the relevant constitutional principles if one does not believe there is good reason, political or moral, for the community to concern itself with the production and consumption of obscenity. It is that concern, illuminated by what common sense has always had to say about such things, to which we have addressed ourselves. A preliminary survey of constitutional considerations should suffice at this time.

The principal constitutional safeguard here is that of "due process of law" (in the traditional procedural sense)—and, indeed, that in itself places formidable obstacles in the way of any government which would enforce rigorous obscenity statutes. Due process guarantees would require, for instance, that the determination of what is to be used in the classroom and of what is to be available in public libraries should be left primarily to the informed judgment of the bodies entrusted by the community with that duty, that is, the responsible faculties and librarians of those institutions. Due process also requires that the accused, in the ordinary criminal case, be punished only for what he did, having been put on notice about what he should not do, and having had an opportunity to meet the case submitted against him.[24]

"Freedom of speech and of the press," on the other hand, need have very little bearing on this problem, at least as these guarantees are found in the First Amendment and applied to the States by the Fourteenth Amendment. These guarantees are designed primarily to assure that our people will be able to discuss freely the matters that concern us as a self-governing body politic. Most literature is not directed *immediately* to such concerns. Here, too, there is the problem of drawing lines—but again, it seems obvious that most of the material we have been talking about has little or nothing to do with examinations of political issues or with the decisions which we as citizens have to make and which we are entitled to discuss freely.

What we *are* entitled to discuss freely is whether obscenity should be restricted by law and how rigorously, and whether any particular course of action taken by our governments is proper and desirable. We are entitled to discuss, for instance, whether recourse to legal action is, considering the temper of the times, much more likely to hurt than to help matters. Certainly, the prudent community will not want to allow its justifiable distaste for obscenity to mislead it as to what is feasible.[25] Thus, freedom of political discussion must be retained unabridged if citizens are to remain sensibly sovereign : the degree and means of community discouragement of obscenity should be examined from time to time, as circumstances change. This is the way of free men.[26]

Citizens who truly respect freedom should take care lest its good name and good works be repudiated by the confusion of responsible liberty with either insatiable self-indulgence or mere exhibitionism, to say nothing of the restlessness of a fashionable but thoughtless modernity.

Epilogue

. . . "It wasn't for nothing," [Glaucon] said, "that you were for so long reluctant to tell your story."
PLATO, *The Republic* 414e

This citizens' speech, then, can be said to be a speech by

and to citizens in defense of common decency and perhaps the common good. It is, although not without its difficulties, a salutary speech for licentious circumstances, one which stands for (even as it exhibits) restraint and hence civilization. No doubt, another speech would be appropriate for a repressive age. Among the contemporary circumstances to which this speech is tailored is that which finds the country so large and so poorly instructed as to make it hard for anything but the most banal to become truly common, thereby smothering (or at least concealing) what is at the heart of American aspirations.

It is also a speech which, as I anticipated, takes for granted certain fundamental presuppositions of the community, perhaps the very presuppositions which may be at the root of recurring troubles of the nature addressed here. That is, ours *is* (has it always been?) a community in which it is respectable to believe that everyone is licensed and even counted upon to do as he pleases with his own. The primary purpose of the community is seen by many as permitting self-pleasing (which they may be pleased [or is it that they are troubled enough by?] to call self-expression and even self-fulfillment [but without acknowledging a standard which the self should measure up to]). Thus, it is often taken for granted among Americans (and in most Western countries today?) that parents may do with their children pretty much as they please, that lovers may (in the fashion of the Cyclops?) do with each other as they please, and that a man may do with his soul pretty much as he pleases.

Nor do citizens, as citizens, really question their dedication to the particular community in which they happen to find themselves. They, as citizens, are sworn to preserve and defend, not to examine and transform (and, if need be, repudiate), their given way of life. Indeed, they are easily led to believe that they are obliged to be steadfast, even unscrupulous, in its defense. Citizens (of which there are, strictly speaking, fewer and fewer in modernity) are made to feel they would be nothing without the community: their lives would have no meaning; scrupulousness would become empty, and even a mockery. The most they may do by way of radical reform is to call for a return to the principles of the regime which has made them and their forebears, not to what would truly be "first principles." Thus, citizens as such are essentially conservatives.

Conservatives tend to be aware of the limits that the community is entitled to place on the desire for self-expression, especially when such expression takes the form, say, of public obscenity. But they do not like to dwell upon the fact that the question of obscenity is intimately related to the question of property, to the question of what one may legitimately do with one's own, and indeed to the question of what *is* really one's own. One may sometimes wonder, as one considers contemporary passions, whether Americans as a people still have anything in common but a devotion to the principle of unlimited acquisition and to the principle of unimpaired enjoyment of whatever happens to be acquired. One may also wonder what all this means: Are private property and genuine citizenship ultimately irreconcilable? What should be done when some want to acquire (and to "share," once acquired) what others insist should be kept private? Does not the community have to determine what should constitute "acquisition" and "enjoyment"? What is for these purposes the authoritative community? What standards should it use in making the required determinations? Does the trafficker in obscenities emerge as the true capitalist? Or is he really a prophet of comprehensive socialism?

Thus, the problem of obscenity may have at its core unsettling questions about the deference of private property to private desires. Still another, and perhaps the most critical, challenge ignored by citizens is that which questions the fundamental presupposition that it *is* legitimate for a community to regulate, on the basis of what seems reasonable, a variety of attempts to intensify and enjoy the motions of the soul. Do we not find concealed here the enduring question which underlies any serious debate about the regulation of obscenity? Political men claim the right to judge what the artist may say and how he may say it. The artist, on the other hand—and this includes the greatest—insists that only he is equipped to determine what he should say and how, even whether obscenity should be employed by him (especially in comedies) to achieve the effect sought for.

Citizens, although their principal arguments usually do not recognize this fully, need not limit themselves to the regulation of obscene publications: their fundamental concern really is with *any* literature (whether or not obscene, whether trash or a classic) which may have a harmful effect in the circumstances in which the community happens to find itself. That is, one challenge to citizenship is, in its most elevated form, whether the philosopher-king (that peak on which human reason and political power meet) is equipped and entitled to judge the social utility of art. One has indeed risen from the "low swamps" of obscenity when one addresses oneself to this question and its corollaries:

Socrates speaks of an ancient quarrel between philosophy and poetry, between reason and art. How is this ancient quarrel to be understood inasmuch as both parties to it sincerely pursue the good? Both poetry and philosophy are touched by *eros:* one sees truth in beauty, the other beauty in truth. Both recognize the role of chance in human affairs, but in different ways: it may be a matter of chance whether philosophy emerges in the community, but its course thereafter is, in principle, prescribed; poetry, on the other hand, can be said to be always in language and with mankind, but the courses it follows depend on chance.

Thus, all philosophers may be considered, in their essentials, identical (just as there is, for beings with our natures, one best city which reason can discover): to be right-thinking is to arrive, upon serious inquiry, at the conclusions of others like oneself— at the conclusions others have come to or would come to in like circumstances. (Cf. *Hamlet,* I, v, 164-167.) Discrepancies in conclusions require investigation, reconsideration, and correction on one or both sides.

The poet, however, may not care whether he contradicts another poet. (Cf. *Republic* 349b-350d.) He seems to cherish—or, at least, is often cherished for—individuality : he strives to create, to make something *his* way, thereby making manifest something which may never have been evident before about man, about the poet himself, or about the world.

The philosopher, in order to associate himself with timeless thought, abstracts from material things; poets, in making the most of and out of themselves, delve into—sometimes even revel in—the material, at least into how the material happens to appear to them at the moment. The diversity among poets is related to the flux in that matter by which they must take their bearings : the ebb and flow of their inspiration may reflect the shifting stimuli emanating from constantly changing matter.

The poetic activity which is regarded by poets as creative is discerned by the philosopher to be essentially imitative. The philosophic activity which is regarded by the philosopher as discovery is dismissed by poets as sterile. Poets see the philosopher as fettered, but nevertheless tyrannical. The philosopher cautions the poetical against willfulness, if not even anarchy. One seems to stand for liberty (spiritual as well as social), the other for virtue (intellectual as well as moral) : poets are, in inclination, moderns, whereas the philosopher is, if anywhere, an ancient.

The thoughtful observer may be moved to conclude that there can be no bridge across the timeless gulf which divides poetry and philosophy—but then he remembers Plato and Shakespeare and is obliged to reexamine his conclusions.

Notes

1. The citizens' speech is adapted from a lecture, "How to Begin to Think About Obscenity: Ends and Means," delivered April 24, 1965 before the Senate Club of Shimer College. The Notes were added subsequently. The Prologue and Epilogue have been added at this time. ("Obscenity" and "pornography" are used interchangeably.)

See, for further examinations of many of the points touched upon in the citizens' speech: George Anastaplo, *The Constitutionalist: Notes on the First Amendment* (Dallas: Southern Methodist University Press, 1971), e.g., chapter 5, note 126; Anastaplo, "On Civil Disobedience: Thoreau and Socrates," *Southwest Review* (Spring 1969); Anastaplo, "Law and Morality: On Lord Devlin, Plato's *Meno* and Jacob Klein," 1967 *Wisconsin Law Review* 231 (1967); Anastaplo, "Preliminary Reflections on the Pentagon Papers," *University of Chicago Magazine* (Jan.–Feb., March–April, 1972); 117 *Congressional Record* H12557.

See, also, for useful discussions subsequent to the 1965 lecture: Leo Strauss, *Socrates and Aristophanes* (New York: Basic Books, 1966); Harry M. Clor, *Obscenity and Public Morality* (Chicago: University of Chicago Press, 1969); Walter Berns, "Pornography vs. Democracy: The Case for Censorship," *Public Interest* (Winter 1971); Joseph Cropsey, "Radicalism and Its Roots," *Public Policy* (Spring 1970); Alexander Bickel and others, "On Pornography: Dissenting and Concurring Opinions," *Public Interest* (Winter 1971); Irving Kristol, "Pornography, Obscenity, and the Case for Censorship," *New York Times Magazine* (March 28, 1971); Harry M. Clor, ed., *Censorship and Freedom of Expression: Essays on Obscenity and the Law* (Chicago: Rand McNally, 1971). See, as well: *Report of the Commission on Obscenity and Pornography* (New York: Bantam Books, 1970); Allan Bloom, "Interpretive Essay," in *The Republic of Plato* (New York: Basic Books, 1968); Leon R. Kass, "Making Babies—the New Biology and the 'Old' Morality," *Public Interest* (Winter 1972); Willmoore Kendall, *Contra Mundum* (New Rochelle, N.Y.: Arlington House, 1971), pp. 544ff; "What Alternative Society?" (an editorial), London *Telegraph*, August 7, 1971, p. 10. See, on pollution, nature, and the seeming verities of economics: George Anastaplo, R. Stephen Berry, Ronald H. Coase, Harold Demetz and Milton Friedman, *The Legal and Economic Aspects of Pollution* (Chicago: University of Chicago Center for Policy Study, 1970); cf. Plato, *Republic* 341c, 346 and Aristotle, *Politics* 1257b4ff. See, on the natural limits of "gainful . . . commerce": Edward Gibbon, *Decline and Fall of the Roman Empire* (New York: Modern Library, n.d.), I, 778. See, for a review of recent litigation in the Supreme Court of the United States with respect to both obscenity and its commercialization: "The Supreme Court, 1970 Term," *85 Harvard L. Rev.* 229–237 (1971); and, for a review of recent English developments, see the series, "The Abuses of Literacy," beginning in the *Times Literary Supplement*, January 14, 1972.

The perennial (and, in a sense, natural) lure of the obscene is suggested by what should be the choicest ribald lines of the year:

No one who sees us will deny
It is the only way to fly.

The naughtier reader will be able to imagine the subject of the "poem" from which these lines are taken. The more prosaic will have to resort to the *New Statesman*, August 13, 1971, p. 196. Cf. Plato, *Republic* 408c–409e.

It should be kept in mind, in thinking about what widespread indulgence in obscenity might imply, that a remarkable lack of *political* self-restraint among respectable leaders contributed in Greece to the coming of the colonels' tyranny in 1967. See Anastaplo, "Military Men and Political Questions," *Congressional Record*, vol. 117, p. E6129 (June 17, 1971). Consider, also, what the contemporary recourse to obscenity might imply about the soul of America: "As Steven Marcus has remarked, even the new pornography that emerged in American mass entertainment and art could be understood as 'a form of pseudo-radicalism' tied to this sense of loss of moral authority in the formal structure of society." William Pfaff, "Vietnam, Czechoslovakia, and the Fitness to Lead," *New Yorker*, July 3, 1971, pp. 33–34. See Harry Kalven, Jr., "Introduction," *Contempt* (Chicago: Swallow Press, 1970), on "contemporary tensions between decorum and justice." Or as a notorious Chicago pornography peddler protested, upon being harassed by the police, "After all, this is still the United States, and we still should fight for the things that made our country great." Chicago *Sun-Times*, January 5, 1972, p. 16. (The notes which follow, including the remainder of this first note, pertain directly to the citizens' speech.)

"Obscenity," George Orwell observed, "is a very difficult question to discuss honestly. People are too frightened either of seeming to be shocked or of seeming not to be shocked, to be able to define the relationship between art and morals." *Critical Essays* (London: Secker and Warburg, 1954), p. 142. See note 12, below.

When we concern ourselves with the problem of obscenity today are we really concerning ourselves, in a secular manner, with the now unfashionable but nevertheless politically vital problem of piety? See, for example, *Exodus* 3:6; *Deuteronomy* 34:4. Consider also, with respect to piety, W. E. B. DuBois, *Souls of Black Folk* (Chicago: A. C. McClurg & Co., 1903): ". . . all in all, we black men seem the sole oasis of simple faith and reverence in a dusty desert of dollars and smartness." (pp. 11–12) Cf. p. 8: "To be a poor man is hard, to be a poor race in a land of dollars is the very bottom of hardships." Cf., also, Anastaplo, "Neither Black nor White: The Negro in America," in *Notes on the First Amendment* (University of Chicago doctoral dissertation, 1964).

However offensive public obscenity may be, we should be careful not to bring government and law into disrepute by relying upon force and the criminal courts, in lieu of other more appropriate social measures, to remedy (or would it be to mask?) our most pressing deficiencies as a community. "After some lesser business they discussed the reconstruction of the South. . . . 'No one need expect me,' said Abraham Lincoln, 'to take any part in hanging or killing these men, even the worst of them. Frighten them out of the country, open the gates, let down the bars, scare them off.' 'Shoo,' he added, throwing up his large hands like a man scaring sheep. 'We must extinguish our resentments if we expect harmony and union. . . .' " Lord Charnwood, *Abraham Lincoln* (Garden City: Garden City Publishing Co., 1917), p. 450.

2. Aristotle, *Nicomachean Ethics*, I, ii; X, ix. See Euripides, *Rhesus* 105; *Suppliant Women* 160–162, 195ff, 334ff, 1227ff. See, also, notes 13 and 25 below. Cf. Homer, *Iliad*, III, 64–66 (where Paris instructs Hector about the gifts of Aphrodite). Cf., also, Aristotle, *Nicomachean Ethics* 1162a16ff, 1177a12ff. But see Gibbon, *Decline and Fall*, I, 50–53, on the effects of a people settling into and for their private lives.

3. Thus we see in the opening sentences of John Milton's *Areopagitica* a movement from the advancement of "the public good" to the promotion of his "country's liberty" as the primary duty of the public-spirited citizen. See, also, note 26 below.

4. *Leisy* v. *Hardin*, 135 U.S. 100, 158 (1890) (a dissenting opinion by Justice Gray, endorsed by Justices Harlan and Brewer). Cf. Montesquieu, *The Spirit of the Laws*, XXI, xx, "How Commerce Broke through the Barbarism of Europe."

"The end of all political struggle is to establish morality as the basis of all legislation. 'T is not free institutions, 't is not a democracy that is the end, —no, but only the means. Morality is the object of government. We want a state of things in which crime will not pay; a state of things which allows every man the largest liberty compatible with the liberty of every other man." Ralph Waldo Emerson, *Complete Works* (Boston: Houghton Mifflin, 1911), XI, 540–41. See note 13 below. Cf. Averroes, *On Plato's Republic* 27. 14ff.

5. July 13, 1787; *Documents Illustrative of the Formation of the Union of the American States* (69th Cong., 1st Sess.; Hse. Doc. 398) (Washington: Government Printing Office, 1927), p. 373.

See, also, Article 45, Pennsylvania Constitution of 1776 ("Laws for the encouragement of virtue, and prevention of vice and immorality, shall be made and constantly kept in force . . ."); note 1 above (on piety).

6. See, for example, Clarence Darrow's suggestion about the influence of Friedrich Nietsche's writings on an impressionable college student. *The Plea of Clarence Darrow in Defence of Richard Loeb and Nathan Leopold on Trial for Murder* (Chicago: R. F. Seymour, 1924), pp. 77–86. Cf. Montesquieu, *The Spirit of the Laws*, XII, xii.

7. Plutarch, *Lycurgus*. Milton, in *Areopagitica*, explains that Lycurgus "sent the poet Thales [to Sparta] from Crete to prepare and mollify the Spartan surliness with his smooth songs and odes, the better to plant among them law and civility . . ." See, also, on Thales, his connection with Onomacritus, the central figure in the "history" of lawgivers found in Aristotle, *Politics*, II, xii. Consider the significance of the discordance at the end of Plato's *Crito*, a discordance which protects from rational examination the "argument" of the single-minded laws. Consider, also Plutarch's *Pericles* (particularly the

relations of Pericles with Damon and Anaxagoras); Francis Bacon, *The Advancement of Learning*, in *Selected Writings of Francis Bacon* (New York: Modern Library, 1955), p. 244 (on the uses of poesy and feigned history). Consider, as well, Euripides' deliberate exposure to public gaze, at the end of his *Orestes* (on the eve of his "exile" from Athens), of the desperate dependence of the gods, the family, the city, and the moral order upon the poetic art.

Gibbon, in his *Decline and Fall* (I, 10, n. 39) suggests, "There is room for a very interesting work, which should lay open the connection between the languages and manners of nations." See, also ibid., I, 33–35; Plato, *Laws* 656c–657c; *Prose Works of John Milton* (London: J. Johnson, 1806), I, pp. xi–xii; Kurt Riezler, *Man, Mutable and Immutable* (Chicago: Henry Regnery Co., 1950), pp. 94–109.

Whatever may be said about the legislation of morality, it should not be expected that the very best can be legislated but, at most, the conditions for the emergence of the very best. Consider, for intance, the compromise with the very best implied in Xenophon, *Cyropaedeia*, 1.2.7 (describing criminal processes among the Persians for ingratitude). Such a compromise is reflected as well in the kind of statute assessed in *Beauharnais* v. *Illinois*, 343 U.S. 250 (1952).

8. Harry Kalven, Jr., "Metaphysics of the Law of Obscenity," 1960 *Supreme Court Review* 1, 3–4 (1960).

9. Ibid., p. 4. Compare the respect shown for conventions by ruthless leaders as divergent as those quoted in note 17 below. See, also, note 12 below. (Does ruthlessness mean a denial of nature and hence even greater reliance than usual on convention, on what happens to be decreed? Charlotte Bronte [in a preface to *Jane Eyre*] argued in opposition to those "in whose eyes whatever is unusual is wrong": "Conventionality is not morality. Self-righteousness is not religion.")

Is not too much made today of the qualification, "a voluntary audience" (or, as we often hear, "consenting adults")? What induces more and more adults *to* "consent"? And may not this undermine, by a kind of seepage, the entire community, without the community as such really having had an opportunity to consent?

Do not "consent" and "voluntary" imply that the consenter understands what he is doing? Compare the "consent" of the taste buds to foods which harm the heart. See Shakespeare, *Coriolanus*, I, i, 99–150.

10. Compare a nineteenth-century appraisal of political offenders: "It may be expedient to prosecute political delinquency, even to the death, but certainly not necessarily on account of the moral iniquity of the accused. Amidst conflicts of opinion, each half of the community is seditious in the sight of the other. When governments are unsettled, it has often been doubtful, with the purest characters, whether treason itself was not a duty. The English revolution made traitors *in law* of men of the highest personal honour; nor was it till things got solid, by the subsidence of the loose matter connected with that event, that personal integrity and political innocence became the same. To see no difference between political and other offences is the sure mark of an excited or of a stupid head. . . ." Henry Cockburn, *An Examination of the*

Trials for Sedition Which Have Hitherto Occurred in Scotland (Edinburgh: D. Douglas, 1888), I, 68. See note 26 below.

See, on licentious words, Plutarch, *Moralia* 28A (Loeb Classical Library edition); Aristotle, *Politics* 1336b5.

11. ". . . But let us not flatter ourselves that we shall preserve our liberty in renouncing the morals which acquired it." Jean Jacques Rousseau, *Letter to M. d'Alembert on the Theatre*, in Allan Bloom, trans., *Politics and the Arts* (Glencoe: Free Press, 1960), p. 113. Does not a community's liberty depend on its morale as well as on its morals? See, on morale, note 21 below. Cf. Plutarch's *Pelopidas* (on the Sacred Band).

See, with respect to the epigraph for the citizens' speech, Plato, *Republic* 466e, 537a; Dante, *Inferno*, xxx, 130–148; Charles Darwin, *The Expression of Emotions in Man and Animals* (Chicago: Phoenix Books. University of Chicago Press, 1965), p. 293; Orwell, *Critical Essays*, pp. 142–43. See, also, Charnwood, *Abraham Lincoln:* "The words of [Lincoln's] political associate in Illinois . . . may suffice. He writes: 'Almost any man, who will tell a very vulgar story, has, in a degree, a vulgar mind. But it was not so with [Lincoln]; with all his purity of character and exalted morality and sensibility, which no man can doubt, when hunting for wit he had no ability to discriminate between the vulgar and refined substances from which he extracted it. It was the wit he was after, the pure jewel, and he would pick it up out of the mud or dirt just as readily as from a parlour table.' In any case [Charnwood continues] his best remembered utterances of this order, when least fit for print, were both wise and incomparably witty, and in any case they did not prevent grave gentlemen, who marvelled at them rather uncomfortably, from receiving the deep impression of what they called his pure-mindedness." (p. 13)

12. Edward Albee wrote, in a preface to *The American Dream* (New York: Signet Book, New American Library, 1961): p. 54: "Is the play offensive? I certainly hope so; it was my intention to offend—as well as amuse and entertain. Is it nihilist, immoral, defeatist? Well, to that let me answer that *The American Dream* is a picture of our time—as I see it, of course. Every honest work is a personal, private yowl, a statement of one individual's pleasure or pain; but I hope that *The American Dream* is something more than that. I hope that it transcends the personal and the private, and has something to do with the anguish of us all." (p. 54) (Cf. *The Selected Letters of Gustave Flaubert*, ed., Frances Steegmuller, [New York: Vintage Books, 1957], pp. ix ["No lyricism, no comments, the author's personality absent!"], 148, 165–166, 194, 266.)

It is not suggested here, of course, that Mr. Albee should have been prosecuted for anything he has written. Instruction would have been more appropriate. See *Heraclitus*, ed., Philip Wheelwright, (Princeton: Princeton University Press, 1959), p. 69 ("Their processions and their phallic hymns would be disgraceful exhibitions, were it not that they are done in honor of Dionysos."); Ovid, *The Art of Love* (New York: Universal Library, Grosset & Dunlap, 1959), p. 160 ("The laws of modesty"); Moses Maimonides, *The Guide of the Perplexed* (Chicago: University of Chicago Press, 1963), pp. 432–36, 573, 604; Sigmund

Freud, *A General Introduction to Psychoanalysis* (New York: Washington Square Press, 1960), p. 194 (on due regard for that which is "most intimate in the personality"); Bertrand Russell, *Why I Am Not a Christian and other essays* (New York: Clarion Book, Simon and Schuster, 1957), p. 173 (emphasis added) (". . . The conception of the obscene has its roots deep in human nature. We may go against it from a love of rebellion, or from loyalty to the scientific spirit, *or from a wish to feel wicked,* such as existed in Byron; but we do not thereby eradicate it from among our natural impulses. No doubt convention determines, in a given community, exactly what is to be considered indecent, but the universal existence of *some* convention of the kind is conclusive evidence of a source which is not merely conventional. In almost every human society, pornography and exhibitionism are reckoned as offenses, except when, as not infrequently occurs, they form part of religious ceremonies." See note 18 below, for the passage immediately preceding this one.).

Also instructive is Flaubert's lament, "Ah! Ce qui manque à la société moderne ce n'est pas un Christ, ni un Washington, ni un Socrate, ni un Voltaire, c'est un Aristophane." Quoted by Ortega y Gasset, *Meditations on Quixote* (New York: Norton, 1961). pp. 162–63.

13. Leo Strauss, *Natural Right and History* (Chicago: University of Chicago Press, 1953), p. 323. Mr. Strauss continues, in this passage, "[Edmund] Burke himself was still too deeply imbued with the spirit of 'sound antiquity' to allow the concern with individuality to overpower the concern with virtue." See, also, Strauss, *The City and Man* (Chicago: Rand McNally, 1964), pp. 41–45; Anastaplo, "Human Being and Citizen: A Beginning to the Study of Plato's *Apology of Socrates*," in *Ancients and Moderns: Essays on the Tradition of Political Philosophy*, Joseph Cropsey, ed. (New York: Basic Books, 1964), p. 16; Anastaplo, "Natural Right and the American Lawyer," 1965 *Wisconsin Law Review* 322 (1965).

The transformed status in modernity of "individuality" is suggested by two radically different conceptions of the role of law. The orthodox ancient teaching can be said to have been that whatever the law (in the broadest sense of "law") does not command, it forbids. See Aristotle, *Nicomachean Ethics* 1138a4–8. Certainly, one of the critical purposes of the law was understood to be that of promoting virtue. On the other hand, ". . . [T]he prevailing view is that . . . State interference is an evil, where it cannot be shown to be a good." Oliver W. Holmes, Jr., *The Common Law* (Boston: Little, Brown, 1881), p. 96. Francis Bacon remained enough of an "ancient" to believe, "I am of his mind that said, 'Better it is to live where nothing is lawful, than where all things are lawful.'." *Apothegms*, No. 69. See Aristotle, *Nicomachean Ethics* 1094a27, 1103b3, 1109b33, 1113b22, 1130b8, 1130b28, 1178a8, 1179b31, 1180a33; *Politics*, 1253a2, 1253a19, 1276b16, 1280b5, 1293b3, 1309b31, 1328a17, 1329a29, 1332a33, 1335b13, 1337a1, 1341b33. Cf. Aristotle, *N. Ethics* 1141a29, 1143b33, 1145a10, 1162a16, 1177a12; *Politics* 1271b1, 1287b19, 1324b5, 1333b22. See, also, Leo Strauss, *The City and Man*, pp. 30–31, 41–45;

Harry V. Jaffa, "Aristotle," in Leo Strauss and Joseph Cropsey, *History of Political Philosophy* (Chicago: Rand McNally, 1963), p. 67; Laurence Berns, "Thomas Hobbes," in Strauss and Cropsey, *History of Political Philosophy*, pp. 362, 366; notes 2 and 4 above. Cf. Thomas Jefferson, *Notes on the State of Virginia* (New York: Harper Torchbooks, 1964), Query XI, p. 90: ". . . were it made a question, whether no law, as among the savage Americans, or too much law, as among the civilized Europeans, submits man to the greatest evil, one who has seen both conditions of existence would pronounce it to be the last; . . . the sheep are happier of themselves, than under care of wolves . . . ."

14. This appetite for novelty is reinforced by the shamelessness which modern democracy seems to encourage. (See, also, notes 16 and 22, below.) It may be seen as well in the emphasis we now place on the value of artistic self-expression. Thus, one of Oscar Wilde's characters (in chap. 19 of *The Picture of Dorian Gray*) assumes art to be "simply a method of procuring extraordinary sensations." Consider the "unbounded passion for variety" which Gibbon describes. *Decline and Fall*, I, 74. (Are not the unexpurgated poems of a Catullus valuable for mankind to have and to leave in the original Latin?)

Is not the identification of the artist with the bohemian life (or with the life of the expatriate) essentially modern? See, for example, James Joyce, *Portrait of the Artist as a Young Man*. Cf. Laurence Berns, "Aristotle's *Poetics*," in Cropsey, ed., *Ancients and Moderns*, p. 70.

One sees all too often today the man of genuine talent descending to fabrication of the merely shocking and sensational, thereby exhibiting the affliction which has paralyzed his artistic sense. That is, whatever talent he does retain unencumbered is employed to make something which is no more than ingenious. One can hope that that which is deep within him remains untouched by such exploitation. When a man of genuine talent desires to shock, it is the polemicist or the sick man or the hostile man in him who seeks expression, not the true artist. It is the "self," not his art, which is thus mobilizing his talents. Such distortions are applauded by the petty and the disenchanted—by those, that is, who were always beneath the vision he had had and who sense he has now come down to their level. Do not most artists depend on the guidance and discipline of a healthy community in order to do their best work? Does not Plutarch (in *Pericles* 13.3) regard the Acropolis at least as much Pericles's as Phideas's work (or, as we would say, "creation")? See note 20 below.

See, on the lure of novelty, Homer, *Odyssey*, I, 351–352; Aristotle, *Nicomachean Ethics* 1154b20–30. Cf. Aristotle, *Politics* 1336b27–36.

15. It has been suggested that exposure to the most blatant obscenity can sometimes be therapeutic. Perhaps a physician's prescription could be made available in appropriate cases. But the healthy reader or the serious writer should not require more eroticism than what Homer says of Odysseus and Calypso or of Odysseus and Circe. See *Odyssey*, V, 225–27; X, 333–35. Cf. ibid., XXIII, 300–309, 321–25, 333–37. See, also, ibid., VIII, 266–369. Cf., also, Plato, *Republic* 607d. (The contemporary reader could well be diverted, for what is legitimate in

what he seeks for in obscenity, to the restrained portrayals of modern love in the novels of Graham Greene and to the adventure stories of John Buchan and Geoffrey Household [stories which have their excitement heightened by portrayals of heroes who are pursued both by the police and by evil men]. Cf. John Donne, "The Extasie.")

Compare the vantage point at which Jonathan Swift places the poet in "A Description of a City Shower."

16. Richard Weaver, *Ideas Have Consequences* (Chicago: University of Chicago Press, 1948), pp. 27–28. See note 22 below. The first chapter of Weaver's book, "The Unsentimental Sentiment," is particularly valuable for the student of the problem of obscenity.

The following announcement, posted by the "Management," has been observed on a law school bulletin board: "*Playboy* at the Law Club Store. Also various other 'mags' which may appeal to your 'prurient interest.' We know when we see it, and this is it." Cf. "the dreams all men carry in their loins" (John Vieners, "For Jan," in Paris Leary and Robert Kelly, *A Controversy of Poets* [Garden City: Doubleday, 1965], p. 480); "for this is a goodly thing, to listen to a minstrel such as this man is, like to the gods in voice" (Homer, *Odyssey*, I, 370–71); "This aptness of language is one thing that makes people believe in the truth of a story . . ." (Aristotle, *Rhetoric* 1408a20).

17. We should be reminded of the retort of J. P. Morgan to the associate who complained that Morgan was angry with him for doing in public what others did behind closed doors, "That's what doors are for!"

"It was Zhdanov who reported Stalin's observation on the book of love poems by K. Simonov: 'They should have published only two copies—one for her, and one for him!' At which Stalin smiled demurely while the others roared." Milovan Djilas, *Conversations with Stalin* (New York: Harcourt, Brace & World, 1962), p. 158. See, also, the next paragraph in the Djilas text.

And it was Nikita Khrushchev who protested, upon having can-can dancers thrust upon him in Hollywood in 1959, that "humanity's face is more beautiful than her backside." See note 9 above.

18. *Regina* v. *Hicklin*, L.R., 3 Q.B. 360, 371 (1868). Cf. Judge Hand in *U.S.* v. *Kennerley*, 209 Fed. 119, 120–121 (1913); Lord Birkett, in *Does Pornography Matter?* C. H. Rolph, ed. (London: Routledge & Kegan Paul, 1961), pp. 8–9. Lord Cockburn's opinion in *Hicklin* continues: "Now, with regard to this work, it is quite certain that it would suggest to the minds of the young of either sex, or even to persons of more advanced years, thoughts of a most impure and libidinous character . . . I take it therefore, that, apart from the ulterior object which the publisher of this work had in view, the work itself is, in every sense of the term, an obscene publication . . . . But, then, it is said for the appellant, 'Yes, but his purpose was not to deprave the public mind; his purpose was to expose the errors of the Roman Catholic religion especially in the matter of the confessional.' Be it so. The question then presents itself in this simple form: May you commit an offence against the law in order that thereby you may effect some ulterior object which you have in view, which may be an honest and even a laudable one? My answer

is emphatically, no. The law says, you shall not publish an obscene work. An obscene work is here published, and a work the obscenity of which is so clear and decided, that it is impossible to suppose that the man who published it must not have known and seen that the effect upon the minds of many of those into whose hands it would come would be of a mischievous and demoralizing character. Is he justified in doing that which clearly would be wrong, legally as well as morally, because he thinks that some greater good may be accomplished? . . . I think the old sound and honest maxim, that you shall not do evil that good may come, is applicable in law as well as in morals; and here we have a certain and positive evil produced for the purpose of effecting an uncertain, remote, and very doubtful good . . ." (pp. 371–72)

Obscenity cases presuppose and thereby reaffirm a community's dedication to a good society, however vague, uninformed and even misdirected that dedication may often be. It is such vagueness which sometimes puts a prosecutor in the awkward position of having to urge a jury to revive and apply a standard alleged by him to be *the* community standard. But, on the other hand, is it not unreasonable to suppose that there was no good reason heretofore for virtually all communities imposing restraints upon what may be said publicly about certain things? Consider, for example, the quotation from Bertrand Russell in note 12 above, a passage which is immediately preceded by his observation, ". . . Modesty, in some form and to some degree, is almost universal in the human race and constitutes a taboo which must only be broken through in accordance with certain forms and ceremonies, or, at least, in conformity with some recognized etiquette. Not everything may be seen, and not all facts may be mentioned. This is not, as some moderns suppose, an invention of the Victorian age; on the contrary, anthropologists have found the most elaborate forms of prudery among primitive savages." *Why I Am Not a Christian,* pp. 172–173. Consider, also, Shakespeare, *Macbeth,* V, i.

19. *Smith* v. *California,* 361 U.S. 147 (1959), Transcript of Record, Supreme Court of the United States, pp. 81–83. The principal book in question (which has long been unavailable) was *Sweeter Than Life* (New York: Vixen Press, 1954) by Mark Tryon (a pseudonym).

A useful discussion of *Smith* v. *California* may be found in William B. Lockhard and Robert C. McClure, "Censorship of Obscenity: The Developing Constitutional Standards," 45 *Minnesota Law Review* 5, 43–47, 103–108 (1960). The authors described the case as one in which the Supreme Court "added a requirement of *scienter* for criminal prosecutions to the battery of constitutional requirements that the Court had already established, and thus seemed to jeopardize the widespread use of abrupt criminal prosecutions as a means of suppressing materials thought to be objectionable." (p. 43) See note 24 below.

20. Or rather, "adverse" publicity emanating from whatever journals do notice such books can usually be depended upon to promote sales.

Is it not both selfish and dangerous for intellectuals to insist, without regard for its effect on the moral opinions of the community at large, upon every minority's right to "express" itself as it pleases? See Plutarch's *Nicias* and *Alcibiades*. See, also, notes 25 and 26 below. Is it significant that that which is a "duty" for the judge in *Smith* v. *California* is no more than a "job" for defense counsel? It should be noticed that defense counsel's concluding comment about "whims of fate" (does he mean "chance"?) suggests that the making and preservation of virtuous men are considered by him essentially beyond the control of human reason. See the opening passage of Plato's *Meno* and the closing chapter of the *Nicomachean Ethics*. See, also, note 23 below. Cf. the beginning of Plutarch's *Dion*.

It should also be noticed that the judge sometimes confused in his remarks a description of how someone is corrupted with a description of something which would contribute to the corruption of readers. The former kind of description may not corrupt readers. Indeed, it may even be salutary to be shown how someone is corrupted, especially someone for whom the reader can be taught to care. Consider, for instance, the sort of thing Flaubert uses to attract us to Emma Bovary: "Country-style, [Emma] offered [her future husband] something to drink. He refused, she insisted, and finally suggested with a laugh that he take a liquer with her. She brought a bottle of curacao from the cupboard, reached to a high shelf for two liquer glasses, filled one to the brim and poured a few drops in the other. She touched her glass to his and raised it to her mouth. Because it was almost empty she had to bend backwards to be able to drink; and with her head tilted back, her neck and her lips outstretched, she began to laugh at tasting nothing; and then the tip of her tongue came out from between her small teeth and began daintily to lick the bottom of the glass." *Madame Bovary* (New York: Modern Library, 1957), p. 25. Cf. ibid., p. 357. Cf., also, ibid., pp. 216, 277–279, 369–370. See *Selected Letters of Flaubert*, F. Steegmuller, ed., pp. 136–137, 140, 148, 162–164, 170–171, 177–179, 181, 184.

Does the "liberation" of artists, with the attendant demands of the "market," make it likely that bad literature will tend to drive out good? Would a Flaubert, for example, be obliged, lest he be ignored as "too tame," to be much more "explicit" than even he thought would be good for his art? See the text at note 12 above, See, also, note 14 above.

21. To "care" about such matters is to seem (and perhaps even to be) somewhat naive. See Plato, *Republic* 414d. See, also, Thomas Hobbes, *Leviathan*, chapter 10 ("To speak [to another] harshly, to do anything before him obscenely, slovenly, impudently, is to dishonor [him].")

Consider, on the relation of naivité and caring, the 1904 letter of the revered University of Chicago football coach, Amos Alonzo Stagg, to the president of the University:

It is with the greatest pleasure and satisfaction that I herewith send you a check for $1000 as a gift to the University. It was just a year ago during my sickness, you will remember, that the thought of making this gift came to me. I was greatly depressed and worried by the spirit shown by our team in the Thanksgiving Day contest, and in casting about for possible helpful things, my mind went back to my own college days at Yale. The sweet chimes of Battell Chapel have always been an inspiration to me, and I recalled the many, many times during the period of my training that that cheery, hopeful ten o'clock chime had led me to fall asleep with a quiet determination for a greater devotion to duty and to my ideals.

The thought came to me and filled me with the deepest satisfaction, "Why not have a goodnight chime for our own athletes? to let its sweet cadence have a last word with them before they fall asleep; to speak to them of love and loyalty and sacrifice for their University and of hope and inspiration and endeavor for the morrow."

Whenever, therefore, the Alice Freeman Palmer chimes are installed, it would be my wish to have a special cadence rung for our athletes who are in training—perhaps five to ten minutes after the regular chimes at ten o'clock.

University of Chicago Maroon, April 26, 1957, p. 5.

Consider, also, the implications of Prime Minister Jawaharlal Nehru's remarks, in a letter of June 28, 1959, to Shri Bimal Roy, "I am glad to tell you that I liked your film *Sujata* . . . . It is a good film with good photography, and the story is interesting. There is always a danger in films which have too obvious a moral purpose, to become dull . . . ." See Averroes, *On Plato's Republic* 32.44ff, 49.14ff.

22. "This failure of the concept of obscenity has been concurrent with the rise of the institution of publicity which, ever seeking to widen its field *in accordance with the canon of progress,* makes a virtue of deseeartion." Weaver, *Ideas Have Consequences*, p. 28 (emphasis addcd).

Two photographs in the May 28, 1965 issue of *Time*, at pages 22 and 28, are examples of such desecration. Such pictures, especially since they *are* related to political discussion, are (and should be) hard for the law to deal with. See note 26 below. Cf. the quotation from *Regina* v. *Hicklin* in note 18 above.

If the traditionally (and obviously) obscene should come to be considered illegitimate for the community to discourage, the more critical instances of harmful publication and display are not going to be addressed either. That is, permissiveness with respect to obscenity both implies and reinforces the opinion that the character of its people is not a proper concern of the community. That which is not believed to be a proper concern is not likely to be dealt with properly.

23. We would take more seriously the concern often expressed about the possible temporary discouragement of the public sale of an occasional good book (because of restraints upon obscenity) if we could believe that the truly great books we already have were being seriously studied among us. If serious programs of undergraduate study, of which St. John's College is probably the best in the United States today, were generally established, the problem of the effects on the community of a thoughtless toleration of obscenity would become (would have become?) trivial. (See Gibbon, *Decline and Fall*, I, 783–784.)

In any event, it is unrealistic to expect a people to *choose* the better over the worse without proper training. Such training is unlikely either to be available or to be taken seriously if it should become generally fashionable to believe that it is all "but a matter of taste" what one should like. (Does not "matter of taste" come down, in this sense, to little more than "matter of chance"?) Is it not also unrealistic to expect many parents (assuming *they* happen to be properly trained) to be able to train their children in how to make proper choices in the face of whatever corrupting effort may be exerted by "the mass media"? Such parents would be obliged to devote themselves fulltime to the task and to run the risk as well of appearing tyrannical (thereby undermining parental respect in youngsters who see themselves "deprived" of what others are permitted to "enjoy"). It is, upon considering such circumstances, that one becomes aware of how much the family depends on the community to legitimate and thus help establish the moral standards which particular parents may then be in a position to refine further. See note 7 above.

24. We assume that no informed student of these matters in the West today regards with favor a return to any systematic program of licensing and "previous restraint" of printed matter. One problem with "previous restraint" is reflected in George Bernard Shaw's 1899 comment: "What, then, is to be done with the Censorship [i.e., the licensing of plays for performance]? Nothing can be simpler. Abolish it, root and branch, throwing the whole legal responsibility for plays on the author and manager, precisely as the legal responsibility for a book is thrown on the author, the printer, and the publisher. The managers will not like this: their present slavery is safer and easier; but it will be good for them, and good for the Drama." "The Censorship of the Stage in England," in *Shaw on Theatre*, E. J. West, ed. (New York: Hill and Wang, 1958), p. 79.

   A serious due process question can arise from the deliberate harassment of publishers and booksellers resulting from governmental shopping among jurisdictions in which to bring prosecutions most inconvenient for defendants. See note 19 above.

25. See, on the political relevance of circumstances, Aristotle, *Politics* 1288 b22.

   It *is* possible that the best available means for reducing appreciably the appeal and hence the significance of obscenity among us today might be, as some advocate, to repeal (with the proper explanation) all laws relating thereto. (Cf. note 22 above.) But would such advocates concede the right and even the duty of the community to intervene if the experiment should clearly result in a distinct coarsening of public discourse or in a pervasive moral flabbiness? That is, we are obliged to return again and again to what may be for us on this occasion the key question: "What *is* it legitimate for the community to be concerned about?" What answer to this question is implied by the fact that we, as a community, rely upon considerable legislation and tax revenue in establishing and maintaining our public schools? Do we not exhibit by our constant activity as a community the opinion that it is cavalier and shallow to insist that everyone can or should be left alone "to mind his own business"?

Compare the observation that "English Literature towers high above English Drama [which is subject to licensing] because Literature is subject to no judgment but that of its natural masters, the authors." Shaw, "The Censorship of the Stage in England," in *Shaw on Theatre*, p. 77. Who are indeed the "natural masters" of literature? The masters for one purpose (that is, writing) may not be the masters for another (that is, distribution within a community of what happens to be written). See, in Francis Bacon's *New Atlantis*, the regulation of the public use, as distinguished from the private development, of inventions. See, also, notes 2 and 14 above.

26. "For this is not the liberty which we can hope, that no grievance ever should arise in the Commonwealth—that let no man in this world expect; but when complaints are freely heard, deeply considered and speedily reformed, then is the utmost bound of civil liberty attained that wise men look for." Milton, *Areopagitica*. See note 10 above. The government cannot reasonably be regarded, in the typical obscenity case, as trying to suppress grievances or complaints against itself, something which we are properly suspicious of whenever we encounter any attempted suppression of political speech.

One good argument *against* official restrictions upon obscenity is that they might be extended to interfere as well with our indispensable (however occasionally unsettling) political discussion, especially if we have come to equate literary expression with political speech. Would it be an argument *for* moderate restrictions upon obscenity now if it should be shown that the repression eventually provoked by continued licentiousness is likely to threaten freedom of political discussion as well? Besides, does not effective political freedom depend upon a people with a sturdy moral character, something that preoccupation with sensual gratification (or habitual public discourse about it) makes highly unlikely? See note 11 above. Certainly, it is not prudent to believe that such widespread changes in language, opinions, and style as we have witnessed in our time will have no significant political effects. See Aristotle, *Politics*, VIII, v (on virtue consisting "in feeling delight where one should and loving and hating aright"). Nor is it prudent to expect that there will be no eventual massive public reaction (however uninformed and hence self-defeating) against the current licentiousness: a radical change of regime may even begin to appeal to some as the only way out of the swamp. But are not overgrown swamps better than the bleak wastelands of contemporary tyrannies, whether of the Left or of the Right? Cultivated lands are, of course, even better.

We have, in this attempt to suggest and examine first principles, ignored the distinctively American problem of federal-state relations. Much is to be said for allowing considerable local control (and hence variations among localities) in such matters. See *Jacobellis* v. *Ohio* (dissenting opinion), 378 U.S. 184, 204–5 (1964). See, also, Anastaplo, "Freedom of Speech and the First Amendment," 42 *U. Detroit L. J.* 54 (1964); Anastaplo, "Due Process of Law—An Introduction," 42 *U. Detroit L. J.* 195 (1964); "Closing Argument by George Anastaplo before the Committee on Character and Fitness," 19 *Lawyers Guild Rev.* 143 (1959); *In re George Anastaplo*, 366 U.S. 82 (1961).

The Arts of Resistance

D. S. Carne-Ross

> It is terrible that human beings so easily put up with
> existing conditions, not only with the sufferings of
> strangers but with their own.   BRECHT

> And after we have practised virtue together in this way,
> then, if we so decide, we will turn to politics or offer
> advice wherever it seems proper. For by then our advice
> will be worth more than it is now.   PLATO, *Gorgias*

My title may be misleading. This is not a manual of guerrilla
warfare. For although the arts I have in mind are along one-line
skills—skills of "resistance" and perhaps even of survival—they
are also the familiar, the all too familiar and often all too boring,
fine or beautiful or liberal arts of tradition and the humanities
classroom. But what have these arts to do with resistance? And
what has to be resisted?

I can best suggest the region into which this essay seeks to
move by recalling its origin in my own life. The themes I am
concerned with are public themes, but the approach is, deliberately, personal, though not I hope private. The starting point was
something persistent, even obsessive, but quite vague. Call it a
sense of constraint or confinement. A sense that certain roles
cannot now be played, a sense of unused or denied possibilities—
possibilities in man and also in things: as though a tree or even
a table were no longer all that they might be. A sense that certain elements have fallen out of experience. A sense that, amid
the glaring plenty of our culture, something is missing. But not
recognized as missing.

Culture, the great human artifice, proposes itself to us as
reality. It allows us a mitigating private realm, where its writ

does not run, to play truant in. And we know, theoretically, that other peoples have created and still to some extent inhabit quite different realities. Nonetheless, the reality of our own culture takes pride of place. It *allows* us our truancies and can account for them; it can handle all the other cultural realities. Some it has defeated or superseded or simply swallowed up; or it comprehends them by finding a niche for them in one of its imaginary museums. Our culture stands all about us and inside us, confronting us at every point with its dense and bristling facticity. It *is*.

And yet it is possible to feel confined there and to sense that "something is missing." Though fragile and easily argued into silence, this sense is potentially very subversive, for reality—to deserve the name—must claim to be all-inclusive. If this sense is allowed or encouraged or *trained* to grow, it may lead to what I am calling resistance. By resisting our cultural reality I mean, to begin with, questioning its absoluteness and inevitability, learning to see it as, after all, a fiction and then little by little dismantling it. I mean trying as it were to stand outside culture, trying to find a perspective from which to look in and observe what we are doing here, the way we live now, what is happening to us. From inside culture, the way-we-live-now is opaque. It can be, and constantly is, criticized, but only in its own terms; it can be changed, but only in accord with its own laws. That our present way of living is not altogether satisfactory many people seem to agree, but standing where we do—inside culture—we cannot discover what is wrong with it, let alone what should be done about it. To do so, we need a standing point (an Archimedean point, if you like) outside culture.[1] I am concerned, then, with cultural transcendence and my argument is that our powers of transcending culture are now dangerously limited.

Two quick objections suggest themselves, from different sides. First, the freedom I seem to be asking for is impossible—a Utopian or anarchic desire for a state of unconstraint that man renounced when he elected to get up off all fours. A place outside culture is literally Utopia, that is, no place, for every human settlement exists by virtue of the cultural norms it imposes on its members and even the cultural drop-out is still enacting a myth provided by the culture he seeks to reject.

Yet, culture's totalitarian claims can, or could, be answered. The Christian had, possibly still has, the solidest answer. For his religion told him that there is indeed a place outside culture, not only in the next world but in this one. It offered him the choice of living in the City of God or the City of Man and, more important, of judging Man's City by the standards of God's. In its flourishing days, the Church recognised and even institutionalized man's right to reject culture. The Catholic radical movement is trying to recover the antinomian status which the Christian knew before Constantine made the Church part of society; courageous men like the brothers Berrigan are translating this old freedom into political action.

From the other side I meet the objection that this is a foolish, an untimely time to talk about the need to stand outside culture: a time when cultural disaffiliation is so modish and so dangerously easy. A troubled conservative—Quentin Anderson, in his recent book *The Imperial Self*—sees America and now Europe engaged in what he calls "coming out of culture," withdrawing "affect from the collective life . . . and [from] the fostering and authenticating offices of the family and of society." [2] The central, "official," reality of our culture, weakened from within by multiple fractures of nerve and jostled from without by contending counter-realities, no longer has the power to contain us. Everyone is free to worship in the reality of his choice.

And yet this apparent ease of disaffiliation may indicate not the weakness but the strength of the official reality. The center may be holding well enough, despite the rumpus on the periphery. The whole may be large enough to contain the dissenting parts, elastic enough to expand and find room—and sanction—

for the supposed deviations, and strong enough to let them play in the wilderness of their fancy. Our pluralism, in other words (in itself the notion is common enough), may be less plural than it looks and conceal massive agreements that prevent the centrifugal tendencies from being genuinely disruptive.

For true cultural disaffiliation—or resistance—is, unlike the showier forms of protest, very difficult. To go against culture is to go against nature, against that second, human, nature which leads man to create shared realities that bind together the discrete moments of his individual existence and insert them into a meaningful common world. To resist culture means moving outside the social and conceptual framework which guarantees the persistence and assuring solidity of that world and transforms the chaos of biological existence into human life in society.

Our cultural reality, it seems to me, is very well equipped to withstand the assaults made upon it. Far from falling apart, it is growing stronger and more pervasive. Using the enormous powers which science and technology have provided, it is reaching out in pursuit of its *mission civilisatrice* to every corner of the earth, and now further out, into space; it is laying hands on the heavenly bodies, as they once were called; it has designs on the oceans. To take possession of the elements, culture must first deaden them and deprive them of independent status. The earth becomes a source of raw materials, a neutral field for man's activities; the oceans are there to be colonized and exploited once we have the required skills. It has even been suggested, I don't know how seriously, that outer space might be used as a dumping ground for the mountains of trash we ingest and excrete every day.

All this is proposed in the interests of man. And yet culture reaches not only outward but inward, into every moment of our conscious and soon of our unconscious lives. Culture, the great human artifice, acts back on its creator and fits him into its design. In this sense it regards man too as raw material, to be reshaped in whatever ways may prove necessary. To take an extreme instance : as space trips grow longer and more taxing, the human organism may be unable to sustain them and the pilots of the future may have to be not so much trained as constructed. We hear of plans to construct a new kind of man called a Cyborg. A Cyborg would have "many artificial organs and thus would be better able to cope with harsh and novel surroundings." Other such creatures are apparently on the drawing board : there was talk a while ago of a proposal by the U.S. Navy to produce "gillmen" whose lungs would be surgically adapted to allow them to breathe under water. And far beyond these modest hybrids are the possibilities held out by rapid advances in biochemistry and molecular biology that "in a few years" may permit us to redesign man's biological and psychological nature.

The lay person has little means of gauging the immediacy of the threat to man, to the humanum of man. More serious, it is doubtful how far our culture still allows us to recognize a threat here at all. In what terms, except those of a sentimental humanism, can we establish that to Cyborg a man is to violate him, or determine the point past which a genetically reconstituted man ceases to be a man? Paul Ramsey, in a book on the ethics of genetic control, may speak of "elements in the nature of man which are deserving of respect and should be withheld from human handling or trespass." [3] But Ramsey is a theologian and as such does not speak with today's voice. He draws his concept of "the nature of man" from a system that has only an honorary place in our culture. Today's voice is more likely to be heard saying, for instance : "If we decide that something is lacking in all men, there is no reason why we should not set about introducing it, even if this makes us into something new." [4]

But perhaps it is a mistake to frighten ourselves with these science-fictional prospects. To see clearly what is happening to man here and now, under "existing conditions"—should not this be enough?

II

One problem today is that even things that touch us closely are hard to take hold of and possess because they are so rapidly by-passed and left behind in the wastelands of cliché. (by-pass: "a road built for fast traffic to pass by, and not through, a town"—*Penguin Dictionary*.) My argument so far will appear trite enough and to beckon in an all too predictable direction: to some form of "spiritual revival," presumably, with the usual anti-scientific bias. In which case, why all this talk about resisting culture? Spiritual revivals are quite the thing nowadays; we have our culturally accredited mystagogues. However, to the extent that they (and all the other counterculturists) merely reverse culture's values, offering black for its white, "spiritual" for "material," and so forth, they are still part of culture, still joined in dialog with what they seek to oppose. And it is still culture that calls the tune. A resistance movement, to be worth the name, would somehow have to take the initiative and propose its own terms. And it would be very chary of employing the ready-made adversary terms now so easily available. (It may have been culture that made them available in the first place.) It would require adversary terms, certainly; there would have to be a principle, even a doctrine, of resistance; but this doctrine, while making use of what it found on the surface of contemporary life (an hour spent watching TV, a drive into any American city), would need to grow from below and be nourished by some pure source of refusal. It would have to grow in ground not under culture's direct control.

But what does this mean? And where is there such a ground?

It came to me, dimly, one day in class. I am an academic of sorts and my business is with literature and on this occasion I was trying to talk intelligibly about the Italian poet, Leopardi. The passage I was concerned with began *Vivi, tu, vivi, o santa natura?* The words ask if nature is alive, and they may be taken to ask or imply a second question: Is nature sacred? There are plenty of ways of handling both these questions, but I realized that I did not want to "handle" them, I wanted to *ask* them or rather stand open to them and let them ask me. It struck me that the ways of approaching literature which I had been taught, by my culture, were so many ways of silencing the questions it raises, or at least of containing them within the conventions of the classroom or the research paper or the rehearsed academic response. But what if one tried not to contain them but to *release* them? Suppose one tried to release Leopardi's question (in the purity of its saying, protecting it from the instant satisfactions of the latest earth religion), taking it out of the class room and into the marketplace, into the supermarketplace and the air terminal and onto the highway and into the living room in front of the television screen. Suppose one put it smack in the middle of the way-we-live-now. What would happen to it there? And what would happen to the supermarket if somehow one contrived to confront it with this alien question?

It asks about nature, or earth, and about the sacred. Without violence to its intention it can be rearranged, to yield the question in a different form: Has sacred nature died? A pointer to the more famous death that Nietzsche spoke of? No, it is a harder question than that. It is not the God of Abraham and Isaac and Jacob and the Christians that Leopardi's words have in mind; it is the *parva religio*, the local pieties of place, the immanent sanctities of earth; the death, or departure, not of God but of the gods. And "the gods" are not part of our culture. The words may also be taken to ask about man and the world he lives in. What is there in man that prompts him to ask such questions? And what is there in his present world that may prevent him from asking them? Once you open it out, it is a very large question; it asks almost everything. But can it be asked now?

Not only asked but answered, someone says. If we want to know in what sense it is or is not proper to speak of nature *(physis)* as alive, the "natural" science of physics can tell us. If we want to know about the sacred, there is someone in a department of comparative religion who knows all about it— if the churches have forgotten. Yet every question points in a particular direction and expects a certain range of answers, positive or negative, and the answers we are likely to get from physics or *Religionswissenschaft* (or the churches) do not come from the region which the poet's question faces, and so it remains unanswered, and unasked. A Greek, of the earlier, "pre-Socratic" period, would have understood it at once and perhaps an American Indian still can. Both would reply that nature is very much alive, ensouled from top to bottom, and eminently sacred; everything is full of gods. Within the Christian order the question would also have made sense and a Christian would have replied (a Catholic more hesitantly than a Protestant) that although nature may in some sense be alive it cannot be called sacred. It is God's handiwork, but sacredness can be ascribed only to God. When Moses led the children of Israel out of Egypt, he led them out of the old sacred universe in which heaven and earth were bound together by sympathy within a great vital continuum; the West has, with some backsliding here and there, stayed out ever since.

We are so far out today, in our scientifically measured, technologically ordered world, that the question can only sound fanciful. It presupposes the existence of a sacred realm, to which nature may or may not belong, which in turn presupposes the existence of a profane realm. But we have neither sacred nor profane. It is not as though the sacred were known to have been

lost, or replaced—or expelled—by the profane, for in that case
we should still have at least a memory of the sacred and could
say : This which was once sacred is now profane. But we have
no profane either, no category of the profane to point to the
missing sacred.

My insistence on this question may be found tiresome. A
rather special interest, surely—why does it matter so much? It
matters, for my argument, because this is one of those topics
which culture (as Mr. Empson said about death) "feels very
blank upon." It thus provides a way of catching culture out and
showing that its claim to be all-inclusive does not hold up. Here
is an instance of something that has fallen out of experience, as
I put it, something that is missing and yet is not recognized as
missing. (A good question about death could be even more subversive.) As though a letter fell out of a line of type without
leaving a gap, for the other letters closed in and rearranged themselves so as to make perfectly good sense, a consistent, impene-
trable sentence on which doubt can get no hold. And yet one
feels doubtful.

The question matters (far beyond the terms of my argument) because if it is true that we no longer stand open to what
is asked there, this means that a human possibility, a way of
being man, is now no longer possible. It means that a perspective
on to a region where man has always moved is now closed to
him. And what came to meet him in that region now comes no
longer. Within the reality of our culture, the loss of this perspective and of this region is not felt as loss—though we can
admit to having outgrown some old habits. By standing outside
culture, you will not necessarily recover the perspective that gives
on to this region, but you may come to recognize that it has
been lost, and this is a first step. A place outside culture is one
where loss can still appear as loss, not as gain or inevitable
change ; and where the questions that culture has settled, or
shelved, can still be raised.

III

A place—to which a line of poetry innocently, or insidiously, directed us where loss is still felt as loss, is *preserved* as loss. Where the blanks on our map, the absences, are still marked as presences. This is not very helpful, though. To get any further we need better directions than this.

To find them we have to look outside our culture and outside the modern Western world. A brief detour—to Japan, for instance—might provide what we need. Not the religious Japan to which some people are turning, but the Japan that has proved itself the West's most brilliant pupil and in a century or less moved from its semi-feudal, traditional past into the full glare of the technological, universalist present. As a result, Japanese society seems to the outsider to reveal with special clarity contrasts or rifts that here are blurred, or blocked in. Here are two passages which, if I have chosen them well, will show not the elements that we have lost but rather the process, the moment, of loss.

The first is a statement by a Japaneses student comparing the modern celebration of Christmas, a recent cultural import, with the traditional Japanese festival of the New Year:

> Of course I celebrate Christmas but I don't necessarily find it pleasant. It is just an excuse to go out and drink *sake*. . . . Christmas doesn't matter much to me. . . . But the last night of the year, when people eat what we call *toshikoshi soba* [New Year's noodles], some of the real feelings of the old days come out. . . . I used to go to the shrine on that night together with my family, with a solemn feeling. . . . There would be a priest, and it would be very quiet around the shrine grounds. Then at the time of the night when the moon hovered above us, when the frost made the ground transparent, the priest would offer us sacred wine *(omiki)*. I would clap my hands and, standing in the dark in dim candlelight, I would ring the bell and throw offerings. . . .

These mystical feelings I had during my childhood I no longer feel toward the New Year, but when I look at my mother and father I have the impression that they still feel them.[5]

The second passage comes from the *New York Times* for December 24, 1969:

The secular approach to Christmas produces an occasional exotic touch in Tokyo, such as a manger scene showing one of the Wise Men holding out a gift of Suntory whisky, or scantily clad chorines in a nightclub singing a jazzed-up version of Silent Night in Japanese.

What we find in these two scenes (giving them as representative a quality as possible) cannot simply be called the transition from a "religious" to a "secular" way of life. Neither term has retained enough meaning to render the qualitative change that is taking place here. A whole complex of beliefs and usages and symbols is falling apart, and is being replaced by another complex that will quickly solidify and shut out all memory of the former one. A movement that in the West took several centuries is here compressed into a single generation. The world that to us is all literally second nature, so massively extended in space and time that we can hardly imagine it has ever been otherwise, is here in the process of formation. This Japanese student stands between two wholly discontinuous realms; both are still part of his experience, though one is closing to him. It appears that he can still feel what he is losing, but soon he will forget and feel no pain. The flesh around the wound will grow numb and he will not know that anything is missing; he will be content.

What is he really losing? Something intangible that we vaguely call the religious dimension of his former life? That, yes, and also *things*, the known, lived, lived-into, loved things that belonged to him and belonged to a particular place and people and tradition (the grove, the sacred wine). What the great Welsh poet David Jones calls "the remembered things of origin and streamhead." In their place he is being given the things that we know, the only things that we know, the interchangeable token-things, mass-things of the universalist world market, the throw-away things that surround us at every point and in their dead proliferation compose our lives.

When this Japanese is deprived of his New Year festival and given a bogus Western Christmas instead, when he is deprived of his sacred wine and given nightclub whisky instead—when this happens, something very terrible and indeed irreparable is being done to him. And what is most terrible is that he does not know that anything is being done to him. On the contrary, with most of his mind he believes that he is moving into a more enlightened and privileged way of life. He will learn to think that what he had before is unfitting to a civilized modern man and any twinges of regret he may feel he will write off as nostalgia, the regressive desire for a simpler world into which he sometimes projects a goodness and wholeness it did not really possess. If he continues to be troubled by these regrets, he can go to his analyst and be cured. Everything in his new life will stand solid against the old one and tell him that there is no other way of living, that "everyone lives like this now."

This Japanese student is instructive, exemplary even, because he is so much closer to his loss than we are. Though he cannot return to it, he still knows of another realm that stands outside and *against* his everyday experience and transcends that experience. We have no Other of comparable purity, for the Western analogs are buried in far deeper oblivion. Still, and for a little while yet, he knows *that* he has lost something and he knows *what* he has lost. He has thus an essential and existential knowledge that is denied to us. For we no longer know—only occasionally and with difficulty do we even feel—that we have lost anything, let alone know what we have lost.

IV

A place where loss is preserved as loss, I said. But if this is to be more than an exercise in nostalgia, there must be a *knowledge* of what has been lost. The knowledge of others ways of being man, of being man on earth, and of other ways of earth's being. If my program is to make any sense, an alternative knowledge must somewhere be available, something akin to the Japanese student's access to different realms of experience. Where is this knowledge to be found? I have already implied or hinted at my answer. It is to be found in—of all places—the arts, the humanities, and most articulately in literature.

The place where literature is taken seriously—taught and studied, anyway—is the university. If literature is to provide what I am apparently hoping for, the elements of a doctrine of resistance, this involves thinking of the university as, potentially, a kind of third force. A paradoxical concept, all things considered. A role the university is scarcely qualified and certainly not anxious to play.

Even odder will the timing of this large claim for literature appear. For literature today has lost its former prestige. It is no longer, Susan Sontag tells us, "the model for creative statement. . . . The primary feature of the new sensibility is that its model product is not the literary work."[6] The status not merely of literature but of literacy itself has been called in question; the old confidence in the word has failed, the belief that language is somehow congruent with the structure of reality. So Marshall McLuhan can usher us into the new world of post-literate electronic technology, the global village where we will all be speechlessly at one. George Steiner reminds us that when the test came, the humanities were found wanting; no longer can we affirm their power to humanize. "We know now that a man can read Goethe or Rilke in the evening, that he can play Bach and Schubert, and go to his day's work at Auschwitz in the morning." [7] Marcuse tells us that the higher culture has lost its power not because it has been rejected but because it has been so massively accepted, incorporated wholesale into the established order. The instant availability of the world's best literature and thought in paperback has rendered that thought and literature innocuous.[8]

I don't propose to argue the truth of all this. Suppose it is true, or partly true. The question is, rather, does it matter very much if our old house of cards *has* finally collapsed? And if it does, *why* does it matter? Specifically, what honest claims can we still make for literature, for the study of literature, in this day and age, with so much else to be done? Not just the stuff written now but the long backward stretch, the ranked shelves?

Borges, in his economical way, imagines the death of the last man who has heard the name of Helen. Literates, separatists of the print culture, men of the book and the word, are not a very numerous company and promise to dwindle still further. Literacy, opposed by powerful interests in the modern world, its traditional resources gravely threatened, looks to be a minority affair in any foreseeable future. Would it matter, though, if literacy, in the old sense, disappeared altogether? Would it matter if the world of the day after tomorrow were one in which no one had any longer heard of Plato and Dante, in which the plays of Shakespeare and the novels of Stendhal were—not banned or burned, but simply consigned to a few libraries which no one was any longer moved to visit? But this is science fiction and does not carry the force of the question I am trying to ask. By *Helen* and *Shakespeare* I mean a region, a reach of the mind, a meditative openness where whatever we intend by those great names grew into possibility. We might forget Helen. Very well, so long as we kept the power of myth and metaphor that created her fable. The text of Shakespeare could disappear and be imagined all over again, better imagined, perhaps: so long as we kept that power of imagining. But what if that power were lost? What if the meditative openness that is its region and condition for some reason closed to us?

And literature has another function, humbler perhaps but indispensable: it bears witness. It points with an evidence we cannot altogether deny to what is missing, a gap, a hole in the middle of experience. It holds, preserves, what was once presence and now is absence and might at some great though unimaginable noontide become presence again. Bearing witness is not what literature is happiest doing—it has other ends in view, this is merely a sideline—but this is what we have to ask from it at present. Literature bears witness to man, not just man as he is now but as he has been, through the long backward stretch. It thus saves the memory of man at a time when everything inclines to forgetfulness. David Jones, speaking of the work of some notable contemporary artists and writers, remarks that the arts as practiced by these men are, "for all their contemporaneity, *signa* of man as such. They show forth, recall, discover and re-present [re-présent] those things that have belonged to man from the beginning." [9]

But literature does more than this. A purely humanistic (or moral or psychological) reading does not exhaust it. "Poetry is the image of man *and nature,*" Wordsworth said. Its subject is man and his doings and also the region where he does them. It is concerned with nature, or earth, the place of man's sojourn. And if earth is most often shown in this humanized perspective, literature knows of another earth that is rapidly disappearing: earth as or in itself, earth as the other, the not-man, even earth the sacred. (*Vivi tu, vivi, o santa natura?*) It may be that this response to earth has gone for good. Now that we are on the point of becoming, in Descartes' phrase, the "master and possessor of Nature," we may only be able to see earth as ministering to our needs, as so much raw material submitted to our transforming will. The rift that has opened between ourselves and the earth that presents itself to us, between the *res cogitans* and the *res extensa,* may be impossible to close. We may be permanently alienated from earth. Yet literature still holds the old vision, for whatever use we may be able to make of it, and it could one day help us to learn a way back to a more creaturely sojourning. Certainly if we are going to "save the environment" it will be by recovering this vision of earth, not by tinkering with our technology.

And literature does—or knows—more than this. It speaks of God and the gods (not only the God of Christian theology or the "pagan" gods of mythology) and of what may be apprehended as the sacred or, more philosophically, as the ground of things, reality, or being. Under long pressure from the opposition (for whom literature lies or at best fancies), we have kept rather quiet about this and tended to hedge. Yet we know that when it puts forth its full powers it speaks what is true. Edgar, confronted by the spectacle of Lear mad and his father blinded, says

I would not take this from report; *it is*—

and this is how we respond to great literature, whether we go on to say, with Edgar, "and my heart breaks at it" or whether the heart rejoices. We acknowledge this truth with what Richard E. Palmer in his book on hermeneutics calls a flash of ontological recognition,[10] by saying, "Yes, this is how things are, this is so."

In its concern with man, then, *anthrôpos,* literature is an anthropology; in its concern with nature, *physis,* a physics; in its concern with God or the gods, a theology; in its concern with reality or being, an ontology. More exactly, it "is" none of these things, yet it touches all their territories.

It is in this sense I would claim that literature provides not simply experience but *knowledge,* a knowledge moreover that is not directly given or controlled by culture—and can thus point to a place outside culture. Partly this is so for the obvious reason that much of our literature is old and comes from across the border, from its extracultural sanctuary in the past. (Where it lies inert unless we learn to read the work of earlier ages, that is, to stage an encounter between the text's Then and our Now which preserves the rights of both parties. Neither hauling the old text into our Now and challenging it to demonstrate its "relevance," nor destroying the very possibility of a true encounter by trying to project ourselves into the text's Then and see it "as it really is.")

More importantly, literature is outside culture because in one sense it is always *against* culture, it transcends culture. It does so through its power to pass beyond the given, social frame of reference and confront our everyday lives—*The Marriage of Figaro* no less than *Oedipus Rex*—with alternative images of the human condition, heights and depths and ranges of experience that "take us out of ourselves" and out of our cultural situation and thus *alienate* us from culture. In Marcuse's phrase, art is "the Great Refusal—the protest against that which is."

That the transcending, oppositional powers of literature make very little mark on the stronghold of culture I am not at all concerned to deny. But then, we have asked so little of literature and preferred to turn it into an academic parlor game where we run through the tricks of our professional trade. From the point of view advanced here, the professional academic humanist has with more or less elegance, and usually less, devoted his best energies to selling the pass.

V

This contentious stuff aside, though, even a reader disenchanted enough with academe to indulge my persuasions this far is bound to wonder how they could possibly be translated into classroom practice. And what bearing they have on a "liberal education," however refashioned. At this point I can afford to make a few concessions. To the literary person who objects that so salvational an approach offends against critical manners and is likely to lead too bluntly through the text's necessary indirections in pursuit of its "message"—to this objection I yield gladly, merely putting in a strong plea for what I take to be a necessity of the time. Certainly a good text does not want to be put on a pedestal; it asks you to attend to its formal properties and delight in the cunning of its making.

To the more academic person (who is probably beyond reassurance) I would say that I hold strongly with a good deal of old-fashioned discipline—mastering the necessary languages, getting a sense of fact and getting your facts straight, setting your reading in a solid historical or philosophical setting, and so forth. The trouble with some of the more "innovative" educational programs—those seeking to bring education closer to life—is that they risk making To Learn an intransitive verb almost synonymous with To Live. Finally, learning means learning to live, but mediately it means a great deal else. It means learning, transitively, much that may seem to have no direct bearing on life today and may therefore be discarded, innovated away into limbo. To Know's end is Know Yourself, but if going to school means going to school to yourself you will not reach this end and education becomes a process in which the self feeds on the self and that is a thin diet. To Know has got to stay transitive.

However, I agree with innovators who believe that the humanities, to keep their virtue, must lose some of their purity or exclusiveness and submit to infusions from outside. What is needed is not so much some special "cross-disciplinary" mix with other academic subjects as a ready openness to extracurricular urgencies. And not just the headline urgencies.

Imagine a course of this sort, for sophomores or even freshmen. Call it Literature X (Yale's property, I believe) or some variant on Santa Cruz' History of Consciousness. The course might begin in the Third World, in Africa, and take as its first text a book by Doris Lessing called *Nine African Stories*. In the introduction Mrs. Lessing quotes a news item about the chief of a small tribe near the Portuguese border fighting in the courts for the privilege of remaining on the land where his people had lived long before the Europeans came. He is reported as saying : "Our land is regarded by European law as part of a vast European-owned ranch, so that we are squatters in the country which our forefathers occupied since before man can remember. Our ancestors are buried there. Their spirits are in these hills." [11] It would be easy to bring home the reality of this by means of parallels from the American Indians who have suffered so many similar instances of territorial eviction and whose response carries the same accents of piety and pride and loss.

Familiar enough, no doubt. Yes, if you stop there and consider merely what *we* have done to *them,* a perspective which may lead, through penitence (perhaps not untinged by paternalism), to remedial action on the practical or political level. The *educational* power of such material only begins with the reflection that we have done very similar things to ourselves. There is a perspective from which we too, fat and applianced as we are, may be described as squatters in the country which our forefathers occupied since before man can remember. The class would hardly buy this—and in America it could only be a figure of speech—so for a more intimate sense of what deracination means, the instructor would turn to Western literature, to the novels of Thomas Hardy, for instance, with their many side glances at rural depopulation and the complex human loss it entailed.[12]

Hardy could lead naturally into nineteenth-century social history. But history, for many students, even quite recent history, is not peopled by flesh-and-blood figures, so to bring the whole matter nearer home, further into focus, the instructor might turn next to a passage written in the mid 1950s by Heidegger, a man as rooted in his own Black Forest region as Hardy was in Wessex.

In an address delivered to the people of his native village of Messkirch, Heidegger said :

> Many Germans have lost their homeland, have had to leave their villages and towns, have been driven from their native soil. Countless others whose homeland was saved, have yet wandered off. They have been caught up in the turmoil of the big cities, and have resettled in the wastelands of industrial districts. They are strangers now to their former homeland. And those who *have* stayed on in their homeland? Often they are still more homeless than those who have been driven from their homeland. Hourly and daily they are chained to radio and television. Week after week the movies carry them off into uncommon, but often merely common, realms of the imagination, and give the illusion of a world that is no world. Picture magazines are everywhere available. All that with which modern techniques of communication stimulate, assail, and drive man—all that is already much closer to man today than his fields around his farmstead, closer than the sky over the earth, closer than the change from night to day, closer than the conventions and customs of his village, than the tradition of his native world.[13]

And Heidegger goes on : "We grow more thoughtful and ask : What is happening here—with those driven from their homeland no less than with those who have remained? Answer : the *rootedness,* the *autochthony,* of man is threatened today at its core." But what does this concept of rootedness, *Bodenständigkeit,* really mean? The complaint that we have "lost our roots" is tiresomely familiar and serves, at a popular level, to explain some of our discontents. Does it in fact explain anything—do we have any real sense of what it means, or meant, to be rooted? And if it does or did mean something, is not such a concept, in today's world, nostalgic and unrealistic, a harking back to earlier forms of life that have gone for good? Under the impulse of a common technology and the thinking that goes

with it, the world is growing together. Using the same tools, it
increasingly lives in the same way and soon perhaps will think
the same thoughts. We have been uprooted from our parishes.
Should we not seek to put down new roots in the world and
become, not simply Americans or German or Japanese, but men,
united in a common world-citizenship? Or is world-citizenship
another word for world-homelessness? Are roots inevitably local?
Should we, whatever the apparent imperatives of our technology,
be looking for what Heidegger calls "a path that will lead to a
new ground and foundation," a ground where we are truly
grounded and not mere vagrants, a foundation from which to
grow?

Literature, I conceive, could create the space, the extracultural space, what I call a region of meditative openness, in
which these questions might come to seem real. If the instructor,
through his texts, were able to lay such questions truly open, he
might help a few students (and help himself, heaven knows) to
do what is now so difficult, to stand momentarily aside from
their lives and look, in a kind of wonder, at the quality of their
lives, look down to the regions, the springs, out of which they
live, and ask themselves what life-sustaining powers still harbor
there. How de we endure, living as we do, lacking so much that
men have always needed? The sense that something is missing,
even something all-important, will not bring it back. Yet to
sense, and then to *know*, that it is missing—might not this be a
first step, a step toward a path that could lead to a new ground?

VI

I began by talking about a sense of loss. I can now be more
specific and speak not of loss but of deracination, or homeless-
ness. At this point, the class I am imagining might turn again to
the Indians who have been here before us and are now, some of

them, seriously facing the question: Are we too to be absorbed into the American melting pot, and through America into the world's melting pot; or are we going to remain local, rooted, Indian? The Navajo people, in Arizona and Utah, are particularly instructive here. They have, I believe, the largest reservation in the country; in the last century it has increased over tenfold, from about 7,000 to nearly 90,000 population. They have their own educational institutions, the Navajo Community College at Chinle and the Rough Rock Demonstration School. At Rough Rock they are very deliberately taking hold of their tribal past and reshaping it to allow it to survive in the present and grow into the future. They have learned a way of writing their language and are building up a curriculum based on written versions of Navajo myth and history; they offer programs in shamanistic training and are retraining the Navajo medicine men. In other words, they are transforming their tribal arts into arts of resistance in order to preserve their historical identity and being.

The political or economic expedience of separatism—or the degree to which it would incommode the smooth functioning of the modern state—is not at all the point. If a man decides that he needs to be, in some sense, "separate," then political and economic expediences must accommodate themselves to this necessity as best they can. The argument of this essay tells me that the Navajos (and the other separatists here and abroad) are making the correct decision. But of course the choice is much more clear-cut for them than it is for us. The world which they see as alien and threatening is *our* world; we made it, we are at home here. On this note the class would be plunged into the thorniest literature of our time and the instructor's task would be to play up for all it was worth what Trilling calls "the adversary intention, the actually subversive intention, that characterizes modern writing" and reveal how profoundly we do *not* feel at home here. An easy lesson for today's supposedly already alienated youth? No, for they would be shown that they are not nearly alienated enough, that they fit far too snugly into culture's encasement and allow far too readily its claim to constitute an acceptable reality. Systematically the instructor would knock away their props and break down their assurances and cut the ties that bind them to their social surround until, by term's end, they would scarcely dare show their faces in the street.

Having broken down, he would then proceed to build up. This is merely the prelude, the unsettling or *aporia* needed to prepare the ground for the program itself, a program of studies based on *our* tribal arts transformed into arts of resistance designed to preserve and renew our historical identity and being.

VII

I have spoken, or will have seemed to speak, in terms of a regular academic course. And earlier I brushed in the notion of the university as a third force. But plainly it is quite unfitted to play such a role. Often accused for being too cut off from the wider social life, it is in fact integrated far too closely into society, and the "values" it holds apart from society are mostly quite trivial. It is at best a place where education (in any more than formal sense) can sometimes still happen—on the margins, in the interstices, of its official operation—and it is hard not to believe that education could happen more happily elsewhere, away from the ritual distractions of the campus. Certainly the kind of program I am sketching could not easily fit there. It presupposes a small, dedicated group, perhaps something akin to the "house church" that Catholic radicals are talking about ("the periodic meeting of friends" rather than "the Sunday assemblage of strangers"—Ivan Illich), or even the early Christian monastic cell which (in a historian's words) was "capable of survival in the oddest places and in the worst times, like a seed in the winter *detritus* of Nature. . . . Every cell was independent. If one perished, others survived. If all but one perished, the system could yet be re-created from one survivor." [14]

The analogy is helpful, at this point, for the note of quiet extremism that it sounds. It proposes a clean break (and implies the need for such a break), a resolute withdrawal from culture's good and bad, but without any of the self-advertising gestures of protest, the whole thing carried through modestly, seriously, the tone a shade penitential no doubt and inevitably ascetic but with a gay asceticism, an easy, ironic farewell to our cultural triumphs, our crowding technological easements. There is no need to think in terms of an elite (since this good word has a bad name in America), but everything suggests that I must be speaking of a small minority group. The sociologist Peter Berger talks of a *cognitive* minority and this suits my book very well. "By a cognitive minority," he writes, "I mean a group of people whose view of the world differs significantly from the one generally taken for granted in their society. Put differently, a cognitive minority is a group formed around a body of deviant 'knowledge.' " [15]

This knowledge is found in literature : in the sense, to begin with, that it provides a region (the region of meditative openness) where our first misgivings about the great artifice of culture, our incipient motions of resistance, can take shape and develop. To this "region" we must bring, in all its purity, our sense of loss and dispossession, the sense that we live like aliens in temporary, indifferent places surrounded by dead, voracious things. This is our condition, our birthright. Literature cannot free us from it, offers no refuge from it. What it can do is help us to take hold of our condition and possess it (instead of being possessed by it), to live dispossession until, very slowly, not overnight, not in one year or one generation, scarcely in a single lifetime, the faint outlines of what has been lost may begin to take shape again.

In the meantime, we practice resistance. Culture keeps us always on the move, shifting from place to place, from notion to notion; it teaches us to be the man the credit card catches for, "The Card for the man who cannot stay in one place." We resist culture, in the most practical way, by resisting these solicitations, by learning to stay in one place, in one thought, and digging in somewhere—it hardly matters where, we belong nowhere. We can resist culture by gradually learning a respect for things, by learning the contours, the feel, of a particular place, tentatively rehearsing the old gestures of attachment and very slowly recovering a sense of natural piety. In the poets we find the grammar of piety, and the appropriate devotional exercises.

A forlorn hope? Yet there may be grounds for hope, paradoxically, in the very extent and enormity of the outrage we are committing. To contemplate a row of sturdy trees being bulldozed down to make room for another stretch of highway; to drive on that highway past the dead animals killed by people going nowhere in particular very fast; even to be offered, in place of bread, cellophaned pulp that tastes and feels like cotton wool—everyday experiences of this sort could I think be *developed* from the negative sense of violation to a positive sense of what it is that is being violated. From such seeds a reverence for natural forms could grow and for those ancient makings of man's hands that are filled with his sense of the holy.

The student would next be brought to see that the region where he has settled belongs, or belonged, to a larger whole, to what was once a particular country (before it was degraded into a mere nation-state) which in turn belonged to a still larger whole, to Western civilization. Does this have anything to do with him? To be Western by the biological accident of birth means nothing. Nor is he Western by inheritance, for here too the old attachment has failed. Tradition, which once bound together and handed down, is now merely a repository of stereotypes, a flag-word. However, though he is not (in any meaningful sense) born Western, he is free to choose to *become* Western. Driven by some obscure homing instinct, he may decide to explore the famous territories that belonged to his fathers.

He begins to recognize that Western civilization extends in time as well as space and he starts coming to terms with the Western past, which involves recovering a *sense* of the past. For the past is now very weak. He learns to see the past not as a chronicle of dead devices but as a living force that pushes through the present into the future. He may be helped here, paradoxically, by the failure of tradition. This failure, if it has endangered the very existence of the past, may also, as Hannah Arendt has argued several times, have *liberated* the past. "It could be that only now will the past open up to us with unexpected freshness and tell us things no one has yet had ears to hear." [16] This *new* past is not something over and done with, but something that still has to be faced.

I spoke of "coming to terms" with the Western past and this is not, should not be, easy for there is much there that is destructive, even monstrous. Thucydides described the Athenians in the fifth century b.c. as a people "who think that the further they go the more they will get. . . . They are by nature incapable of either living a quiet life themselves or of allowing anyone else to do so." [17] If we could look at our past through the eyes of an outsider, we would see more clearly than we ordinarily do how much there is immoderate and exorbitant, not only in our actions, our worldly empires, but in our all-embracing systems of thought, our world-mastering poems : a compulsion to take hold and transform, a restless will to perfection, a discontent with the human condition that has its glories but also its infamies. Stillman and Pfaff, in their interesting book *The Politics of Hysteria,* speak of "a tradition of excess—of violence for transcendental and essentially unattainable goals—that is as much a part of the West as our tradition of regard for individual destiny and worth." [18]

The student, feeling his way into this excessive Western past and reading its consequences in the present, might well find himself turning away, in hatred and guilt, and wishing to reject it altogether. And yet in so doing he might discover that hatred and guilt only reaffirm the tie he is seeking to sever. Sartre, writing at the height of the Algerian war, dwelt on the disaster that has befallen this "fat, pale continent," Europe, that is now at death's door. Our boasted humanism was "nothing but an ideology of lies, a perfect justification for pillage," and our only defense is that "we, at least, feel some remorse." He goes on: "What a confession! Formerly our continent was buoyed up by other means: the Parthenon, Chartres, the Rights of Man, or the swastika." [19] A hateful collocation. And yet Sartre may be right. Perhaps there is a deeper connection between what we were and what we are than is normally allowed. A Southeast Asian peasant would have no trouble interpreting Thucydides' description of the Athenians. The forces that drive our culture relentlessly onward, what Stillman and Pfaff call the "truly Faustian ambition . . . to transform by physical action not merely the earth, but the qualities of the creatures who dwell upon it, an ambition related to the modern quest for the breaking down of mountains, the escape from the bounds of earth, the control and reform of human genetics, the manipulation of life itself" [20]—this ambition is empowered by new scientific and technological tools, but its origins lie deep in our past. It has perhaps been able to grow so powerful because we turn a blind eye on that past and thus hide from ourselves the nature and goal of our action.

The student in time comes to see the past, *his* past, not as culture would have him see it, as something over and done with, nor as it was proposed to him in college, as an "object" of dispassionate study, but as a living force, and he finds that he cannot reject it. For better or worse, his ancestors are buried there. Nor can he simply accept it. His task is rather to take over the

past and transform it—into a future. At this point he will have
to come to grips with Heidegger's crucial concept of *Wiederholung* (retrieval). By retrieval Heidegger means making present
the "possibilities" of the past in the light of one's resolute projections into the future. I am a futural creature standing in the
present who has inherited, who has *chosen* to inherit, the past
(not the world's past but the past of my particular historical
region). As I confront this past, I find there not simply completed events, actions, texts, but the possibilities present in, even
hidden in and never completely expressed through, those actions
and texts, and my task is to take them over and transform them
and hand them on to the future. (Impossible shorthand. Kierke-
gaard expressed the germ of the concept when he said that "the
knower cannot know a historical reality until he has resolved it
into a possibility.")

For Heidegger, the past that matters most is the origin, the
beginning, the foundational period (the "sign years," in David
Jones' phrase) when the form of a civilization is first revealed.
This, for Heidegger, means the early Greek world—the first
words uttered by Western man, through the mouths of the pre-
Socratic philosophers, when he stood open in astonishment
before the miracle of being. In his life-long attempt to re-found
Western thinking and put it on the way to a new beginning,
Heidegger has sought to retrieve and transform the possibilities
hidden in the words of the earliest Greek thinkers.

My own program is also centered on Greece—the Greece
primarily of the poets. I can now reveal that the literature in
which I hope to find the strongest elements of my doctrine of
resistance is the literature of Greece. I go to Greece not at all as
a refuge from the present but because I can find there what I
have been looking for, a place outside culture from which to
look in at the way-we-live-now. The obvious approach is via the
fifth century. The historical parallel between the moral world of
late fifth century Greece and the modern world has been fami-

liar since Nietzsche and is even more striking now than when he
proposed it. Much that characterizes and afflicts our culture is
present there in an already developed form : the restless laying
hands on everything, the compulsion always to be *doing* something, which the Athenians called *polupragmosunê;* the trans-
gressive need for new territories—on earth or in space or in our
own genetic structure—to explore and exploit *(huperbasia);*
the aggressive reach for more, more, more *pleonexia (Haben-
und Mehrhabenwollen,* in Nietzsche's inspired translation); the
whole violence of excess, *hubris,* the will to pass beyond the
human condition. In an age ravaged by a faceless yet boundless
libido dominandi, there is everything to learn from a people who
suffered egregiously from this disease and confronted its symptoms a great deal more frankly than we do. Like my Japanese
fable earlier, but far more powerfully, late fifth century Greece
offers a means of studying, at the right distance, our own world
in the process of formation.

However, it is not primarily for these salutary lessons that
I turn to Greece, but for the principle of a new foundation.
Sartre coupled the Parthenon and the swastika. It sounds shocking, yet a great Greek poet was moved to speak of that shining
monument to Athenian imperialism in not dissimilar terms at
the very moment when it was rising. Pindar—in whom, a critic
writes, "one catches sight of what Greece and the West might
have become if there had been no Athens, something closer to
the symbolic and formal cultures of the Orient, less analytical,
more conscious of the enfolding whole" [21]—Pindar said of
Athens, of the restless Athenian spirit :

> ᾇ τὸ μὲν λαμπρὸν βιᾶται,
> τῶν σ᾽ ἀφάντων κῦδος ἀντείνει σαυρόν.

"It does violence to splendor, and lifts a flawed glory for men
[or things] better hidden." [22] And from the other end of time, our
end, our own great poet who in his youth spoke of "our kinship

to the vital universe, . . . the germinal universe of wood alive, of stone alive," and in his age has come upon a sacred universe that can be embodied in poetically convincing forms—Pound, who has rounded back to a new, recovered sense of the enfolding whole, brings his huge poem to rest with the answering words :
> A little light, like a rushlight
>> to lead back to splendour.

VIII

And the end, the goal, of all these tribal studies? The bachelor of the arts of resistance might be asked to parse this word resistance. Latin *sisto,* he would say, the reduplicated form of *sto, stare,* to stand, is related to Greek *histemi,* stand or make to stand, and to Sanskrit *stha,* a place (the place outside culture). And the prefix *re-* holds the sense not only of opposition but, the dictionary tells us, of "a restoration of a thing to its original condition (e.g., a freeing or loosing from a state of constraint)"; it can also have the sense of "repetition" which one may understand in Heidegger's way as retrievel, *Wiederholung.*

And for the doctorate in resistance? The candidate would simply be asked to speak some lines by Yeats. If he could do so, with right accent and good conscience, then—? Well, then I suppose he would be ready to start on the way, ready to turn to politics or offer advice wherever it seemed proper. For by then his advice would be worth something. The lines at any rate are these :

> I am content to follow to its source
> Every event in action or in thought;
> Measure the lot, forgive myself the lot !
> When such as I cast out remorse
> So great a sweetness flows into the breast

We must laugh and we must sing,
We are blest by everything,
Everything we look upon is blest.

Notes

1. This notion, or image, derives ultimately from Lionel Trilling, though I have developed it in ways that its author would scarcely approve. See, for example, his essay on Freud where he remarks that Freud "needed to believe that there was some point at which it was possible to stand beyond the reach of culture." *Beyond Culture* (New York: Viking, 1968, p. 108).
2. Quentin Anderson, *The Imperial Self* (New York: Knopf, 1971), p. 8, vii-viii.
3. Paul Ramsey, *Fabricated Man* (New Haven: Yale University Press, 1970), p. 31.
4. Gerald Feinberg, *The Prometheus Project* (New York, Doubleday, 1969), p. 114.
5. Cited in Robert Jay Lifton, *History and Human Survival* (New York: Random House, 1970), p. 65; Lifton uses the quotation for purposes quite unlike mine.
6. Susan Sontag, *Against Interpretation* (New York: Farrar, Strauss & Giroux, 1969), pp. 298–99.
7. George Steiner, *Language and Silence* (New York: Atheneum, 1967), p. ix.
8. Herbert Marcuse, *One-Dimensional Man* (Boston: Beacon, 1968), p. 57.
9. David Jones, *Epoch and Artist* (New York: 1959), p. 140.
10. Richard E. Palmer, *Hermeneutics: Interpretation Theory in Schleiermacher, Dilthey, Heidegger, and Gadamer* (Evanston: Northwestern University Press, 1969).
11. Doris Lessing, *Nine African Stories* (London: Longman, Green, 1968), p. 6.
12. See, for example, *Tess of the D'Urbevilles*, chapter 51.
13. Martin Heidegger, *Discourse on Thinking*, trans., John M. Anderson and E. Hans Freund (New York: Harper & Row, 1969), p. 48.
14. Hugh Trevor-Roper, *The Rise of Christian Europe* (New York: Harcourt, Brace & World, 1968), p. 88.
15. Peter Berger, *A Rumor of Angels* (Garden City: Doubleday, 1969), p. 7.
16. Hannah Arendt, *Between Past and Future: Six Exercises in Political Thought* (New York: Viking, 1968), p. 94; see also pp. 25–29. This is, of course, a central theme in Heidegger; see, for example, *Being and Time*, Introduction, II.6.
17. Thucydides, *History of the Peloponnesian War*, 1.70.
18. Edmund Stillman and William Pfaff, *The Politics of Hysteria: The Sources of Twentieth Century Conflict* (New York: Harper & Row, 1965), p. 13.

19. Preface to Frantz Fanon, *The Wretched of the Earth* (New York: Grove Press, 1968), pp. 25, 27.
20. Stillman and Pfaff, p. 29.
21. J. H. Finley, Jr., *Pindar and Aeschylus* (Cambridge: Harvard University Press, 1966), p. 189.
22. The possibility of understanding this as an allusion to the Parthenon depends on an unorthodox dating of the poem, *Nemean* 8, after 446 B.C. rather than around 459, once proposed by Norman O. Brown ("Pindar, Sophocles, and the Thirty Years' Peace," *T.A.P.A.* 82 1951 i-28). This and the Finley reference above I owe to a dissertation by my friend William Mullen.

The Reformed University as a Third Force in American Life

William Arrowsmith

"All mapmakers," says Saul Bellow's wise old Sammler, "should place the Mississippi in the same location, and avoid originality. It may be boring, but one has to know where he is."

The Indians usually knew where they were before we uprooted them from themselves and from the land. They stood simply on the earth of their convictions, resisting as stubbornly as they could the outrageous benevolence of government policies and the gospel greed of the land-hungry whites. Exploitation, we have been told, cannot be seen as such by those who do it; it must be mystified and viewed as benevolence. It was in this spirit that the government tried a century ago to persuade, or otherwise compel, the Shoshones of Utah and Wyoming to renounce their ancient Earthmother, sell their arable land to the invaders, and retire to semideserts where—such was the white man's mystifying logic—they would learn the art of farming under conditions that doomed them to failure. The Indian agent explained his progressive proposals, and the tribe debated them.

This essay has been slightly abridged from its publication as "Teaching and the Liberal Arts: Notes Toward an Old Frontier," in *Liberal Arts and Teacher Education*, ed., Donald Bigelow (Lincoln: University of Nebraska Press, 1971) and reprinted with permission.

Then Chief Washakie rose to summarize. Mustering what little English he had, he said tersely but effectively, "God damn a potato !"—and with these "winged words" he sat down, adjourning the council. He meant, of course, that buffalo hunters had better things to do than grub for tubers like a lot of Irishmen or Paiutes. But that was not all. He also meant what Smohalla, the great prophet of the Columbia, said in answer to the same demands :

> It is a bad word that comes from Washington always.
> . . . You ask me to cut grass and make hay and sell it
> and be rich like the white man. But how dare I cut my
> Mother's hair ? Shall I take a knife [a plow] and tear
> my Mother's breast ? Then when I die, she will not
> take me to her bosom to rest. My young men shall
> never work. Men who work cannot dream, and
> wisdom comes in dreams.

Aristocratic words. Too aristocratic for the whites, who characteristically mistook the disdain for drudgery as nothing more than Indian shiftlessness. But they are much more than contempt for menial labor. Behind these words of Washakie and Smohalla lies all of Indian life, the very heart of Indian culture. They are statements of the spirit, and the spirit's priorities, and they spring from a natural piety that merely practical or vulgar men could never hope to understand. Washakie, I suppose, had nothing against potatoes. He was a prudent man, a chief, and even Shoshones must eat. But there are some things a man, a true man, will not eat, even if he starves for his refusal. To the Indian the dream was the bearer of his identity, his name, just as it also conferred his citizenship—his membership in the great community outside himself to which he was forever linked, to the friendly dead, to the genius of the place, the Great Spirit overhead, the powers of nature, and all those things which we should now view as the voices of our unconscious and our past. In the dream he encountered the Other—something he recognized as kin to himself, but larger and unmistakably there. For it he felt the awe and aspiration of the limited for the unlimited. And in the dream he found a self by transcending himself.

I do not mystify. The young Indian on the verge of manhood waits, tense with promise, in the wilderness. He does not eat or sleep or drink. Because he invokes a higher power, he purifies himself; he is all aspiration. The dream comes like a revelation inward yet also outward. It suddenly speaks his name, tells him who he is and what his ripening powers are—the grace of the otter, the badger's courage, the gravity of the elk. It makes him a man among men. The dream seals the maturing powers of the dreamer with the tutelary welcome of the larger world, the great chorus of the others. And what is true of the boy's vigil is also true for his people, whose sachems and shamans dream the great collective dreams of the tribe's fate, just as the Greek seer understood the voice of the oracular earth and the gods in it. Everything the Indian meant by his humanity and its fulfillment, every link with the great world of the others, was violated and annulled by that stupid word from Washington. And the word got the answer it deserved: "God damn a potato!"

I

There, my Mississippi is on the map. Education is a spiritual affair, a matter of fulfillment, a fatal business. An old and familiar text, it might seem, dressed up in topical Indian guise. Perhaps. The same convictions can be found in Plato, or Nietzsche, or Emerson, or in any ordinary commencement address. It is boring, but it is true. And perhaps it is not boring at all. But it is where we begin.

> "The mind of this country," said Emerson, a contemporary of Smohalla, "being taught to aim at low objects, feeds on itself. Young men of the fairest promise . . . are hindered from action by the disgust

which the principles on which business is managed
inspire, and turn drudges or die of disgust. . . . Our
culture has truckled to the times. It is not manworthy.
If the vast and spiritual are omitted, so are the practical and the moral. It does not make us brave or free.
We teach boys to be such men as they are. We do not
teach them to aspire to be all they can. We do not give
them a training as if we believed in their noble
nature. . . . We aim to make accountants, engineers,
but not to make able, earnest, great-hearted men." [1]

Smohalla and Washakie tell the same miserable story, but they
tell it more forcefully, from the viewpoint of the victims who
suffered the arrogance and inhumanity of the failed education
Emerson describes. For Emerson the failure is mostly a matter of
low ends, of making spiritual aspiration subservient to merely
practical purposes. There is no hint in his words, as there is in
Smohalla's, of the critical role played in education by the external community, the great world of "other" powers the youth
encounters in his vigil. For Emerson, as for Nietzsche, it is a
matter of individual aspiration which needs to find cultural
accommodation. The individual is isolated in his heroic individualism, and his transcendence is a matter of imposing his will
upon himself and the world.

This tradition of intense individualism and voluntarism,
blended with and compounded by ideas of Manifest Destiny and
the all-American "melting-pot," is the source of that arrogance
and solipsism, that mindless assumption of white superiority, that
Smohalla so resented. The conviction of cultural superiority was
itself simply a national expression of the individual's immersion
in his own will.[2] Multiplied and magnified, the individual's
egotism became the nation-state, but not a society, which implies
a concord of discrete individuals, a civic sense of the "other." A
society is precisely what we would not manage to create; citizenship was merely self-assimilation. And the evidence is all around
us: will and isolation turned intolerant and violent; an absent-

minded rage to expunge all difference, to annihilate the "other."
The result is that syndrome of disease whose deadliest, most
prevalent form is racism. Yet this racism, as ruthless or merely
mindless acculturation, is still our standard educational practice.
I think, for instance, of my own state of Texas, where Spanish-
speaking children must go on strike in order to speak Spanish on
their own schoolgrounds. Or of our unspeakable—our divine—
arrogance in Vietnam.[3] Or of the Alaskan Eskimos, who by
means of *Dick and Jane*—an instrument more lethal than the
carbine—are being compelled to deny their own immemorial,
working culture for one which has proven a miserable failure in
suburban America. My point, however, is not to recite mal-
practices that are now notorious, but to point out the epidemic
range and symptoms of the disease.

What cannot be tolerated, what must be always shunned, is
the direct experience of difference, the naked, unassimilated
encounter with the "other." When school children study foreign
countries, it is not China or Pakistan or Chile they study, but
Switzerland, Norway, or France—that is, the always assimilable,
the not-so-strange. The practice is defended on grounds of peda-
gogical necessity, but its real purpose is to evade encounter by
domesticating the alien texture of reality.[4] It is the same with the
past as it is with the world. Programs in the humanities are
anemic because humanists mindlessly view the past not as a great
source of "otherness"—what we no longer have, the skills we
have lost and need now, what we never knew we lacked—but as
cultural reinforcement for the present. The past justifies the
present; we teach students, not how we might become different
or better, but merely how we became what we are. In the
schools and universities the languages are being "phased out,"
apparently because their central educational purpose—the access
they provide to alternate ways of being human, and hence to our
undiscovered selves—is no longer understood.[5] In the schools
condescension and stultifying benevolence prevail: we teach

Midsummer Night's Dream or *As You Like It* or even *Macbeth* (all of them badly for the most part), but not *Hamlet* or *Lear;* and the reason is not only their "difficulty" but our desire to spare the young the brush with the terrible, with the uncontrollably tragic. And so we puerilize them; we deprive them of the encounters, literary and human, which might educate them, and we then wonder why this process does not produce compassionate or greathearted men. Even youth culture, with its declared affinity for minorities and the outcast, is all too often hostile or indifferent to any curriculum or study that does not reinforce or reiterate its cardinal perceptions. No less than the "straight" culture, it excludes whatever it cannot cope with or somehow assimilate to itself. It is a closed, not an open, culture.[6]

A classicist would call this disease simply *hybris.* Inaccurately translated "pride," *hybris* has a constant aura of violence or violation. It suggests processes that have gotten out of hand, the luxuriance of things spilling over their natural limits, violating the physical space or the rights of others, their very right to exist. It is a denial, an annihilation, of the "other"; a violation of nature and natural law. Thus in fifth-century Attic law *hybris* means "rape"; imperialism is simply *hybris* on a grand political scale. A garden which is "lush" is said to have *hybris*—which means a discontented garden, a garden with megalomania, aspiring to be a jungle. Finally, there is a positive form of *hybris*— the metaphysical discontent of the hero, the obdurate, cross-grained perversity needed to accomplish great tasks. The opposite of *hybris* is *sophrosyne.* This means, not "moderation," but "the skill of mortality"—the self-knowledge of the man who knows that he is doomed, who accepts his limitations. He has encountered "the other," whether as god or man, and he therefore treats other men with the compassion his own doom claims from them. Now, in the Greek view, *hybris* can be met in only two ways. First, by the actual experience of disaster, the bitter tragic doom that teaches the man of *hybris* who he really is, his miserable anonymity and transcience and nothingness. The second way is by education, which teaches *sophrosyne* through the tragic spectacle of doomed *hybris*. I believe that the essential purpose of Greek tragedy—which was deliberately subsidized by the state for the instruction, not the amusement, of the people—was to educate a proud people, a people prone to *hybris,* in *sophrosyne.* Euripides in his *Trojan Women,* for instance, is visibly trying to elicit and to strengthen in his audience the feeling of compassion and humanity so achingly absent in the play and in Athenian foreign policy.

Hybris, then : an expansive, sometimes aggressive, sometimes mindless, solipsism, in which the assertion of self is a godlike denial of the other. Immured in folds of self-sufficiency, the man of racist *hybris* is almost unreachable; almost, it seems, unteachable. He can kill with something like negligence—with the barbarous but bland irritability of the massacres at My Lai and Wounded Knee. You can recognize his features in Ortega y Gasset's description of modern "mass man," the new man who claims to rule the world :

> Heir to an ample and generous past—generous both in ideals and in activities—the new commonalty has been spoiled by the world around it. To spoil means to put no limit on caprice. . . . The young child exposed to this regime has no experience of its own limits. By reason of the removal of all external restraint . . . he comes actually to believe that *he is the only one who exists,* and gets used to not considering others. . . . Whereas in past times life for the average man meant finding all around him difficulties, dangers, wants, limitations of his destiny, the new world appears as a sphere of practically limitless possibilities. . . . If the traditional sentiment whispered, "To live is to feel oneself limited, and therefore to have to count with that which limits us," the newest voice shouts : "To live is to meet with no limitation whatever and, consequently, to abandon oneself calmly to oneself. Prac-

tically nothing is impossible, nothing is dangerous, and,
in principle, nobody is superior to anybody." Ingenu-
ously, without any need of being vain, as the most
natural thing in the world, he will consider and confirm as good everything he finds within himself :
opinions, appetites, preferences, tastes. And why not,
if . . . nothing and nobody force him to realize that he
is a second-class man, subject to many limitations. . . ? [7]

The ancient world knew mass man, too; but as a universal
phenomenon, he is essentially modern. And no wonder. We have
maximized *hybris*. Anything is now possible, and the possible is
always desirable. It is that simple. There is no saving skill, no
sophrosyne, no natural piety available to resist it with, or school
it. What was once a chronic and dangerous human tendency, is
now an almost certain fate. If only we could find or set a limit to
our unimpeded wills, if we could only encounter the other,
whether god or man. . . . But America is no longer a country
where the "other" is to be encountered. We have brushes, but
few encounters. The past is being systematically erased; the earth
has few powers we respect. As for other men, other men in their
tangible conditions, they are almost all unapproachably isolated.
"No man is an island, entire of himself," said John Donne, who
could not have imagined *this* America. Even the stages of human
life have lost their continuity, their old sequence and proximity.
Young and old simply fail to meet any more. Therefore they
cannot qualify each other, cannot compose a sense or arc of
common humanity. Florida, like Phoenix, is one vast geriatric
spa, rabid with fear and hatred of the young, feeding on its own
desperate isolation. The public schools, the high schools, are
peer-group prisons, patrolled by armed adults and terrified
teachers. Everywhere ghettos. Old and young, rich and poor,
black and white, living and dead—not sensible pluralisms, but
segregated parts of a once common life, fragments of a single
condition! If there are encounters, they occur at the barriers,
and they are violent or cold. And meanwhile in Washington the

elected warlocks and warlords turn human differences into antagonistic blocs, chanting of unity but exploiting divisiveness in an orgy of bad faith. Never a healing word. "It is a bad word that comes from Washington always. . . ." And as the encounters grow rarer and colder, as the "other" disappears from embrace and sight, the demonologies become more virulent and explosive. Outside the prison enclosure any evil can be believed of anybody, because there is nobody human there. Inside the barrier reef, the coral *hybris* grows.

As it swells, it takes its toll of the psyche, the inward man, fragmenting him like the world outside. And we suddenly discover in ourselves the shambles R. D. Laing has described so vividly:

> Bodies half-dead; genitals dissociated from the heart; heart severed from head; head dissociated from genitals. Without inner unity, with just enough sense of continuity to clutch at identity—the current idolatry. Torn—body, mind, and spirit—by inner contradictions, pulled in different directions. Man cut off from his own mind, cut off equally from his own body—a half-crazed creature in a mad world! [8]

Hybris nearly incorrigible, nearly hopeless! What then can educators do? Are we doomed to go on toiling forever behind, like Homer's goddesses of healing Prayer, in the wake of Ruin, trying in vain to undo the desolation and the hurt? Perhaps that is our modest, monumental job, the most we can do. There are many—an increasing number—who believe our crisis is so vast and so complex, and our margin of time so pathetically short, that we must turn all our energies to politics. I share their fears. If ever we desperately needed real political vision and leadership, the time is now. But there is not the slightest sign of either anywhere. And even if we had vision and leadership, we would still need educators who believed in the value and goodness of what they do, who still see their work as a necessary task of the spirit. Our permanent business is human fulfillment and the liberation of the mind—the great project of creating a larger humanity or simply preserving what human skills we still possess. The opportunities, the contexts, exist. The hunger for true education is everywhere. The schools and colleges are one of the last places in the society where real encounters can occur; here youth and adult, past and present, rich and poor, still meet. Here there is still a hope of making a self in collaboration with others. This is why the failure of education is so utterly killing—because the amplest and most generous expectations are still focused there, the last high hopes of the species.

II

There, my Mississippi is on the map. If we have maximized *hybris*, how can we enable and enlarge *sophrosyne*? Clearly, by making those reforms it lies in our power to make.

Not everything is possible. Politics is one thing, education another. And formal education is an awkward instrument for effecting major political change. What it can do, however, is to shape the sensibility of the age—its hopes, its aspiration, its maturing consciousness of human life and meaning—and to that degree radically affect the form of any future culture, including its political life. A truly liberal education does not politicize; it has almost nothing to do with revolution or reaction, and its relevance is moral and metaphysical, not political. It liberates because it sets us free to become ourselves, to realize ourselves; it frees us to learn, slowly and painfully perhaps, our limitations and our powers, and to recognize our real modalities, undeafened by the overwhelming Muzak of the social and political enterprise. Liberally educated, we are free to become political at last, without risk of being captured and possessed by our politics. And this freedom, this ripeness of self, is the indispensable element in all true teaching, simply because it speaks so compellingly to those who hunger to be free—that is, presumably, to all men. . . .

The stakes are high. The most revolutionary risk ever run by this country was its decision—an act of positive, heroic *hybris*—to dedicate itself to universal education. True, no such decision was ever actually taken; it was a decision reached by indirection and degrees, by incremental drift. Yet the drift was implicit in the national character—an evident *daimon* from the beginning. From the beginning we were aiming to make all men spiritually as well as socially and politically free. Only one other society in the history of mankind has taken a similar course, and that was Athens, which in the fifth century B.C. deliberately tried, by means of a curriculum of poetry and drama, to democratize a great aristocratic *ethos* and to impose on every citizen the burden of heroic *arete*. Ultimately that effort was a failure, but it was one of the most brilliant failures of human history.

Our own commitment to universal education is now in real jeopardy. On the one hand, it has been betrayed by an insidious elitism—the elitism of the learned professions—which has made liberal education the servant of merely professional ends and disavowed the needs of those students who lack scholarly or professional interests. On the other side, it has been betrayed by a class of pseudoprofessionals who, by means of their own illiteracy, have turned the public schools into nurseries of a massive illiteracy—an illiteracy which, in combination with that national *hybris* I see everywhere, now threatens to destroy the republic.

"No amount of reflection," wrote R. P. Blackmur with remarkable prescience two decades ago,

> has deflected me from the conclusion that the special problem of the humanities in our generation . . . is to struggle against the growth of the new illiteracy and the new intellectual proletariat, together with the curious side-consequence of these, the new and in-

creasing distrust of the audience by public and quasi-public institutions. All three of these are the results of the appearance, in combination, of mass societies and universal education. . . . We deal not with ignorance but with deformities of knowledge. . . . The old illiteracy was inability to read; as the old literacy involved the habit of reading. The new illiteracy represents those who have been given the tool of reading without being given either the means or skill to read well or the material that ought to be read. The habit of reading in the new illiteracy is not limited to, but is everywhere supplied by, a press almost as illiterate as itself. It is in this way that opinion, instead of knowledge, has come to determine action; the inflammable opinion of the new illiterate is mistaken for the will of the people, so that arson becomes a chief political instrument.[9]

Against *hybris, sophrosyne;* against the new illiteracy, a new literacy; against the arson of deformed knowledge, a renewal of the liberal arts. To educate a nation: it is the incomparable priority of the age. And it requires active mind at the top of its bent, flexible intelligence, a positive appetite for complexity and sympathy, and, most important of all, an openness to these terrible times in which we no longer know how to act in the confusion of being human. Youth culture, for all its quick compassion and its generous humanity, is not enough; it has no heart for the long haul, and it is increasingly anti-intellectual. Nor are the traditional liberal arts, with their impoverished parish of reality and their decorative scholars, any longer adequate. We simply cannot survive if we go on puerilizing and barbarizing the young with a hollow technical mockery of true knowledge. The humanist's *hybris* is his distrust of the audience, his habit, in Blackmur's phrase, of believing that the audience is not up to what he has to say and therefore ending up inferior to the potential response of his audience. We deny the student's hunger to be more than he is when we tell him he is not ready for Homer or *Lear.* And the consequence of this stultification, multiplied millions of times, is an illiterate electorate, militant *hybris,* and a racist society.

In an illiterate society the teacher's literacy may be the only literacy in sight; the teacher's *sophrosyne* may be the only approachable evidence of achieved humanity. Without the liberally educated man, as witness and seal of what he is, education will become more and more a mug's game, a trade school, a vulgar racket for privileged illiterates. Professionalism, scrappy or fastidious, will not do. Vulgarization deforms both student and citizen.

My *first* proposal is simplicity itself. Let the liberal arts colleges take as their primary function—their highest priority—the training of teachers—teachers for the primary and secondary schools. Over six years ago James Conant, in *The Education of American Teachers,* made his valuable proposal that the liberal arts colleges should have the right to train and certify teachers. His unspoken purpose was to challenge the colleges of education to reform themselves; to make them recruit better students and to educate them better; to put content and rigor back into their programs. The threat of competition was the spur. But the suggestion was met by the colleges with small enthusiasm and token programs. A few colleges responded, and the M.A.T. programs were a notable step forward.[10] Yet no really serious or massive effort has yet been made, or even considered, by any leading university. This is not surprising since the universities long ago renounced the training of schoolteachers for the greater prestige of pure research and graduate instruction. The disdain academicians felt for the training of teachers was wholly in keeping with their own headlong professionalization. Later, not content with writing off the lower schools, they effectively renounced all undergraduate instruction which could not be accommodated to their professional routines. As for the liberal arts colleges, they were snobbishly skeptical of programs which might detract from their major effort, the preparation of students for graduate

schools. The training of teachers, in both colleges and universities, was simply not then regarded as a serious intellectual
operation. But if Conant were to renew his proposal now, it
would meet, I believe, with a very different response.

It will doubtless be objected that this is grandiose folly,
that there are now too many teachers for the jobs available; that
there are so many teachers the market cannot absorb, only
insanity would propose preparing more. But this is a quantitative,
not a qualitative, objection. There are undoubtedly too many
aspiring teachers; but the bulk of these are the badly trained
and generally inferior products of the colleges of education. They
are simply not a base upon which any real reform of American
education can be undertaken; they are simply unworthy of our
crisis, of our desperate need for superlative teachers of high
intellectual gifts and generous human skills. And of well-trained
paraprofessionals there is no overabundance at all, but rather an
appalling shortage, simply because the problems of minorities
and of bicultural education are not problems to which either
colleges of education or higher education generally has been in
the least responsive.

The decisive fact is the satisfaction *this* generation might
find in teaching the very young. Their complaints of their own
education apply after all with even greater force to the primary
and secondary students. Here, in the terrible bleakness of the
schools—not merely ghetto schools, but almost all schools—is
where the generous, lively talents of this generation might really
flourish. *Here,* if anywhere, is where the future will be created or
destroyed. Here is where we will change ourselves or not at all.
Generosity of spirit is crucial. But so is bright, clear, nimble,
trained intelligence. Teachers have for too long been recruited
from the ranks of the not-too-bright, and then stultified by their
education. If the material rewards are poor, this should hardly
matter to a generation that has largely turned its back on business and the comforts and certainties of American affluence.

What is needed now is a signal, a strong one, from a major university or college. The response, I am convinced, would be almost overwhelming. . . .

III

I am not sanguine about the survival of the official, formal humanities, the liberal arts curriculum as it exists now in American universities. It will persist, of course : an imposing academic husk, respected and even revered. And there will still, I hope, be a place for its nobler scholars. But the real spirit of the liberal arts will vanish—is already vanishing—elsewhere, into the arts and the professions and perhaps the sciences, to reappear as an *ethos* rather than a discipline or subject matter. And everywhere the sensibility of the excluded non-Western world and the cultures of poverty is pressing for a place in the sun—a development which should stimulate and challenge and perhaps reinvigorate the traditional liberal arts.

The loss of the official humanities does not, I think, greatly matter. The texts and curriculum go underground, to reappear in new guises; the texts may change, but the spirit persists. What matters is that this new humanistic *ethos* should find congenial ground for growing. The greatest obstacle is still the vanity and stupidity of the established disciplines : moribund but as monstrously *there* as a dying whale. Disestablishment is what they deserve ("After such knowledge, what forgiveness?"), and disestablishment is their almost certain fate.

The liberal arts have not yet suffered the last of their humiliations. The groundswell of public opinion that condones neglect of students in the name of mostly worthless research is still building. It will end by compelling drastic revision of educational priorities. Neither conscience nor economy can tolerate a system that, in order to produce a tiny elite of professional scholars, stultifies thousands of potential teachers and perhaps millions of students, that makes the past and the great liberal arts merely decorative culture. It is just possible that poverty may bring the humanists to their senses; to a valid sense of the difference between curriculum and culture. Who hasn't heard professors of English heatedly argue that Melville and even Faulkner could not be really read without their mediation? Monstrous! What is still actively alive in the culture is deadened or destroyed by being curricularized before its time. Common ground—common culture—enclosed by a scholar or critic is lost ground. Losses surround us everywhere. After ten years of being worked up into courses and syllabi, black studies will be as useless to black pride as the Renaissance is useless to contemporary Italians. A few years of genteel poverty might encourage concentration on essentials, but one wonders why poverty should work when the threat of extinction has failed.

Paradoxically, the greatest present hope of liberal education, now a nearly desperate enterprise at all levels, is the crisis of all the social—not the academic—professions. The unnameable convulsion of our society— the convulsion for which we have no words, no skills, no styles of coping—has brought all professional certainties into dispute and even anarchy. We simply do not know whom to train for what contingencies or society, in what numbers, or how. Professional establishments have served us badly, and we confront chaos with the pat and selfish routines of professional classes incapable, in numbers and vigor and humanity, of coping. The consequence has been, at the point of contact between society and the professions, to create demands which will profoundly affect the academic disciplines. The most immediate result is a growing demand for the collapsing of all structural barriers between the professions and the disciplines, for doing away with the separate colleges of law, medicine, art, architecture, and communications, and merging them in new ways with the arts and sciences. And the reason is simple necessity.

We have integrated problems and disintegrated skills. And the alienation of knowledge and the liberal arts from the crisis of the professions is no longer a tolerable luxury. If the liberal arts attempt to maintain their traditional aloofness, their devotion to pure research and contemplation, their subject matters will simply be appropriated. The professions have no alternative; they are too close to society, to the convulsive chaos around us, to escape responsibility for change, for rational and humane action. The professions, I am suggesting, have encountered the "other"; a new humanism is already taking shape among younger professionals in response to the desperation of those who depend upon the professions. And because the professions cannot do without the arts of knowledge and the liberal arts, their encounter will eventually spread to education too.

The liberal arts may be radically changed in the process. It is their liberating and humanizing functions, not their curriculum, that are permanent. But it is from *outside* that reform will come. Not through existing discipline where old routines and professional interests make fresh response nearly impossible. Rather from the world of the professions, from the public schools, from the communities, from the sciences, from all those encounters between crumbling ethical codes and the necessity to act *now,* even at the risk of having to improvise your values as you go. If conscientious, the lawyer faces the obsolescence of his statutes, of the very assumptions of law perhaps; the doctor is trapped in an agony of choice for which his traditional code provides only uncertain and inadequate answers. Whether they like it or not, the professions are doomed to the agony of value, to metaphysical danger, to a leap of faith. From these encounters may emerge a sense of someone there, of conscience and care. This sense of care then comes to the university, where professionals are trained, in quest of company, solutions, validations, help. But help is not to be expected from academic humanists, nor is it forthcoming. It comes, if at all, from the professions themselves, which thereby take on the burden of reforming themselves, humanizing themselves, adjusting to these new problematics of value. And the consequence, profession by profession, is an involvement in choice and purpose which slowly, gropingly, uncertainly improvises a new *ethos,* an attitude toward the use of professional skills arrived at by hunch and instinct and maturing meditation. In this new community of amateurs lies, I am convinced, the future of the liberal arts.

This community is of course much larger than the immediate professional community. It includes all those who feel, however incoherently, that the great task of the times is to create a new breed of professional as well as new institutional forms— above all, new schools and universities—to cope with the problems of scale and value imposed by the new mass society. The formal humanism of the old university failed because it could not connect its theory with its practice; because it pretended to be only discipline, it lost its power as *ethos.* Behind all demands for new educational institutions is the notion of the liberal arts as an attitude everywhere informing an *engaged* intellect; the very engagement, it is hoped, will sharpen and define the emergent mission. Where these demands have not been merely demands for direct political action, their effect is to make of schools and universities a secular church. They are spiritual demands and should be recognized as such.

An example. A year or so ago the chairman of the board of regents of the University of Texas authorized the chopping down of a dozen magnificent live oaks in order to make room for a culvert. Resisted by droves of student Druids perched in the doomed trees, the chairman himself, for all the world like a Texas Xerxes, cheered on the bulldozers with idiot glee. But he miscalculated : his opposition was not merely outraged students, but a sudden, large, angry coalition of townspeople, faculty, and students. He had failed to observe a critical fact : the feeling for the environment is an extremely potent form of feeling, a force that will soon, it seems, be chartering universities and even churches. And the reason is that unmistakably religious and scientific feelings find here something like respectable scientific status. Beneath all the talk of ecosystems lies a new intimation of natural law, a muddled but powerful feeling of kinship with the life of earth and a new reverence for the cosmos. Of a fresh *sophrosyne*. So too, in student revolt, one senses the presence, beneath all the hokum, of religious feeling that have, as yet, no institutional home or focus.

The demand for a new reformed university is potent because the intent behind the demands is to make education the home of those orphaned religious feelings. The suddent felt antagonism between society and its schools conceals, I believe, the ancient quarrel between secular and spiritual institutions. Certainly the universities are being asked to assume tasks that once belonged to family and church, but which those institutions now lack the intellect—and also the moral courage—to perform. And this suggests that the major problem for the liberal arts in our time may be to recognize and *re*define, in study and conduct, the metaphysical and religious ground of our motives and meanings. I write, I should explain, as a secular intellectual. These are not for me easy or comforting conclusions. But I am driven to them by events and pressures I cannot otherwise explain.

We cannot yet say whether the effort to create a new university (or new schools)—that is, structures in which a new humanism might be defined and embodied—will succeed. The obstacles are formidable. But so are the stakes. It would be a disaster if, in the struggle over the university, either the radicals or the conservatives won a clear-cut victory. If the university and schools are politicized according to radical doctrine, they will forfeit their potential as spiritual institutions and become merely another set of (probably impotent) political lobbies.

IV

My *second* proposal is therefore that we deliberately set about creating what I have elsewhere called a "university of the public interest." [11] By this I mean a university dedicated to the advocacy of just those public interests—in education, in health, in population control, in social justice, in the environment—that are now endangered by organized greed, professional mindlessness, miseducation, and policies of "benign neglect." In short, a modern Socratic university for a mass society, an organization of concerned professionals determined to apply their skills as effectively as possible, and to educate their students by enlisting their efforts in the same mission. By "Socratic" I mean to suggest both power of mind and the conscience of knowledge. A university of the public interest would educate by the power and example of its advocacy; because it addressed itself, with the full power of active mind, to the public's sense of justice, compassion, beauty, in the hope of thereby eliciting or strengthening the moral skills, the literacy, that now seem paralyzed or lost. Lost because unaddressed; because daily diminished; made illiterate by half-truths and politic lies, by deliberate arson, by being always addressed in terms of its basest, least generous powers. A teacher appeals to the powers he hopes to enlarge. The spirit must be visible or it will not be believed. And in a mass society the individual tends to become invisible; this is why we need spiritual institutions and concerted commitment.

Creating a university of the public interest means above all to reform the major professions. The nation has no future worth thinking about unless we can produce, swiftly and in quantity, a different kind of professional: a lawyer whose client is the public interest, an architect who is more than the cagey flunkey of his client, an engineer sensitive to other factors than cost. The problem is not talent. Talent abounds. What is lacking are institutions that demand or permit a talented man's best work, that encourage gifted men to exercise their compassion and conscience. Professional education is now in a ferment of reform. But the pace needs quickening. And this can best be done, I believe, by chartering the university itself as a corporation for the public interest. It would provide, for instance, an institutional shelter for the public-interest lawyer, or a base for systematic criticism of professional performance in the society at large : the work of architects, the projects of engineers. It would attempt to publish a national newspaper. It would actively sponsor and protect the economic and cultural interests of those minorities too small or weak to help themselves. That is, the university would house and train the conscience of the professions, and proceed to give that conscience tangible and active expression. It would also seek to provide the public education, and the ramifying reforms, which programs affecting the public interest must have.

I assume that the public interest will be served by such projects, and that such service should best be pluralistic. An orthodoxy of benevolence would be intolerable. The educational benefits, I would argue, are extraordinary. First, a context in which knowledge, applied in a spirit of service, could be made moral; in which skills and values could be enlarged and refined by significant use. Second, an overriding mission in terms of which men might pool specialized skills, simply because there is no other way of getting their task done; in short, a context in which interdisciplinary work would occur naturally, as it now does not. Third, the community such collaboration might create—the community we do not have. Fourth, the possibility of recruiting generous human energies which now have almost nowhere to go—energies which, turned rancid and frustrated, make education impossible. Finally, the hope of restoring the authority of reason and intelligence by virtue of their *visible* pertinence to the task in hand.

The purport of this proposal is to make the university a

third force in American life—a force that is neither government nor industry, but rather a new form of spiritual institution. I offer no apology for the phrase. No great society has yet managed to survive without powerful spiritual institutions, whether subversive or established. They are made up of men who, in Chapman's words, sound a certain note: "They hold a tuning fork and sound A, and everybody knows it really is A, though the time-honored pitch is G flat. The community cannot get that A out of its head. Nothing can prevent an upward tendency in the popular tone so long as the real A is kept sounding." It was the intent of the founding fathers that family and church should speak for the spirit in American life. They could not have foreseen the dreadful eclipse of both those institutions, nor the ominous concentrations of wealth—and hence of political power—in recent years. To some degree the spirit survived in the courts and the foundations; but Congress has now emasculated the foundations, and the courts have been gutted. The spirit is not in good health or odor. Many think it a myth. And with good reason. Unselfishness in American life is unincorporated; it has no coherent party or program, no normalized institutional home. And the absence is as tangible as the absence of God. Indeed, the demands now being made of the university are, I believe, as unappeasable as they are because they are unrecognized demands of the spirit. The university is being asked to act as a spiritual institution. But because nobody believes in spiritual institutions, the demands come disguised as intransigent political demands.

The critical problem is to make the university a *potent* institution of the spirit. Otherwise it will not have the kind of influence needed, in a mass society, to affect the quality of life. The difficulty is transcending old habits. So long as the university community believes its true constituency is the classroom, it is doomed to the custody of increasingly dissatisfied and ungrateful students. Our schools and universities now have a mandate to educate everybody. But we cannot confine all the young to institutions. And the consequence is that the classroom becomes the country. But you can't educate a country by classroom techniques, by formal instruction. You educate rather as an artist does, by what you say and do, by rational persuasion; or, like a pre-Socratic, by embodiment and example. You address your audience without condescension, with the fineness and complexity reality requires; you refuse to collaborate in extending the new illiteracy. That is, the university shows, *as an institution,* what men might be if they were *free* to be what they wanted. It liberates because it *practices* the liberal arts. It embodies conscience because it trains conscientious professionals; compassion, because only compassion could explain its strange and generous behavior, and so on. Its potency derives not only from the spirit, but from its institutional elan, the energy and modernity of its action.

A university of the public interest is not, I believe, a visionary project. It is already emerging everywhere around us, in random experiments and programs, the shape of the future institution looming unmistakably behind the confusion and frustration and anger. Abortive as the efforts to reform education have been, the efforts take a common direction, and it is important to name it. Otherwise we are apt to miss what is positive and see only anarchy and trouble. We are on the verge of creating, here in America, a great new social and educational institution, a new form of the university and perhaps the school too, adapted to the needs of a new society and the agony of our present condition.

V

Let me close, and come full circle, with the words of still another Indian. The speaker is Chief Seattle; the occasion is his response to the demand of the whites that he and his tribe retire to a small reservation on Puget Sound.[12] Seattle's statement is one of the very greatest of American speeches—all radiant *sophrosyne,* a tragic charity that includes even the white oppressors in the range of its understanding. You have to go to the *Iliad,* to that supreme moment in the final book when Achilles speaks to Priam across every conceivable gulf of condition—age, culture, and fortune—to find anything quite like it. To us, now, Seattle speaks as a voice of that great community of the "others," which all education hopes to knit into our lives, until listening to it and heeding it become conduct and a second, larger, nature. Seattle is a great teacher. Listen:

> *Brothers:* That sky above us has pitied our fathers for many hundreds of years. To us it looks unchanging, but it may change. Today it is fair. Tomorrow it may be covered with cloud.
>
> My words are like the stars. They do not set. What Seattle says, the great chief in Washington can count on as surely as our white brothers can count on the return of the seasons.
>
> The White Chief's son says his father sends words of friendship and good will. This is kind of him, since we know he has little need of our friendship in return. His people are many, like the grass that covers the plains. My people are few, like the trees scattered by the storms on the grasslands.
>
> The great—and good, I believe—White Chief sends us word that he wants to buy our land. But he will reserve us enough so that we can live comfortably. This seems generous, since the red man no longer has rights he need respect. It may also be wise, since we no longer need a large country. Once my people covered this land like a flood tide moving with the wind across the shell-littered flats. But that time is gone, and with it the greatness of tribes now almost forgotten.
>
> But I will not mourn the passing of my people. Nor do I blame our white brothers for causing it. We

too were perhaps partly to blame. When our young
men grow angry at some wrong, real or imagined, they
make their faces ugly with black paint. Their hearts too
are ugly and black. They are hard and their cruelty
knows no limits. And our old men cannot restrain
them.

Let us hope that the wars between the red man
and his white brothers will never come again. We
would have everything to lose and nothing to gain.
Young men view revenge as gain, even when they lose
their own lives. But the old men who stay behind in
time of war, mothers with sons to lose—they know
better.

Our great father in Washington—for he must be
our father now as well as yours, since George has
moved his boundary northward—our great and good
father sends us word by his son, who is surely a great
chief among his people, that he will protect us if we do
what he wants. His brave soldiers will be a strong wall
for my people, and his great warships will fill our har-
bors. Then our ancient enemies to the north—the
Haidas and Tsimshians—will no longer frighten our
women and old men. Then he will be our father and
we will be his children.

But can that ever be? Your God loves your people
and hates mine. He puts his strong arm around the
white man and leads him by the hand, as a father leads
his little boy. He has abandoned his red children. He
makes your people stronger every day. Soon they will
flood all the land. But my people are an ebb tide, we
will never return. No, the white man's God cannot
love his red children or he would protect them. Now
we are orphans. There is no one to help us.

So how can we be brothers? How can your father
be our father, and make us prosper and send us
dreams of future greatness? Your God is prejudiced.
He came to the white man. We never saw him, never
even heard his voice. He gave the white man laws, but
he had no word for his red children whose numbers
once filled this land as the stars filled the sky.

No, we are two separate races, and we must stay separate. There is little in common between us.

To us the ashes of our fathers are sacred. Their graves are holy ground. But you are wanderers, you leave your fathers' graves behind you, and you do not care.

Your religion was written on tables of stone by the iron finger of an angry God, so you would not forget it. The red man could never understand it or remember it. Our religion is the ways of our forefathers, the dreams of our old men, sent them by the Great Spirit, and the visions of our sachems. And it is written in the hearts of our people.

Your dead forget you and the country of their birth as soon as they go beyond the grave and walk among the stars. They are quickly forgotten and they never return. Our dead never forget this beautiful earth. It is their mother. They always love and remember her rivers, her great mountains, her valleys. They long for the living, who are lonely too and who long for the dead. And their spirits often return to visit and console us.

No, day and night cannot live together.

The red man has always retreated before the advancing white man, as the mist on the mountain slopes runs before the morning sun.

So your offer seems fair, and I think my people will accept it and go to the reservation you offer them. We will live apart, and in peace. For the words of the Great White Chief are like the words of nature speaking to my people out of great darkness—a darkness that gathers around us like the night fog moving inland from the sea.

It matters little where we pass the rest of our days. They are not many. The Indians' night will be dark. No bright star shines on his horizons. The wind is sad. Fate hunts the red man down. Wherever he goes, he will hear the approaching steps of his destroyer, and prepare to die, like the wounded doe who hears the steps of the hunter.

A few more moons, a few more winters, and none of the children of the great tribes that once lived in this wide earth that roam now in small bands in the woods will be left to mourn the graves of a people once as powerful and as hopeful as yours.

But why should I mourn the passing of my people? Tribes are made of men, nothing more. Men come and go, like the waves of the sea. A tear, a prayer to the Great Spirit, a dirge, and they are gone from our longing eyes forever. Even the white man, whose God walked and talked with him as friend to friend, cannot be exempt from the common destiny.

We may be brothers after all. We shall see.

We will consider your offer. When we have decided, we will let you know. Should we accept, I here and now make this condition; we will never be denied the right to visit, at any time, the graves of our fathers and our friends.

Every part of this earth is sacred to my people. Every hillside, every valley, every clearing and wood, is holy in the memory and experience of my people. Even those unspeaking stones along the shore are loud with events and memories in the life of my people. The ground beneath your feet responds more lovingly to our steps than yours, because it is the ashes of our grandfathers. Our bare feet know the kindred touch. The earth is rich with the lives of our kin.

The young men, the mothers, and girls, the little children who once lived and were happy here, still love these lonely places. And at evening the forests are dark with the presence of the dead. When the last red man has vanished from this earth, and his memory is only a story among the whites, these shores will still swarm with the invisible dead of my people. And when your children's children think they are alone in the fields, the forests, the shops, the highways, or the quiet of the woods, they will not be alone. There is no place in this country where a man can be alone. At night when the streets of your towns and cities are quiet, and you think they are empty, they will throng with the returning spirits that once thronged them, and that still love these places. The white man will never be alone.

So let him be just and deal kindly with my people. The dead have power too.

Notes

1. Ralph Waldo Emerson, "Education."
2. Cf. Austin Warren, *The New England Conscience* (Ann Arbor: University of Michigan Press, 1966), p. 54: "Much of the falsity of the Protestant ethics lies in just what—whether in its popular or philosophic form—it has prided itself on: its concern with self and subjectivity. Concern with *my* motives, *my* intentions, *my* conscience is always in danger of becoming more concerned with me than with *the whole, vast, other world*. Egoism—refined subjectivity—is morally more dangerous, partly because more subtle, than plain frank egotism of selfishness" (emphasis added).
3. The attitude of the soldiers who massacred Vietnamese civilians at My Lai is revealingly summarized in the words of William Doherty of Charlie Company: "It was pretty disgusting, but it was a different feeling. If they had been Americans, I might have felt different. I never really understood those people." Cf. Seymour M. Hersh, *My Lai 4: A Report on the Massacre and Its Aftermath* (New York: Random House, 1970) pp. 89 ff.
4. Hersh again is pat to the point: "In 1968 the Army's efforts to educate GIs on the rights of prisoners consisted of two hours of instruction a year . . . . The average GI's ignorance of Vietnamese customs was appalling, but even more appalling was the fact that the Army's efforts to give the men some kind of understanding of what they would be faced with were minimal. The Vietnam-bound soldiers were given . . . only one or two lectures on the country and its people while in training . . . . A Canadian nurse described how GIs assigned to pacification projects would often complain that the Vietnamese didn't care about their own children. They would say that the mothers tried to leave them behind when they were being evacuated. 'Saw it with my own eyes,' one GI said. 'A woman hopped up on the chopper after seeing her baby down on the ground. When I picked it up and handed it to her, she shouted and pointed to the ground and wouldn't take the baby from me.' The GI didn't know that a peasant woman in Quang Ngai believes it is unlucky to carry a baby across a threshold, and so she always sets the baby down, steps across, and then reaches back and picks it up. Another GI claimed that 'you can't help these dinks. They like to live like pigs in hovels, and even when you build them new houses, they won't live in them.' What *he* didn't know, however, was that according to the custom in that area, married women had to live in houses with full, double-sloped roofs. The new GI-built units had attached, single-slope corrugated tin-roofed huts. Since most of the

peasant women were married, they refused to move into them . . . .
Even worse than the misunderstandings were the deliberate cruelties
and implicit assumptions of superiority on the part of the Americans."
(pp. 7ff.)

5. This misunderstanding, I should add, is not solely the work of scientists
and engineers. Their rejection of university language study is in most
cases simply a sensible rejection of the argument too often used by
language instructors in favor of languages—that is, utility. For most
scientists, etc., language study really isn't *professionally* very useful;
important discoveries are very quickly translated, and English is now
the scientific lingua franca. Why, then, spend years studying a language
to no practical purpose? The fact is that the defenders of language
study have failed to make the proper case. The study of languages—
and literatures—is a liberal art, a "humanity," because mastery of a
language and its literature gives us an indispensable purchase and
perspective on ourselves and our own culture. The rigorous, close,
disciplined study of difference is both liberating and civilizing. The
humanistic case has not been made, I believe, because the scholars have
abandoned the teaching of the languages (*and*, it seems, the literatures)
to Berlitzers and audio-technicians. And in general they seem to prefer
trying to make facsimile Frenchmen (or Italians, Germans, etc.) out of
Americans to making sensitive and civilized and understanding
Americans through the study of French (or Italian, German, etc.).

6. This at least was the dispiriting conclusion I drew from a conference in
which students at an experimental college were designing their own
curriculum. What I found depressing was the almost routine exclusion
of everything not already contained or implicit in peer-group culture.
Norman O. Brown but not Plato; Hesse but not Leopardi or Goethe;
Ramakrishna but not Iqbal; Cleaver but not Ibn-Khaldun, etc.
Independent work presumably left the door open for curiosity; but
curiosity was not much in evidence, especially where the past or the
rigorous was concerned. If nobody called Homer a "honky" author,
nobody thought he was worth reading. And the sciences, the law—
those great humanistic structures—were not even mentioned.

7. José Ortega y Gasset, *The Revolt of the Masses* (New York: Norton,
1957), pp. 58–62.

8. R. D. Laing, *The Politics of Experience* (New York: Pantheon, 1967),
p.55.

9. R. P. Blackmur, "Toward a Modus Vivendi," in *The Lion and the
Honeycomb* (New York: Harcourt, Brace, 1955), pp. 6–7.

10. In general, the M.A.T. programs were a very distinct improvement.
Almost for the first time, the anti-intellectualism of the colleges of
education encountered the tougher, trained intelligence of the hard
academic disciplines. Nonetheless, the M.A.T. programs were clearly a
halfway house, a means whereby colleges could satisfy their consciences
without seriously disturbing the regular academic programs. They were
also prohibitively expensive, since they added a fifth academic year
and wrote off as pretty much inviolable the four years of the education
degree. And simply because they were a modest and halfway measure,

they failed to provide any real competitive challenge to the colleges of education.

11. William Arrowsmith, "Idea of a New University" in *Center Magazine*, March–April, 1970.

12. Seattle's speech was delivered, in 1856, in his native Duwamish before an audience which included Isaac Stevens, governor of Washington Territory. It was translated on the spot by a Dr. Henry Smith of Seattle, who later published a highly "improved" version of Seattle's speech in the *Seattle Star* (October 29, 1877). Nonetheless, the speech in Smith's version evidently followed the original closely. The version printed here is my "translation" of Henry Smith's Victorian English. What I have done is simply to remove verbal flourishes and obvious Victorian poeticisms; the various embellishments which successive editors gradually intruded into Seattle's speech as reported by Smith have also been removed.

Notes on Contributors

GEORGE ANASTAPLO, with advanced degrees in law and political science from the University of Chicago, is presently professor of political science and of philosophy at Rosary College, River Forest, Illinois and lecturer in the liberal arts at the University of Chicago. In addition to numerous articles on law, American government, ethics, and philosophy, he is the author of *The Constitutionalist: Notes on The First Amendment.*

WILLIAM ARROWSMITH, teacher, translator, editor, critic, essayist, lecturer, and poet, is currently University Professor and professor of classics at Boston University. With advanced degrees from Princeton University and Oxford University, as well as with numerous honorary degrees, he has taught at Princeton University, Wesleyan University, University of California (Riverside), and the University of Texas, and has received several awards for excellence in teaching, most recently the E. Harris Harbison Award. Among his publications are *The Satyricon of Petronius* (translated with an Introduction), the widely read article "The Shame of the Graduate Schools," and a forthcoming volume of American Indian speeches.

ELINOR B. BACHRACH, with degrees from Brown University and the University of Chicago, is presently legislative assistant to Rep. William D. Hathaway (D.-Maine). She has previously held jobs with Senate Subcommittee on Inter-governmental Relations, Agency for International Development, London School of Economics—International Relations Department, O.E.O., Upward Bound, and Maine State Planning Office.

D. S. CARNE-ROSS, with degrees from Oxford University and Cornell University, is currently professor of classics and modern languages at Boston University. He has been a linguistics intelligence officer with the R.A.F., a producer for B.B.C., and editor of *Arion* and *Delos*. He is the translator of two novellas by Tozzi and Calvino and (with William Arrowsmith) of *Dialogues with Leuco* by Cesare Pavese, and the author of numerous articles on ancient and modern literatures.

JOSEPH M. DUFFY, with degrees from Columbia University and the University of Chicago, is professor of English literature at the University of Notre Dame. He taught formerly at the University of Idaho. An American Academy in Rome and a Fulbright Scholar, he is advisory editor of the *Review of Politics* and is a 1971 recipient of the E. Harris Harbison Award for Distinguished Teaching. His publications are principally concerned with 19th and 20th century fiction.

E. A. GOERNER, with degrees from the University of Notre Dame and the University of Chicago, is professor of political theory at the University of Notre Dame and was formerly on the faculty of Yale University. He is a member of the Association des Amis de l'orgue Silbermann de l'eglise St. Thomas, Strasbourg. His publications include *Peter and Caesar, Constitutions of Europe* (ed.), *Democracy in Crisis* (ed.), and "Christendom and the Problem of Justice."

JOHN G. HESSLER, valedictorian of the class of 1971 at the University of Notre Dame and a Danforth Fellow, is presently a graduate student at Stanford University.

DAVID LITTLE, with advanced degrees from Union Theological Seminary and Harvard University, is professor of religion and sociology at the University of Virginia. He has taught formerly at Harvard Divinity School and at Yale Divinity School. His publications include *Religion, Order, and Law: A Study in Pre-revolutionary England,* and *American Foreign Policy and Moral Rhetoric.*

ALLARD K. LOWENSTEIN, with degrees from the University of North Carolina and Yale University, is presently national chairman of A.D.A. In addition to his many years of service in political life, most recently as a member of the 91st Congress, he has taught at Stanford University, North Carolina State University, and City College of New York. His publications include *Brutal Mandate* and *Reclaiming America.*

ROBERT E. MEAGHER, with degrees from the University of Notre Dame and the University of Chicago, teaches philosophy and religion in the School of Humanities and Arts of Hampshire College. He has taught at Indiana University (Bloomington) and at the University of Notre Dame. His publications include *Personalities and Powers* and *Beckonings* (and, forthcoming, *A Question to Myself: A Study of Augustine's Understanding of Person and Nature*).

ROBERT C. NEVILLE, with degrees from Yale University, is currently professor in philosophy at the State University of New York (Purchase) and research associate for the program on behavior control at the Institute for Society, Ethics and the Life Sciences, Hastings-on-Hudson, New York. He has taught on the faculties of Yale University, Wesleyan University, and Fordham University. His publications, ranging from metaphysics and philosophy of religion to social and political theory, include *God the Creator* and *Freedom: Social, Personal, Religious.*

WILLIAM PFAFF, educated at the University of Notre Dame, formerly a journalist, editor, correspondent, soldier, and political warfare officer, is presently senior analyst for the Hudson Institute. In addition to numerous articles, his publications include *The New Politics, The Politics of Hysteria: The Sources of Twentieth Century Conflict, Power and Impotence* (all with Edmund Stillman), and *Condemned to Freedom.*

L. JOHN ROOS, with degrees from the University of Notre Dame and the University of Chicago, is presently on the faculty of government and international studies as well as associate director of The Urban Studies Institute of the University of Notre Dame. His experience in public life includes teaching in a Chicago inner-city school, serving as president of a corporation involved in low income housing, assisting in several mayoral, congressional, and presidential campaigns, and acting as advisor on governmental reorganization to the mayor of South Bend, Indiana. His publications include *Pilot Social Indicators.*

DOUGLAS E. STURM, with advanced degrees from the University of Chicago and post-doctoral studies at Harvard Law School, is presently chairman of the Department of Religion and director of The University Honors Council at Bucknell University. He is the author of numerous published essays in the areas of theological education, political and legal theory, and social ethics, including "Naturalism, Historicism, and Christian Ethics: Toward a Christian Doctrine of Natural Law," "Three Concepts of Law," and "Politics of Inquiry: An Apology for Political Activism by Academics."

ALDO TASSI, a Fulbright fellow, with advanced degrees from Marquette University and Fordham University, is presently professor of philosophy at Fordham University. He taught formerly at Duquesne University. In addition to articles on the political philosophy of John Locke, he is preparing a book on American political philosophy.